JOURNAL FOR THE STUDY OF THE NEW TESTAMENT
SUPPLEMENT SERIES
250

Executive Editor
Stanley E. Porter

Editorial Board
Craig Blomberg, Elizabeth A. Castelli, David Catchpole,
Kathleen E. Corley, R. Alan Culpepper, James D.G. Dunn,
Craig A. Evans, Stephen Fowl, Robert Fowler, George H.
Guthrie, Robert Jewett, Robert W. Wall

PLAYING THE TEXTS
8

Series Editor
George Aichele

Paul's Critique of Theocracy

*A/*Theocracy in Corinthians and Galatians

David W. Odell-Scott

T & T CLARK INTERNATIONAL
A Continuum imprint
LONDON • NEW YORK

Copyright © 2003 T&T Clark International
A Continuum imprint

Published by T&T Clark International
The Tower Building, 11 York Road, London SE1 7NX
15 East 26th Street, Suite 1703, New York, NY 10010

www.tandtclark.com

British Library Cataloguing-in-Publication Data
A catalogue record for this book is available from the British Library

Library of Congress Cataloguing-in-Publication Data
A catalogue record for this book is available from the Library of Congress

Typeset by TMW Typesetting, Sheffield
Printed on acid-free paper in Great Britain by The Cromwell Press, Trowbridge, Wilts

ISBN   0-8264-6966-3 (hb)
       0-8264-7143-9 (pb)

For Lauren, Megan and Paul

CONTENTS

ACKNOWLEDGMENTS

I want to thank the Series Editors of the Journal for the Study of the New Testament Supplement and Playing the Text, Stanley E. Porter and George Aichele, as well as Philip Davies, former Editorial Director of Sheffield Academic Press, and Philip J. Law, United Kingdom Publisher, T&T Clark International, for their interest and support in bringing this work to publication. Special thanks to George Aichele for his helpful discussion and suggestions regarding the manuscript, and Sarah Norman, Managing Editor, for her careful attention to the final manuscript. I also thank William Baird, Professor Emeritus of Texas Christian University, and Professor Daniel Patte of Vanderbilt University for their comments on earlier drafts of Part II. Thanks go as well to Walter Wink for his constructive comments on an earlier version of Part II that I presented to the Colloquium on Violence and Religion at the Annual Meeting at Philadelphia in 1995. I also thank the Bible Translation Section of the Society of Biblical Literature for providing me with a forum at the 1998 Annual Meeting to present an earlier draft of work included in Part I.

I am grateful for the support afforded me by Kent State University for a Faculty Improvement Leave in 1998, and for providing a Summer Research Grant in 1992 from the University Research Council which contributed needed time in the early stages of this research project.

I am grateful to my colleagues in the Department of Philosophy at Kent State University. Their support, useful suggestions and constructive criticism are much appreciated. I am also appreciative of the encouragement for my work from so many of my Kent State colleagues.

My thanks to the editors of *Biblical Theology Bulletin*, David Bossman and the late Leland White, for permission to use 'Let the Women Speak in Church', *BTB* 13.3 (July 1983) pp. 90-93, and the American Academy of Religion for permission to use selections from Chapters 8 ('Re-Plying the Gender Hierarchy'), 10 ('Baptism in Christ') and 11 ('The Reconciliation Fragment') of *A Post-Patriarchal Christology* (American Academy of Religion, Academy Series 78; Atlanta: Scholars Press, 1991), distributed by Oxford University Press, in the Introduction, and Chapters 1 and 10.

I am especially grateful to Lauren, who is my confidante and friend, and Megan and Paul, who fill out my life with joy. I dedicate this work to Lauren, Megan and Paul.

INTRODUCTION

Theocracy n, pl **-cies** [Gk *theokratia*, fr. *the-* + *-kratia* -cracy] (1622) **1:**
government of a state by immediate divine guidance or by officials who are
regarded as divinely guided **2:** a state governed by a theocracy.[1]

The development of modern western social thought was significantly influenced by criticisms of crucial aspects of medieval European theocracy.
The critique of European theocracy came in a variety of moves, including
(but not exclusively through) judicial reforms influenced by Voltaire and
the establishment and free exercise clause of the Bill of Rights. Democratic secular governments do not admit *hierarchy*, at least not formally,
for no one, no office, no place is privileged as having sacred authority.

Yet theocratic hierarchy continues to influence, if not dominate, most
Christian political institutions. Further, Christian theocratic aspirations
continue to influence 'ecclesial' social policies in otherwise more or less
secular societies. To assess that theocracy persists in Christian thought and
action may be to state the obvious. To persist in doing so is to continue
firmly, if not obstinately, especially against opposition. Many Christian
churches obstinately maintain that they enjoy 'sacred authority' in opposition to the authority of the secular state or other institutions and societies,
religious or secular. The persistence of 'hierarchy' so permeates modern
Christian social thought and practice that to act, let alone think, in other
than a theocratic way with regards to issues of Christian authority is
assessed as a threat not just to a system or theory of authority but a threat
to Christianity. That Christian theocracy persists in churches in otherwise
secular societies may bespeak the continued influence of medieval European institutions upon western cultures, albeit morphed, as well as the
continued influence of biblical theocratic design and aspirations.

But theocratic convictions and aspirations are more than an obstinate

1. *Merriam-Webster's Collegiate Dictionary* (Springfield, MA: Merriam-Webster,
1996).

refusal to accommodate secular modes of authority. Christian theocracy continues not simply as persistence but also as a disposition. Theocratic convictions and aspirations appear as 'natural' within Christian social values. The disposition towards theocracy or, more precisely, the cultured habits of theocratic ordering may quickly yield to the force of persistence when hierarchical authority is challenged. But these contemporary issues and concerns are not the subject of this work, although their denial may belie their influence.

The complexities of Christian theocracy are complicated by the index of Christian social terminology. The terminology of Christian 'belonging' is often employed as if key words were synonyms. But terms such as church, congregation, assembly, kingdom and temple, which are often employed in formal social self-identifications, would hardly survive if the terms did not provide significant and helpful differentiations. Other terminology, such as the use of 'ecclesia', has all but disappeared as communal designations except among academic theologians. Ecclesiastical terminology has come to designate ritual objects (ecclesiastical garments) and institutional offices that belong to the 'church' rather than designate Christian belonging. ·

'Church' has come to be the most common term associated with Christian belonging.[2] It is a curious designation. The modern term 'church' and its many renderings, like Scottish *kirk*, are believed to be related to the Greek *kuriakē*, meaning 'belonging to the Lord'.[3] To belong to the Lord is to be a member of the Lord's house (*kuriakon*). Such belonging often plays upon inchoate images of family and household in which the Lord is master (*kurios*). The vague and meaningful images of belonging to the Lord play out some of the most powerful themes associated with Christian life and experience. To belong to the Lord is to be saved, to enjoy immortal security and well-being.

---

2.   It would not be uncommon for an inquiry 'Where do you go to church?' to be answered, 'I attend the Assemblies of God', or 'Kingdom Hall', or 'God's Temple', or 'the Christian Family Center', or 'the Chapel'. However, it would sound odd for someone to ask of a Christian, 'Where do you go to assembly, or kingdom, or temple?'

3.   '*kuriakon*, properly adj. "of the lord" (from *kurios*, "lord"), cf. Latin *dominicum*, dominical, which occurs from the third century CE at least, used substantively (sc. *dōma*, or the like) means "house of worship". The earliest citation is 300 CE in *Apostolical Constitution I* (II: 59). Constantine named several buildings of Christian worship *kuriaka* (Eusebius, De Laud. Const. xvii)', *Oxford English Dictionary* (ed. C.T. Onions; Oxford: Clarendon Press, 1966), VI, p. 403.

I am not concerned in this study with the processes by which any group of Christians proceeds to identify and assess whether a particular course of action, including the selection of persons as leaders, is a proper exercise of God's will. The issue is not whether one rightfully discerns God's intent or faithfully represents the Lord in the exercise of political authority in a given instance. My point is that 'authority' in Christian communities is 'theocratic' and 'hierarchical'. Divine authority is exercised by a person or persons who are believed to serve on God's behalf. When the theocratic authority of any particular person or group is called into question among Christians, rarely is the legitimacy of theocratic authority per se called into question. Rather, the issue is whether a particular person or group are the worldly proprietors of God's authority. The classical criteria for Christian theocratic authority provided resolution to proprietary concerns through apostolic succession, purification, and belief (orthodoxy).

One of the means by which Christian communities substantiate their theocratic authority is through the composition of a narrative that draws upon fragments from the books of Christian scripture. These text fragments are deployed to substantiate the integrity of the particular 'church' as the self-realization or self-realizing 'original' *church*. The narrations of different origins produce different ends. Different ends seek origins that substantiate their end. Some of the lines of text drawn from Christian scripture most commonly employed include the calling of the twelve disciples, or when Jesus granted Peter the keys to the kingdom, or the story of Pentecost. In other words, the various 'origins' of the various 'churches' are traced in texts. Those who identify themselves with the Petrine tradition trace their authority to the story of Peter receiving the keys to the kingdom from the Lord. Whoever the Petrine Church receives is received into the everlasting kingdom of God. Whoever the Petrine Church releases is forever outside the kingdom of God. Communities that oppose those who legitimate their authority by identification with Peter appeal to the Lord's declaration that Peter is Satan within the story that the Petrine Church deploys for legitimating its authority. The selection of different fragments serves to substantiate different narratives in the contest over sacred authority. But this process of textual fragmentation, of interpretive inflation in the production of a founding narrative, serves not so much to elucidate the *textus* and nuances of a particular text so much as to employ fragments in the composition of a text that serves to legitimate or question the theocratic legitimacy of a particular Christian institution.

Particular texts avail themselves to such manipulation, especially when fragments are taken out of context. Those who employ the available texts to substantiate the formation or maintenance or defense of a particular communal institutionalization often deploy text-fragments from the Pauline corpus. The customary reading of the introduction of 1 Corinthians suggests that in response to the divisions within the community, expressed in the quoting of the contentious self-declarations in 1 Cor. 1.12, Paul puts forward a self-declaration ('I belong to Christ') that serves as the resolution to the social fragmentation of the Corinthian community. The declaration 'I belong to Christ' enjoys much that is similar to the phrase 'I belong to the Lord'. And as we noted, the Greek *kuriakē*, commonly translated 'belonging to the Lord', is an etymological ancestor of the modern terminology associated with the Christian social designation 'church' common in the Germanic languages. The church is that which belongs to the Lord, or those who are members of the church are those who belong to the Lord. The common, established reading of the introduction to 1 Corinthians is that Paul offers to the fractured Corinthian community a proper 'creed': if they will say and believe the right thing, then (so goes the interpretation informed by credo convictions) the promise is that Christians will enjoy social unity and peace.

It is customary to interpret the Pauline Epistles as critical of theo-epistemic claims such as 'I know God', yet theocratic claims such as 'I belong to Christ' and 'We are the temple of God', or that 'man is the icon and glory of God' while 'woman is (only) the glory of man', and the conviction that the sacred community is the family of God the father are on the whole received by Christians as proper. Emergent orthodoxies could identify Paul's critiques of theology as a rejection of *other* theologies that they judged to be heretical, even if such identifications were unfounded, inadequate or simply wrong. In the centuries that followed Paul's letter-writing, claims like 'I belong to Christ' and 'We are the temple of God' found in the Corinthian corpus were judged to be appropriate professions of faith to guide Christian society. The family metaphors and the gender hierarchy must have seemed appropriate as well for those who came to fashion Christian theocratic institutional life in the centuries that followed.

I contend that it is not so much what Paul has written regarding authority that has drawn the criticism of so many contemporary readers, as it is what has been done and is done with the Pauline texts by and in the service of various Christian 'communities' (if we can use the term 'community' as a generalization for 'whatever' social arrangements). One of the many things I find disconcerting in the history of Pauline interpretation is that the Epistles have been 'overinterpreted', so processed that there is surprisingly very broad agreement between interpretive parties as to the content or thesis of any particular section of a canonical letter. For instance, with respect to the conception and political status of 'woman', defenders and critics of male hierarchy and female subordination concur as to Paul's position on the matter as expressed in 1 Corinthians. I find such shared assessment troublesome for many reasons, not the least of which is the careless disregard for the complexities of the texts, and the need for critical separation between text and interpretation.

An emphasis in the critical study of the Corinthian letters is the 'collecting' of the 'collection', the processes by which editors gathered and copied the occasional letters from Paul to the congregations in Rome–Corinth into the canonical texts of 1 and 2 Corinthians. Under the sway of this critical approach to the canonical 'letters', textual problems are often considered to be the product of an editor or editors who mismatched material from the earlier occasional letters by Paul or who, in their editorial workings with the Corinthian correspondence, included other material (intentionally or unintentionally) not authored by Paul and presumably written later than the occasional letters. I argued, first with respect to 1 Cor. 14.34-36, and in subsequent works with respect to several passages of the Corinthian letters, that the 'interpolation' hypothesis is an inadequate method for resolving many, if not most, of the significant textual problems. The emphasis upon editorial activity as the cause for apparent textual abnormalities presupposes that the occasional letters to the Corinthian congregation(s) imitate the overall structure of Paul's letters to the Romans and the Galatians. But it is my contention that the letters to the Corinthians are different in one significant and, I think, obvious way from the other letters by Paul. Paul's letters to the Corinthians were 'occasioned' according to material presented in the texts by (i) letters from the Corinthians delivered to Paul and (ii) verbal reports about situations in the congregation conveyed by those who delivered the letters from Corinth to Paul. Paul in turn not only wrote in response to the Corinthian letters and the verbal reports but incorporated bits of the verbal reports and pieces, and in some instances extended quotations from the letters, in his replies. Paul's letters to the Corinthians were not just responses to the Corinthian letters and reports. Paul's letters to the Corinthians were, in the strongest sense of the term, *replies* to the Corinthian communications.

Etymologically, the text is a cloth: *textus*, from which 'text' derives, means 'woven'.[4]

Roland Barthes reminded us that the term 'text' comes from Latin *textus*, which is derived from the past participle (*text-*) of the verb *texere*, meaning 'to weave, to plait, to fit together'. A *textus* or 'text' is quite literally 'that which is woven or fitted together; a texture, structure; context'.[5]

The history of interpretation has been dominated by a hermeneutic of explication. To 'ex-pli-cate' means to 'ex-' ('un-') 'ply' ('fold'). In other words, to explicate means to 'un-ply', to 'un-twist'. Thus, to explicate means to 'un-weave', to 'un-construct', the text. It has been assumed that the meaning of a text can be discerned only by unraveling. As such, the process of finding the meaning is atextual. So long as the text is textured, so long as the threads twist and fold and ply, the meaning of the text is hidden from understanding. The task of the interpreter of texts is to explicate, to unfold, unplait, untwist, unravel the *textus*. Explicated, the unraveled text lays before the reader like strands of smooth/untwisted threads. Lines/phrases/words/marks are untwisted from one another and clearly 'un-layered' before the reader. Such a text, a 'de-text-ured' text, is explicated, made level or plain. A leveled surface lies before the examiner exposed (deprived of shelter, protection or care—abandoned), completely illuminated and present. An explained text is exposed without concern for the texture of the text, without concern for the shades and folds of the *textus*. An explained text is not sheltered from the light of inspection. Fully illuminated, the truth of the text is made present. Nothing is hidden. Or, to put it another way, everything is illuminated.

Paradoxically, traditional and critical biblical scholars, who are commonly understood to be at odds, both seek to explicate the text. Traditional readers, having unwoven the text in light of inspired illumination, assert that the meaning of the text is to be found by discovering those threads

---

4.   Roland Barthes, 'From Work to Text', in J.V. Harari (ed.), *Textual Strategies: Perspectives in Post-Structural Criticism* (Ithaca, NY: Cornell University Press, 1979), pp. 73-88 (76).

5.   *Texere* is cognate with terms such as Old Indian *taksati* ('he fashions, constructs'), *taksan* ('carpenter') and *texna* ('art'); Old Slavic *tesla* ('ax, hatchet'); Armenian *t'ek'em* ('I turn, wind, twist'); Old High and Middle German *dahs*, German *Dachs* and Dutch *das*. Klein contends that these terms share a common ancestry from the Indo-European base *tekht-* and *tekh-*, meaning 'to build (of wood, i.e. to carpenter) or to weave'. Klein concludes that 'The original meaning of this base probably was "to plait, to twist"'. E.A. Klein, *A Comprehensive Dictionary of the English Language* (New York: Elsevier, 1966), p. 1597.

which pattern the beliefs or doctrines of the orthodox faith. Critical readers are 'critical' to the extent that they note the discrepancies between what the traditional reader chooses to select from the explicated text and what the traditional reader chooses to leave behind. Critical scholars ask why some threads of the explicated biblical texts that do not cohere or cannot be woven into the pattern of church doctrine are ignored or plucked out. Critical readers, returning to the pile of explicated ravelings from the text, have noted the presence of threads that conflict with or even contradict one another.

The hermeneutics of explication produce by extraction a pile of un-woven individual threads that may then be compared and arranged (depending upon the task at hand). With respect to 1 and 2 Corinthians, explication of the texts has led to the conclusion that the texts are internally incoherent or self-contradicting. But what is often ignored in the process of explication, or worse, what is often obliterated in the process of explication, is the *textus*. The texture, the weave, the patterns are obliterated in the reduction of the explicated text to its constitutive pieces. But the *textus* is not a piece of the text.

Our study of the *textus* of Paul's first and second Epistles to the Corinthians is not an endeavor in the hermeneutics of explication. An explicated text is no 'text' at all. To explicate ('to unfold, unplait, untwist') Paul's letters would necessitate unweaving the *textus*. So unwoven, the explicated text would be 'de-textured', destroyed, reduced to a heap of threads, a pile of trash. Our task is to be sensitive to and curious about the inherent 'texture' and tissue of the work. So we proceed to follow the tapestry, feeling and noting the weaves, the plies, and the craftsmanship in an effort to understand the text as texture, *teknē* and *textus*.

In order to come to an understanding of Paul's writing on the issues before us, we shall engage with the text not as a heap of individual threads with a simple meaning but as a tapestry whose texture and content produce a single context or work. Thus we shall attend not to the single threads that have been removed from the text but to the *textus*, the weave of the 'sheets' or 'plates' or pages of the text.

As we shall see, the complexity of the text and the apparently contradictory threads (contradictory to those who note that some of the lines/threads do not cohere with other lines/threads) that run through the weave will be better understood, will be better read, not by means of a method of explication, but by first attending to the *textus* of 1 Corinthians.

Clearly the Pauline texts are not the presentation of a story in the way a gospel is. Paul is not 'spinning' a sacred 'yarn'. Nor are the texts a collection of treatises on church doctrine or theology. The corpus of Pauline texts is a collection of 'epistles' from Paul to the Christian churches of Rome, Corinth, Galatia and Thessalonia.[6] An 'epistle' (*epistola*) is a letter, a communication between persons who are absent from one another. Such written communication is composed of the 'letters' or 'characters' of the alphabet.[7] A letter belongs (i) to both the one who posts it and to those to whom it is posted, and yet (ii) it enjoys an independence from those for whom it corresponds.[8] For an epistle may be 'diverted' from its path and read by one for whom it was not intended. In what ways are the Pauline Epistles (collected and edited into a corpus and, then, canonized as Christian scripture) 'purloined', put amiss, diverted from their path, prolonged by being sanctified?[9]

We read a correspondence that does not correspond with us. As such, we read the epistle without authority. The author(ity) of the epistle is not simply the individual whose installment of the exchange we have before us. Rather, the author(ity) is plural. All who participate in the exchange author the correspondence.

The Epistles are for us 'literary'. They are pseudo-letters for us. When we forget that the Pauline Epistles lettered a correspondence, an exchange, we forget the sort of text (*textus*, weave) that an epistle is.

But, we may ask, 'What kind of weave or ply is a correspondence?'

The term 'ply' (meaning 'fold, bend, or layer') has dropped from common use in the English language except in compounds or as a technical term. We commonly speak of ply-wood (layered wood), complicate (from Latin *complicare*, 'to fold together'), apply (from Old French *aplier* and Latin *applicare*, ' to fold towards'), explicate (Latin *explicare*, 'to unfold') and implicate (Latin *implicare*, 'to infold, involve, entangle').[7]

In legal terminology, one 'plies' the witness, soliciting response with

---

6.   Old English *epistola*, from which we derive 'epistle', was directly adopted from Latin *epistola*, which was a phonetic representation of the Greek term *epistolē*. An *epistolē* could be transmitted orally as well as graphically.

7.   The English term 'letter' was adopted from Old French *lettre*, which was the phonetic descendant of Latin *littera*. Thus an epistle is the tracing of the letters of the alphabet in such a way as to form a text.

8.   Adopted from Middle Latin *correspondere* (*cor*, 'together, with each other' and *respondere*, 'to answer'), the etymology of the word suggests that 'to correspond' means 'to mutually respond, the answering of things to one another'.

9.   Jacques Lacan, 'Seminar on "The Purloined Letter" '(trans. Jeffrey Mehlman), *Yale French Studies* 48 (1972), pp. 38-72.

persistent questions, petitions, and so on. In a nautical use, 'to ply' is 'to beat up against the wind, to tack, to work to windward'. To tack, to ply, is a going to and fro between certain points. In other words, to ply in this usage is to traverse, ferry and make passage.

To ply is also 'to plaid, braid, interweave'. Ply resonates with Latin *plectere*, which is cognate with Old Indian *prasnah* ('wickerwork basket') and the Greek terms *plekein* ('to plait') and *plokē* ('network'). As we saw earlier, how a text is woven (that is, the difference that is traversed in the twist, the weaving to and fro, the patterning) is the ply of the threads.

The weave of the letters to the Corinthians, the ply of the *textus*, is a 're-ply' or 're-weave'.[10] In the literary sense, a 'reply' is a letter that responds to questions, issues or the like raised by another.[11] It is the mutual addressing of issues, the mutual answering of questions, one to another.[12] The English term 'reply' is derived from Middle English *replien* and the Middle French terms *replier* and *reploier*, meaning 'to fold back, to bend back'. Late Latin *replicare* also meant 'to repeat'.[13] Thus, as a military reply is a return of fire for fire, a literary 'reply' suggest a return, measure for measure, like for like. In other words, to reply is to 'echo' or 'copy'. To reply is to double, to fold back, to exchange and to repeat. It is a bending and folding back, a layering that may fold together (com-plicate) differences that become involved (im-plicated). In a legal sense a reply would be a 'turning of the ply back', to respond to persistent solicitation with counterquestions, counterarguments, counterpetitions, and so on.

Significant for our study are the play of 'ply' and 're-ply' and the com-

---

10. John C. Hurd, *The Origins of 1 Corinthians* (New York: Seabury Press, 1965), p. xii. Hurd notes that Charles H. Buck Jr introduced his students to 1 Corinthians as 'The Corinthian Reply'. My use was arrived at independently from Hurd or Buck.

11. Immediately following the 'greeting' and 'salutation' (1 Cor. 1.1-9), Paul writes (1.10-13): 'I appeal to you…that all of you agree and that there be no dissensions among you, but that you be united in the same mind and the same judgment. For it has been reported to me by Chlóe's people that there is quarreling among you, my brethren. What I mean is that each one of you says, "I belong to Paul", or "I belong to Apollos", or "I belong to Cephas", or "I belong to Christ". Is Christ divided? Was Paul crucified for you? Or were you baptized in the name of Paul?' In these verses, Paul 'quotes' or 'paraphrases' from the Corinthians (1.12) and then returns a 'reply' (1.13). Paul replies to those who have formed divisions in the church with three rhetorical questions whose adversarial manner and sarcastic tone cut to the heart of each faction's position.

12. Klein, *Dictionary*, p. 1329.

13. *OED*, VIII, p. 1329.

pany of terms that accompany the play. A diploma was first a two-fold (once-folded) sheet. A diplomat carried an official diploma (a two-fold sheet) of authority (and possibly had a two-fold purpose in exercising such authority).

One use of the term that is important to our present discussion is the term 'application', which Shipley contends comes to us by way of the French *appliqué*.[14] An *appliqué* is a comply, compliant or reply named for the blank sheet folded in a letter for responses, said to be included in early letters (by which I take it Shipley means early modern European letters). I have not investigated the possible link between early modern European letters with its blank sheet folded in the folded letter with the art of diplomacy and the taking of letters folded and sealed from one head of state by a diplomat to another head of state. No doubt such possibilities might be too perplexing for our consideration. The *Oxford English Dictionary* notes that the use of 'ply' as 'to fold' is rare except as it occurs in compounds. In becoming rare the word has lost many of its figurative meanings. Earlier, 'ply' meant 'to bend in disposition'; 'to bend or be bent'; and 'to yield or to be pliable'. In all of these uses of the term, 'to ply' suggests a reversal, which is in fact one of the rarer meanings of the term.[15] It is also commonly assumed that the negative phrase 'Do you not know?' (*ouk oidate oti*) introduces a question that is 'aimed at the Corin-

14. Joseph T. Shipley, *The Origins of English Words: A Discursive Dictionary of Indo-European Roots* (Baltimore: The Johns Hopkins University Press, 1984), pp. 320-22.

15. Hurd (*Origins*) provides lists of phrases that he and others take to be the presence of quotations from the Corinthians' letter to Paul or phrases quoted from the oral report(s) to Paul in his correspondence with the Corinthians. Hurd's study is too detailed and lengthy to be represented here. For our purposes, we will employ his comments that have to do with the general sense in which 1 Corinthians is a non-literary reply (that is, 1 Corinthians is a letter directed to a particular destination and is not written as a letter to serve some other purpose) which includes quotations from Corinthians (whether they be oral or written), and his remarks about a particular passage which is of interest to our study.

There are differences of opinion among Pauline scholars as to the extent to which the oral reports from Chlóe's people and the letter from Corinth are traced or paraphrased in Paul's reply. There is little or no argument that the phrase 'now concerning' (*peri de*) is one way Paul addresses an issue or answers a question raised to him by the Corinthians. *peri de* is most often regarded as a lead into Paul's reply to the 'letter' from Corinth, as opposed to the oral reports. The phrase *peri de* appears six times in 1 Corinthians (7.1, 25; 8.1; 12.1; 16.1, 12) and twice in 1 Thessalonians (4.9; 5.1). *peri (men) gar* is used once in 2 Corinthians (9.1); Hurd, *Origins*, pp. 65-74.

thians'.[16] The question usually addresses some point of general knowledge about the world or some particular knowledge about the Christians' faith that Paul assumes the Corinthians should have known without their having to be reminded. But apparently, judging from the correspondence or the reports to Paul, it is clear that they in fact lack such knowledge. 'Do you not know?' is thus a lead into items about which they need reminding. Hurd contends that the phrase 'Do you not know?' (*ouk oidate oti*) occurs ten times in 1 Corinthians and once in Romans. It is this sense of bending in reverse, 'to ply', that we shall develop in the sense of 're-ply'. It is the double meaning of 'bending in reverse' and 'response' that we shall use in the term 'reply' to interpret the letters of Paul of Tarsus. I shall argue that the texts of the Corinthian letters 're-ply', reversing and responding. And further, I shall argue that the first fold, the ply that Paul replies, is to be found in the *textus* of the text.

The Corinthian letters are texts that traversed the difference between Ephesus and Corinth, Paul and the Corinthian church. They are texts that plied the distance and thereby ferried the dialogue. The ply of a dialogue, like the lawyer's ply of a witness, is complicated. The Corinthian replies are no simple weave. For in Paul's ply to the Corinthians, in his lettering to them, are traces of their lettering to him. Their ply is woven into his ply, which is his 're-ply'.

Understood as a reply, we will find woven into Paul's letter to the Corinthian church the ply, the *textus*, from their correspondence or reports to him, as well as other texts that are called upon to warrant the positions he takes up in reply to a question by the Corinthians. We must keep an eye open or an ear cocked to see or hear those places in the text in which Paul might be quoting from or paraphrasing an argument or issue from the Corinthian correspondence with him. Such quotes or paraphrases run counter to his proposal. Paul's replies will mark a difference with the plies from Corinth. To engage the Corinthian Epistles without sensitivity to this texture of the text may lead the reader into mistaking what the Corinthians have written and what Paul has traced as Paul's writing (that is, positions). Such a reading may lead the reader to forget that the text has a certain texture.

Given centuries of reading and study, it is to be expected that the Pauline Epistles would have become familiar—commonplace, assumed. And in that familiarity, in the text's becoming obvious, we have become insensitive to their internal *textus*, their internal intertextuality. The edges

---

16. Hurd, *Origins*, p. 85.

of the seams of the various pieces that form the 'epistles' have been worn with age and are so frayed that we no longer sense the various edges within the text. The Epistles are like a well-used patchwork quilt. We no longer see the pieces of a patchwork or feel the seams of the various patches. Instead, the quilt is felt and seen as a whole. So, the Epistle texts now read smoothly—without a hitch or bump. The content is assumed to facilitate, to be without seam, for the seams have been leveled off by the fraying of dogmatic interpretation and familiarity.[17]

The structural differences between the letters written to the Romans and the Galatians on the one hand and the letters written to the Corinthians on the other have to do with the inclusion of extensive quoted material from the Corinthians in Paul's replies, and the general lack of such quoted material in his letters to the Romans and the Galatians. As we re-read the Corinthian letters, we will note the common indicators of quotations, paraphrase or response. However, as we shall see, there are other more subtle marks in the text that alert the reader to the presence of the Corinthian correspondence to Paul or reports from Corinth, including the failure of an argument to flow, or the actual presence of contradictory claims being made within the text.

If, as Ricoeur contends, the discourse is given nowhere else than in and by the structure of the work, then the misidentification of the structure of a text will yield a misidentification of the 'discourse'.[18] Failing to read the canonical Corinthian letters as replies in which Paul incorporated the letters and verbal reports delivered to him from Corinth is a misidentification of the structure of the texts and will yield a misidentification of Paul's discourse. If Ricoeur's contention regarding the dependency of a discourse upon the structure of the work is valid, then I argue that failing to read the Corinthian letters as replies in which Paul incorporated the letters and verbal reports delivered to him from Corinth leads readers to mistakenly identify the quoted material from *Corinth* that Paul critiques as

17. I am of course playing with J. Derrida's sense of *Bahnung*. See J. Derrida, 'Freud and the Scene of Writing' (trans. Jeffrey Mehlman), *Yale French Studies* 48 (1973), pp. 74-117. *Bahnung* is translated by J. Mehlman as *frayage*. *Bahnung* suggests the wearing down of the 'contact-barriers' that mark the seams between things. Fraying is the violent movement that wears down differences.

18. Paul Ricoeur, 'Philosophical Hermeneutics and Theological Hermeneutics: Ideology, Utopia and Faith', in W. Wuellner (ed.), *Protocol of the Colloquy of the Center for Hermeneutical Studies in Hellenistic and Modern Culture* (Berkeley, CA: The Center, 1976), p. 9.

Paul's position. I contend that the misidentification of the structure of the occasioned replies by Paul to the Corinthians is systemic.

The present study is the continuation of a project that began, at least in print, with an article published in 1983 in the *Biblical Theology Bulletin* in which I argued that Paul's letters to the Corinthians have been poorly read because of a failure to take into account the textuality of these occasional letters in which Paul replies to letters and oral reports delivered from Corinth to Paul while he was living in Ephesus.[19] The text under consideration was 1 Cor. 14.34-36. Verses 34 and 35 assert that women are to be silent in the churches and subordinate to men. I argued that v. 36 begins with the negative particle *eta*, which introduces a two-fold negative rhetorical question that calls into question the presumptions by those males who maintain that women are to be silent and subordinate. Paul replies, 'What! Did the word of God begin with you? Or are you the only ones to have received it?' I argued that vv. 34-35 were a quotation from a letter from Corinth or from reports of positions taken up in Corinth which were delivered to Paul, and which he quoted in order to make clear precisely the position to which his reply was a direct, straightforward critique in v. 36.

I explored the usefulness of these strategies for reading the Corinthian corpus in subsequent works that addressed various topics and texts about which there has been considerable disagreement and assessments by critical biblical scholars as to the integrity of the Corinthian texts and/or the mental competency of their author.[20] I argue that if the Corinthian texts are read as epistolary replies in which verses are quoted by Paul from the texts and reports delivered to him to which he replies, often critically, then the *textus* of the text as reply makes the coherence of the work—and, dare I say, the competency of its author—evident.

---

19. D.W. Odell-Scott, 'Let the Women Speak in Church: An Egalitarian Interpretation of First Corinthians 14.33b-36', *Biblical Theology Bulletin* 13.3 (July 1983), pp. 90-93; 'In Defense of an Egalitarian Interpretation of First Corinthians 14.34-36: A Reply to Murphy-O'Connor's Critique', *Biblical Theology Bulletin* 17.3 (July 1987), pp. 100-103; and 'Editor's Dilemma', *Biblical Theology Bulletin* 30.2 (May 2000), pp. 68-74.

20. D.W. Odell-Scott, *A Post-Patriarchal Christology* (American Academy of Religion, Academy Series 78; Atlanta: Scholars Press, 1991), available through Oxford University Press as of 2000, and 'Paul's Skeptical Critique of a Primitive Christian Metaphysical Theology', *Encounter* 56.2 (1995), pp. 127-46.

Chapter 1

EMPTYING HIERARCHY

The question of where to begin is not easily answered and never adequately justified. I choose to begin our inquiry with a consideration of the final few verses located at the end of the first chapter of 1 Corinthians. The text states in a clear and forthright manner a conclusion that the author seeks the reader to draw, 'that no human being may boast in the presence of God'. That the critique of those who seek sacred advantage is the aim of much of Paul's correspondence to the Corinthians is not a novel assessment. Paul sets out in these verses a method of 'overcoming' the claim of those who make sacred boast to establish their own privilege and authority. Paul's encounter is no simple critique but is an attempt to empty all theocratic identifications.

> [26]For consider your call, brethren; not many of you were wise according to worldly standards, not many were powerful, not many were of noble birth; [27]but God chose what is foolish in the world to shame the wise, God chose what is weak in the world to shame the strong. [28]God chose what is low and despised in the world, even things that are not, to bring to nothing things that are, [29]so that no human being might boast in the presence of God (1 Cor. 1.26-29).

Interpreters commonly proceed by differentiating the 'worldly' (the wise and powerful and those of noble birth) and those 'called by God' (the foolish and weak and those of common birth). Those called and chosen by God are presumed to be the *church* that brings the *worldly* to nothing. God's elect is the nemesis of the worldly. On this reading, the conclusion at v. 29 that 'no human being might boast in the presence of God' is taken to mean that Paul is warning those in the church who *are* 'in the presence of God' not to boast about their privileged status.

But this customary interpretation seems distant from the text. Paul's concluding critique does not suggest that those who are in the presence of God should refrain from boasting of their privilege. It is not the case that the church, the elect of God, should keep their privileged status to themselves and exercise humble restraint when in the presence of the less fortunate who have not been privileged by God. Instead, Paul's contention is that since no human flesh enjoys the privilege of God's presence, then no one could possibly make such a boast.

The Greek phrase at 1.29, *opōs mē kauchēsētai pasa sarx enōpion tou theou*, renders a Hebrew idiom, *nāsā pānîm*, 'to lift the face of someone'. The image is of competing supplicants standing with downcast faces to exhibit their humility before a powerful person who, after consideration, steps forward and makes a choice by lifting the face of one of the subordinates with his hand. Only one among the many is selected. Selection is confirmed by the raising of the face of the chosen supplicant to the face of the superior. Thus favor is passed face to face, elevating the face to the superior and the status of the selected over those not 'lifted'.[1] In 2 Cor. 3.7, Deut. 10.17, Job 24.19, Acts 10.34, Jas 2.1, Gal. 2.6 and Rom. 2.11 the image is invoked in order to deny its pertinence with respect to God. No flesh enjoys the 'face' of God. Therefore no flesh may boast of being lifted by God to the face of God. God privileges no one person over another.

The customary differentiation in which the worldly (wise, powerful, noble birth) stand in opposition to the Godly (foolish, weak, common birth) simply does not work. The wise and powerful and those of noble birth refer not to an ungodly *worldly* other but to persons who claim that because of their wisdom, authority and/or noble birth they enjoy God's selection. Paul's conclusion that 'no human flesh might boast in the presence of God' is an *extreme* critique intended to disarm those who assume their election by God.

When Paul critiques a group for being boastful, the situation often reported in the text is that the group has been seeking its own advantage over others. Those who assert their privilege in the Christian community often seek to bolster their status by appeals to exclusive or privileged relations with God and/or the Lord. In the final verses of the first chapter, the boast of being in the presence of God is made not by the foolish, weak and common but by the wise and powerful and those of noble birth.

What is at issue for Paul is whether anyone enjoys social and political power based on their privileged access to the sacred. The charge by Paul that a group is boastful is a serious indictment, and is usually accompanied

---

1.   J. Louis Martyn, *Galatians: A New Translation with Introduction and Commentary* (The Anchor Bible; New York: Doubleday, 1997), p. 199.

by a critique that calls their sacred associations into question in order to disestablish contentious theocratic power.

In these few verses at the end of the first chapter, Paul acknowledges that there are *hierarchies*. 'Hierarchy' is a term with a rich history. The root of Greek *hieros* means 'to be filled with or to manifest divine power; to be a divine thing, sacred; of earthly things that are hallowed or consecrated'. A *hierarchēs* (Greek) names the president of sacred rites, a high priest, while *hierateia* is the priesthood or body of priests. The term *hierateion* designates a sanctuary. And such places are often declared to be under divine protection.

The clear demarcations and stratifications established by the inequities of wisdom/foolishness, authority/weakness and noble/common birth are presumed to be the effect of God's selection, confirmation and distribution of sacred authority. Those who are wise, authoritative and of noble birth enjoy *hierarchy* relative to the foolish, weak and common. Paul begins by acknowledging these differences. But immediately following the acknowledgment, he proceeds to reverse the assumed distribution of privilege by declaring that God has *now* chosen—elected—the foolish, weak and common to 'shame' the wise and authoritative, and to bring to nothing those of noble birth.

This revaluation of theological social privilege is then followed—not by Paul's substantiation or defense of the sudden reverse of fortune—but by a claim that the revaluation serves to collapse the hierarchical system of theistic identification and to disestablish the theocracy. The foolish, in now being chosen by God, shame the wise and bring the wise to nothing. The weak, in now being chosen by God to shame those with authority, bring those with authority to nothing. Those of common birth, in now being chosen by God, bring those of noble birth to nothing. God chose what is nothing to bring something to nothing. When those who are invested with theocratic power are united with their divested opposites, *all* are emptied of theocratic significance. No flesh is in the presence of God.

Thus theocratic identification refers not to the presence of God, lest one boast of standing in the presence of God. Instead, those who enjoy political rank in the theocracy of the church draw upon no *extra*-human, no *extra*-social source for their power. The powerful are powerful only when others are weakened. The wise are wise only when others are assessed to be foolish. Those of noble birth are of noble birth only when others are assessed to be of common birth.

When opposing identifications are understood as *always, already* dependent upon one another, then the identifications are empty. In their inter-dependence upon one another, opposing identifications refer to no other. The wise and the foolish are seen as being mutually dependent upon one another. The wise are wise because they are not foolish. The foolish are foolish because they are not wise. Those who are of noble birth are of noble birth because they are not of common birth. Those who are of common birth are common because they are not of noble birth. And when opposites are united, when each identification is understood to be dependent upon its opposite, those who enjoy contentious identifications in emergent Christian theocracy are found to enjoy their privileged identifications at the expense of others who are disadvantaged or underprivileged. Thus the construction of theocratic identifications and the economy of religious investitures/divestitures are shown for what they are: the securing of one's own privilege at the disadvantage of another. For no one may boast in the presence of God.

Negations

The theme of bringing something to nothing and of overcoming the strife that generates ranked differences is prominent in another of Paul's critical letters written during the brief period of a few years when he also wrote his letters to the Corinthians.

> And from those who were reputed to be something of importance (what they were makes no difference to me; God shows no partiality to humans)— those, I say, who were of repute added nothing to me (Gal. 2.6).

Those who were reputed to be something added *nothing* to him, declared Paul. The phrase *einai ti* is commonly translated 'to be something of importance' (often with the qualification dropped by translators, given that the point about importance is explicit in the parenthetical comment that follows). It is clear that this 'something' refers to a characteristic of or possession by someone. But why is it the case that Paul employs an *indefinite* pronoun when making reference to 'something' about someone instead of forthrightly naming the particular 'something'? What is it that Paul wishes to avoid naming? Clearly Paul has a *definite* something in mind that he alludes to in the parenthetical comment.

The parenthetical comment, *prosōpon [o] theos anthrōpou ou lambanei* is generally conveyed in translation as 'God shows no partiality' (RSV). Translated 'partiality', *lambanō* is a complex term that generally means in an active sense 'to take' or, more passively, 'to receive'. The complexities of such 'taking' may include to grasp or seize, to violently carry off as a prize, to exact a punishment; to the activity of a passion or a feeling or a deity seizing or possessing another; to catch, bind or place; to apprehend by the mind or the senses; to take for granted; to determine or estimate; to take in hand; to take in, hold.[2] Thus the phrase conveys the sense that God shows no taking or selection, no seizing or possessing, no special placing of a human. The use of 'partiality' conveys the nuance that the taking or selection, possessing or placing of a human by God would entail a 'division' followed by God's 'privileging' of the one among the many. Paul's contention is that God does not 'select' one as prized over another. God does not play favorites.

Those who were reputed to be 'something' added 'nothing' to Paul because God has favored no one. The *something* that they were reputed to possess and that Paul apparently lacked was, in the end, 'nothing'. Paul presumes that if they possessed 'something' that he did not possess, then in their meeting that 'something' would manifest itself and Paul would receive it from them. But those who were reputed to be *something* made no difference to him. They added nothing to him.

Paul's parenthetical comment suggests that if God did show partiality, if God had preferences and favorites, then those who enjoyed such selection would be something and could add something to Paul. But since God does not have favorites, does not show partiality, then those who were 'reputed' to enjoy God's preferment in fact do not! Their being *something* is an appearance or reputation that in the end is empty of significance.

If theistic selection and representation were possible for Paul, and at least one individual could be identified with God, and such privileged identification was not the product of human differentiation but God's selection, then Paul could not conclude as he does at 1 Cor. 1.29 that no human flesh might boast in the presence of God, or, as in the case at Gal. 2.6, that God shows no partiality.

The critical use of the foolish and weak and those of common birth as called by God to overcome the wise and powerful and those of noble birth does not lead to a reversal of fortune. Contrary to modern theologies of liberation, in which those devalued or marginalized come to enjoy elevated status as more pure, or having wisdom or knowledge, Paul's valua-

---

2. Henry Liddell and Robert Scott, revised and augmented by Henry Jones, *A Greek-English Lexicon, Ninth Edition with Supplements* (Oxford: Clarendon Press, 1940), p. 1103.

tion of the lowly is that they are identified as lowly in relation to the loftiness of their other.

This sense of differential equilibrium is, of course, quite formal. Each of the identities is the product of differentiation and strife. And when God chooses the lowly, their lowliness nullifies the strife that differentiates the stratifications in the theocratic hierarchy. It is not suggested that the lowly who are chosen to stand to critique and nullify the privileged now come to power. The 'call' of the Corinthians according to Paul is not to call for the redistribution of power and authority so that one group replaces or displaces another in the hierarchy. Rather, the call is to disestablish the structures of *sacred* power and authority. No one, no flesh, stands in the presence of—no one is face to face with—God. No one!

Identity and Strife in the Body of Christ

Fragment 53 ascribed to Heraclitus of Ephesus comes to mind: 'Strife is the father and king of all. Some it makes gods, others men; some slaves and others free.' That strife differentiates and yields identifications entails for Heraclitus that each of the identities differentiated enjoys no status as an identity except in opposition, in strife with its other. Thus, given that the various identifications are mutually originating, then they are also mutually dependent. Identification is differentiation. One might claim, playing upon fragment 53, that for Paul, since no human flesh enjoys the 'face', the presence and selection of God, there are no legitimate theocratic 'identifications'. Instead, strife makes some wise, others foolish; some noble, others common; some something, and others nothing.

1 Cor. 12.12-13 and Gal. 3.27-28 are two obvious texts in which Paul makes a great deal of the mutual dependency of opposite identifications upon one another and their mutual emptiness when united in Christ.

> [12]For just as the body is one and has many members, and all the members of the body, though many, are one body, so it is with Christ. [13]For by one spirit we were all baptized into one body—Jews or Greeks, slaves or free—and all were made to drink of one spirit (1 Cor. 12.12-13).[3]

3.   Lietzmann contends that the phrase 'whether Jewish or Greek' etc. disturbingly interrupts the course of the argument of 1 Cor. 12.12, the reason being, he asserts, that the intent of the section is about unity. But on his terms, v. 12 is about differences. While Conzelmann contends that Lietzmann misunderstands the intent of the passage, it is not very clear what Conzelmann takes that intent to be. See Hanz Conzelmann, *1 Corinthians* (Philadelphia: Fortress Press) p. 212 n. 14. As we shall see, Lietzmann is

[27]For as many of you as were baptized into Christ have put on Christ. [28]There is neither Jew nor Greek, there is neither slave nor free, there is neither male nor female; for you are all one in Christ Jesus (Gal. 3.27-28).[4]

In v. 13 from our first selection, just as the body is one and has many members, and just as all the members, though many, are one body, then the various differences existing in opposition to one another (Jews and Greeks, slaves and free) are baptized into one body. That is, Christ is *one body* into which the *many members* are baptized. The differences persist in their opposition as different members in one body. At first glance, it might appear that in Gal. 3.28 a variety of social distinctions is simply negated. 'There is *neither* Jew *nor* Greek, *neither* male *nor* female, *neither* slave *nor* free.' However, the passage concludes that all of these differences (the differences that were just declared to have been negated) are one in Christ. That is, 'for you are all one in Christ Jesus...' 'There is neither Jew nor Greek...slave nor free...male nor female...' That 'many are one' assumes there are many that are one, not that the 'differences' are simply no more in Christ.

The baptismal passages continue Paul's abolition (by means of a reversal that relativizes and displaces) of all 'claims to privilege' by any and all groups in the church.[5] The triple negation of Gal. 3.28 is not an annihilation of the differences into oneness. Instead, neither one nor the other of each set has a prerogative. Nor is one the origin of the other. The privileged and 'dis-privileged' identifications are presented in order that the construction and valuation of each is understood to be mutually dependent upon its opposite. And Paul accomplishes this not by rejecting the use of hierarchy by some appeal to the 'sameness' of the various differences but by asserting each contentious ranking of the differences in order to bring clarity as to their mutual dependency. What it means to be male is dependent upon what it means to be female. Differences persist. And the tension between opposites is seen as necessary for the construction of identification.

correct in his identification of the presence of difference and unity, but his conclusion as to its not fitting has more to do with his presupposition regarding the relationship of difference and unity than with the logic of the text.

4.   Biblical scholars commonly observe the strong similarities in the content, vocabulary and structure of the two passages. Many believe that the Epistles to the Corinthians and Galatians were written within the two-year period that Paul lived in Ephesus.

5.   See Rom. 2.25-29; 3.1-20; 4.9-12; 9.3-5; 10.2; Gal. 5.6; 6.15; 1 Cor. 7.19; Phil. 3.3.

Such a method of critique empties 'identification' of any theistic, privileged association and significance. Each and every identification is *always* and *already* dependent upon its opposite.

Derived from Greek *baptizō*, 'to baptize' means quite literally 'to dip', 'to immerse', 'to bury' in a liquid. In its preliturgical, pre-Christian usage, *baptizō* referred almost exclusively to 'dipping cloth in dye'.[6] Despite this dominant preliturgical, pre-Christian usage of *baptizō*, baptism came to be understood in the hermeneutical tradition of the institutional church as a ritual cleansing which purifies the person and signifies the 'entry' of the person being 'baptized' into the body of Christ. However, I believe that to conclude that this is the dominant meaning of baptism in the Pauline texts before us is mistaken. I argue that the verse at Gal. 3.27 plays heavily upon the preliturgical themes of 'immersion and dye'.

> For as many of you as were baptized into Christ *have put on* Christ [*my emphasis*] (Gal. 3.27).

First, 'have put on' is offered in translation of *enedusasthe*. From the root *enduō*, meaning 'to put on, to envelop in, to hide in' and thus commonly 'to clothe', *enedusasthe* is an Aorist middle (2nd Aorist) indicative, 'you hid yourselves' or 'you clothed yourselves'. Thus the verse might read:

> For as many of you as were baptized into Christ hid yourselves/clothed yourselves in Christ.

There is a sense in v. 27 that in being dipped in (immersed in) the anointed, one envelops/dyes/covers oneself with the anointed. All who immerse themselves in Christ have endowed (*enduō*) themselves with Christ. They are steeped in Christ; they are soaked, saturated, stained. Paul makes much of the notion of being 'covered' in Christ throughout the corpus of his Epistles.[7]

In our reading of Gal. 3.27 we noted that *enedusasthe* is an Aorist middle (2nd Aorist) indicative which denotes a self-reflexive action. Anyone who is baptized in Christ has 'endowed one's own self with Christ'. Christ is neither the agent who baptizes nor the one who 'endowed'. Christ is that into which one is baptized and with which one endowed oneself in the immersion, but Christ enjoys no causal status in the event. Christ is the medium, the place in which baptism happens.

---

6.   Liddell-Scott, *Lexicon*, pp. 305-306. Baptisia or Baphia names a genus of plant of the pea family used to dye cloth. See Klein, *Dictionary*, p. 147.

7.   Rom. 13.12, 14; 1 Cor. 15.53-54; 2 Cor. 5.2-4; Gal. 3.27.

In the Pauline texts, 'baptism in Christ' is not the means by which some hidden characteristic held in common by various groups is disclosed. Baptism is not the restoration of some previously hidden quality, the washing away of that which covers and conceals some common nature shared by all. Baptism in Christ is an occasion of closure, concealment and disclosure that gathers and preserves those in opposition as opposites. Those in opposition are preserved, sheltered and covered/baptized/dyed in Christ. Their differences are gathered in their differentiation and are preserved as differences. And those in opposition are said to be one in Christ because they were immersed or concealed in Christ. Once immersed in Christ, those who were baptized in Christ are said to emerge saturated, dyed, steeped and soaked. Dipped in their differentiation, they are gathered by the covering of Christ that dyes them all.

It is not uncommon for interpreters to question whether the baptismal passages are symbolic expressions about the identity of Christ or about the salvation of members who unite with the church. For reasons that will become evident below, I argue that the passages are about neither the identity of Christ or about membership in the church.

In 1 Cor. 12.19 Paul asks, 'If all were a single organ, where would the body be?' For Paul, the body of Christ is not a *member*; Christ is not one among the many but is the meeting place in which the differences gather. The body is an *assembly* of the many in which differences are united. But the body is not another one of the members that assemble the rest into a social coherence. In 1 Cor. 12.14-21 Paul raises a variety of questions that serve to illustrate how unthinkable it would be to confuse a member with the body. Who would mistakenly confuse an ear or an eye for the body? It is my contention that Paul's examples serve as counterexamples to any simplistic *identification* of the body of Christ. From the superior to the inferior, the honorable to the dishonorable, all members of the body are *members of the body*, and are not to be confused with the body. Therefore it would be unthinkable for anyone to remove the hand from the body because it is not the head, or to cut off a less honorable member because it is not presentable.

[24b]But God has so adjusted the body, giving the greater honor to the inferior part, [25]that there may be no *discord* [*schisma*] in the body, but that the members may have the same care for one another. [26]If one member suffers, all suffer together; if one member is honored, all rejoice together (1 Cor. 12.24b-26).

Here again Paul presents the differentiations between inferior and superior played out earlier in 1 Cor. 1.28. Those members who seek their own advantage, forgetting that they are mere members, seek to be superior by rendering others their inferiors and cause discord in the body. And like the foolish and weak and those of common birth mentioned in 1 Cor. 1.26-28, God granted the inferior part the greater honor in order to overcome the discord, in order to negate the hierarchical ranking of the members of the body.

One of the points that Paul makes with his use of the analogy of the human body is that the social body of Christ is not an identity but a peculiar assembly. Thus, since Christ is not an identity, no member of the body may identify with Christ. Instead, Christ atones those who are mutually differentiated: male–female, slave–free, Jew–Gentile, wise–foolish, powerful–weak, of noble birth–commoner.

Shortened from the phrase 'at one', to *atone* names the activity of gathering together those who differ.[8] Given Paul's use of the body/members analogy, members may be atoned *to one another*, but the body of Christ is not a member to which a member may be atoned. Individuals are not 'at-oned' *with* Christ. Instead, those who are in opposition to one another are 'at-oned' with one another *in* Christ.

Anyone who claims identification with Christ is mistaken not simply with respect to their own status as a member, but fails to properly differentiate Christ from the members of his body. Identification with Christ is not only boastful but, given Paul's conception of the relation of the body and its members, such identification with Christ would be incomprehensible. A member would never be mistakenly identified as a body. And thus no member should be mistakenly identified with Christ.

Towards the end of 1 Corinthians 4, Paul returns yet again to the three sets of distinctions introduced at 1.26.

> [10] We are fools for Christ's sake, but you are wise in Christ. We are weak, but you are strong. You are held in honor, but we are in disrepute. [11] To the present hour we hunger and thirst, we are ill-clad and buffeted and homeless, [12]and we labor, working with our own hands. When reviled, we bless; when persecuted, we endure; [13]when slandered, we try to conciliate; we have become, and are now, as the refuse of the world, the off-scouring of all things. [14] I do not write this to make you ashamed, but to admonish you as my beloved children (1 Cor. 4.10-14).

Those of noble birth (*eugeneis*) are depicted in 4.10 as *endoxoi*, 'glorious,

---

8.   Klein, *Dictionary*, p. 123.

honored'. And the ignoble are *athimoi*, 'dishonored, despised, insignificant or unattractive in appearance'.

The all-too-common translations of these verses fail to express the ritual significance of the designations commonly rendered *refuse* and the *off-scouring*. It is not simply that 'we have become, and are now, as the *refuse* of the world', in the modern sense of the garbage of the world which is the by-product of production and consumption consigned to incineration, landfills and ocean dumping. Instead, the refuse of the world (*perikathar-mata tou kosmou*) designates the waste that removes and is removed in the rites of purification.[9]

We have become and now are, as the expiation of the world, that which accomplishes the purification, that which by virtue of bonding with the impurity may draw the impurity away. 'Expiate' is from Latin *expiāt-*, whose verbal form *expiāre* means 'to make satisfaction'.[10] The root *piāre* 'to seek to appease (by sacrifice)' is related to *pius* ('devout'), from which we derive 'pious'. To be devout or pious designates to have sought and attained purification from guilt and pollution by religious acts. Thus the expiation is that which in drawing the impurity to itself becomes the vessel or means by which the impurity is carried away. The one expiated—the one cleansed and purified—attains piety through the one who becomes the expiation, the impious one who carries away that which desecrates.

Once the scum is removed what is left is free of impurity. Paul's self-declaration, 'we have become, and are now, as the refuse of the world, the off-scouring of all things', is a declaration that 'we have become and now are as the impure of the world which purifies'. We have become the scape-goats for your purification. Our identification as the 'scum', the 'desecration', is to your purification, your benefit.

Paul immediately states the intent of his severe critique: 'I do not write this to make you ashamed, but to admonish you as my beloved children' (1 Cor. 4.14). Paul's presumption is that upon reading the preceding verses the reader should feel ashamed in hearing that Paul and others are to be identified as the refuse of the world, the very scum of things which, once removed, makes everyone else clean.

The issue is not whether the Corinthians are responsible for the identifications. Paul's point is that those who seek their own advantage assert that with the purging, removal and departure of Paul the community might attain purification. Thus the identification of Paul as the imperfection

9. Liddell-Scott, *Lexicon*, p. 1375.
10. *OED*, III, p. 433.

would suggest that Paul is the desecrating scum. But Paul's point is more critical. He suggests that if it is the case that he is the scum, then he is also the means for their purification. Others benefit from the disadvantage of another. And in this case the Corinthians should be ashamed, because those who seek their own advantage seek their own advantage at Paul's expense. 'For though you have countless guides in Christ, you do not have many fathers. For I became your father in Christ Jesus through the gospel. I urge you, then, be imitators of me' (1 Cor. 4.15-16).

Paul's thinking brings clarity to the mechanics of expiation. A few are identified as the agents of pollution. Others are impure to the extent that they associate with those who are pollutants. The removal of the pollutants renders everyone else clean. Thus, the differentiation between the pure and the impure is brought to nothing by noting the utter dependency of those who are identified as pure upon those who are identified as impure.

Atoning

I argue that Paul's conception of the community as the body of Christ is an extreme critique of the power and harm that the politics of theocracy foster and promote. Bringing identifications to nothing is not an eschatological annihilation. The unity of male and female, slave and free, Jew and Gentile, as well as wise and foolish, powerful and weak, those of noble birth and those of common birth, renders void all sacred identification. For *God shows no partiality and grants no privilege.* Instead, those who stand in opposition may come to 'at-one-ment' in the body of Christ.

Paul's critique of those who enjoy privilege, his contention that the foolish nullify the wise and the lowly empty the lofty, serves to overcome the production of sacred identification by negating the religious value of the strife that produced the various *identifications.* In making evident the dependency of the advantaged upon the disadvantaged, Paul makes evident the very means by which some establish and maintain their claims to sacred privilege. Those who make claims to God's presence in their lives by virtue of their wisdom, power and noble birth are assessed by Paul as boastful.

The unity of those of noble birth who were reported to be 'something' and those of common birth who were presumed to be 'nothing' yielded *nothing.* For when things that 'are' and things that 'are not' are united, then those that 'are not' bring those that 'are' to nothing. When opposing identifications are united, the differentiation, and therefore their identities as opposites, are nullified. God's election of the foolish and weak and those of common birth brings something to nothing, thereby silencing the boastful claims of those who contend that they enjoy the presence and partiality of God. In the unity of the foolish and the wise, the weak and the powerful, the well-born and the common, something and nothing, there comes to be an *emptying* in which there is neither the foolish nor the wise, neither the weak nor the powerful, neither the well-born nor the common, neither something nor nothing.

In all other passages in Paul's letters written in the period of his life when he lived in Ephesus that address the unity of opposites, the location or place of such a gathering is said to be Christ or the Lord.[11] Thus I contend that the unity of the wise and foolish, powerful and weak, and those of noble and common birth is to be understood as occurring in Christ. The wise–foolish, powerful–weak and noble–common birth are references by Paul to members in the body of Christ.

Paul's critique of theocratic privilege yields the social equality not of individuals *free* from identification but the equality of opposing identifications. I will have more to say about this later, but for now it is important to note that Paul makes no appeal to the equality of individuals beyond *identifications*. For instance, the real/appearance distinction is not played out in terms of the real self beyond the social self, or the true individual beyond one's social identifications. Paul's claim that God shows no partiality, and so brings to nothing those reported to be something, does not substantiate the equality of individuals in the cosmos (*pace* the Stoics). Paul's critique of theocratic inequality asserts the unity of opposing identifications without much to say about what (if anything) of a self, autonomy or the individual—or whatever—remains. In so being empty and dependent, the opposing identifications are reconciled; they are 'at-oned', at one with one another in the body of Christ. 'There is neither Jew nor Greek, there is neither slave nor free, there is neither male nor female; for you are all one in Christ Jesus.' For Paul the identifications are empty and therefore exhaustively dependent upon their opposite. In Christ, identifications are simultaneously emptied and reconciled with their opposite. The occasion of the simultaneous bringing to nothing of identifications and the mutual originating and dependence of opposing identifications is named the *ecclesia*. Since all lack sacred identification, no member of the body of Christ may boast of standing in the presence of God. Instead, those who are 'at-oned' are gathered together.

Paul's encounter with those who make sacred boasts goes beyond simple

---

11. 1 Cor. 11.11-12, 12.12-13; Gal. 3.28.

criticism. I contend that Paul sets out in the letters composed during his period in Ephesus a critical means of overcoming sacred identification and disestablishing emergent Christian theocracy. Paul's critique is extreme in that he attempts to *empty* all identifications with God and the Lord, in fact, to deconstruct the making of identification, so that all identity comes to be assessed as a construction in the process of social differentiation. As such, all sacred identifications do not enjoy reference; they do not refer to anything sacred but are the products, the exhaustive outcome, of mundane political and social differentiation that is wrought by those seeking their own advantage.

For Paul, identification is exhaustively yielded by differentiation. An identity is what it is in differentiation from its other, *and nothing more.* Therefore differentiated identifications are mutually originating and mutually dependent upon one another.

Paul's extreme critique has extreme social implications for theocracy. Since all identifications are the product of differentiation, then each and every identification is mutually originating and mutually dependent upon its other. Therefore, in terms of social differentiations, opponents are already always dependent upon one another. The strife that separates one from the other assumes a powerful relation between the opponents, which yields identification. If sacred selection and representation were possible for Paul, and at least one individual could be said to be selected to represent God, and their selection were not the product of mundane human differentiation, then Paul could not conclude that no human flesh might boast in the presence of God. Paul's use of the unity of opposition to overcome the various hierarchies by overcoming power with weakness, wisdom with foolishness and noble birth with common—if not scandalous—pedigree leads not to the establishment or simple reversal of fortune based on a realignment of sacred identification with the foolish and weak and those of common birth. Instead, assuming the mutual originating and mutual dependence of the opponents, the hierarchical social structure decomposes when privilege is emptied of *significance*. The wise, powerful and those of noble birth no more signify God than do the foolish and weak and those of common birth. Instead, opponents are opponents because of the strife between themselves, not because one side represents God and the other does not. And so Paul's extreme critique brings to nothing those who counted themselves something, because on Paul's terms all along they 'stood for' or 'signified' *nothing!* God brings all 'sacred' edifices 'to nothing'.

The political implications of Paul's critiques are innovative. For Paul, the mutual origination and mutual dependency of opponents overcome theocracy. The hierarchy of persons in a theocracy wherein some represent God and are identified with God while others are not is critically dismantled and displaced by the assembly of members atoned with one another in the body of Christ. Hierarchy is deconstructed.

If scholars seem fairly certain that the assumed readership in the Corinthian congregation is more or less adequately portrayed as not wise or powerful or of noble birth in 1 Cor. 1.26, the question remains (and the debate continues) 'For whom were the lowly and common Corinthians a nemesis?' Paul's stated intent to bring to nothing, to empty the means by which some human beings boast that they enjoy the presence of God, would bring to an end the means by which some established their power and authority among Christians. But to whom do the allusions to wisdom, power and noble birth actually refer?

When Paul critiqued those who identified themselves as the body of Christ rather than as members equal with other members *within* the body of Christ, the question is 'To whom is Paul making reference?' Who would—in Paul's terms—boastfully identify themselves with Christ rather than accept their equality with other members of the body?

The letters of Paul are commonly interpreted as prescribing and supporting theocratic authority. In Part I of this book, De/Constructing the Church, I argue that Paul critiques the theocratic authority of the family and disciples who are members of the 'household of the Lord'. Paul's critique proceeds by denying the veracity of any identification with God or the Lord, for all identifications are produced by strife, and God shows no partiality to persons. Therefore, since no one may boast that God privileges him or her, no one has sacred authority. The theme that opposing identifications are mutually produced by strife is played out in a variety of texts in the Corinthian and Galatian Epistles. All opposing identifications that might be employed to warrant power and authority among Christians (e.g. Jew–Gentile, male–female, slave–free, pious–impious) are merely produced by and are dependent upon differentiation made by those seeking their own advantage. Paul's conception of the community as the body of Christ, in which opposites are drawn together, empties identification of sacred significance. No member, no one, is to be identified with the body of Christ.

In Part II, De/Secration, I offer a structural analysis of 2 Cor. 6.11–7.3 in which I argue that 6.14–7.1 (which presents the convictions that those who believe themselves to be God's sacred temple are to seek sacred

perfection by disassociation from those who are desecrations, in fulfillment of the promise that they may become the 'sacred family' of God) is
an extended quotation from a letter sent by a faction in Corinth to Paul
which critiques Paul's ministry of reconciliation as a compromise with
Satan. Paul includes the extended quotation in order to make explicit his
critique of their boastful self-identification as the sacred temple of God.
Those who seek sacred perfection in order to become the temple/family of
God are therefore the agents of corruption who identify, exclude and expel
others as desecrations.

Part I

DE/CONSTRUCTING THE CHURCH

Chapter 2

De/Credo

Introduction

To suggest that there is an intimate association between 'creeds' and 'belonging' may be to overstate the obvious. That Christian communities express with varying degrees of clarity and weight their convictions in terms of 'beliefs' or 'propositions' is an adequate description. Such 'creeds' are often assumed to be true by the laity and just as often enforced and protected as true by Christian social and institutional leaders. In fact, for many centuries, particularly among Reformation Protestants, creedal formulations have served as prescriptions for proper Christian belief and thought, indeed sometimes serving as sentry at the threshold of the church. It is often presumed that social integrity is linked to the coherence and universal acceptance of the primary convictions, beliefs and/or practices of a community. The degree of social integrity may be linked not just to the frequency of creedal presentation but to the degree of conformity in thought and practice within the community. Significant differences of convictions, beliefs and/or practices threaten social integrity. In short, differences of conviction, belief and/or practices denote different communities.

The creedal process proceeds in a two-fold manner by simultaneously pruning and selecting convictions and beliefs. Convictions and beliefs that are assessed to be improper are discarded while convictions and beliefs that are assessed to be proper are selected and allowed to flourish. But the process is not motivated by a desire for the flourishing of diverse convictions and beliefs. The process is one that seeks to diminish the options and divergent convictions, practices and beliefs in the development of a limited set that serve to provide a boundary and therefore delineate the identity of 'the church'.

Seen in this light, the concern to formulate a creed, to clearly and forthrightly state the 'beliefs' that are proper and true for Christians, and to hold that credo is necessary to insure that the church is the representative of Christ on earth, is a master narrative of communal Christianity. Groups and individuals may associate or disassociate themselves over their agreement or disagreements regarding the content of the beliefs, but it is assumed that credo is necessary. For what good or true Christian would admit that they believe in 'nothing' or that a statement of faith is inconsequential? Or that convictions or beliefs do not matter and have no bearing on a person's salvation?

'I belong to Paul, I to Apollos, I to Cephas, I to Christ.'

In the early verses of 1 Corinthians are traces of what have been assessed to be 'creeds'. While there is much to explore and debate as to when these 'self-declarations' were understood to be creeds by those who reportedly uttered them or by the author of the letter who recorded them, it is nonetheless the case that the phrases (quoted above) at 1 Cor. 1.12 have enjoyed the designation as early creeds for at least two centuries, if not considerably longer.

Interpretations of the text may differ over the status of the four 'creeds' with respect to which credo is proper, but the assumption is that the divisions within the community are both expressed and influenced by the multiplicity of 'creeds' and accompanying diverse social alignments. The appeal in v. 10 for the community 'to agree', 'to be united in the same mind and the same judgment and that there be no dissensions' is commonly read to be a call for theological and confessional agreement. The practice has been to string together v. 10 with verse fragment 12e:

> [10]I appeal to you, brethren, by the name of our Lord Jesus Christ, that all of you agree and that there be no dissensions among you, but that you be united in the same mind and the same judgment. [12e]I belong to Christ (1 Cor. 1.10, 12e).

The interpretive conviction has been to assess that the divisions in the community will be overcome when all Christians unite in the credo, 'I (belong) to Christ'. The 'divisions' in the Corinthian congregation are the product of groups who deviate or dissent from the appropriate Christian confession, which is also a statement of social identification: 'I belong to Christ.' Those who do not share the common creed 'I belong to Christ' foreclose the possibility of the community being united in the same mind and the same judgment. So when Paul writes, 'What I mean is that each one of you says, "I belong to Paul", "I to Apollos", "I to Cephas", or "I to Christ"' (1 Cor. 1.12), interpreters commonly assume that a community that makes multiple creeds holds multiple commitments and is divided against itself, thus rendering social unity impossible. The contention that the four self-declarations stand in exclusive relationship to one another and represent distinct factions has been a frequent assessment since the mid-nineteenth century. 'I belong to Paul' is understood as an exclusive declaration that forecloses holding allegiances to Apollos, Cephas or Christ. In turn, each and every declaration has been assessed as being a 'slogan' which stands in disjunction from all the rest. The solution to the divisiveness is for all Corinthians and, by extension, all Christians to make a single confession of faith. 'A house divided cannot stand', as the saying goes. It is all too commonly assumed in the history of Christian thought and practice that a Christian community shares a '*common* discourse'[1] and, further, that creed is necessary to foster social solidarity. 'Uncommon discourses' are assumed to differentiate one community of faith from another. Different discourses, different creeds, differentiate communities. And a community that differs over its creed will soon divide into separate communities.

Confidence in credo conformity to issue communal integrity is a powerful and persuasive force that is not limited to modernity, Christian communities or, for that matter, western civilization. A common assessment has been that Paul offered or accepted the fourth and final self-declaration as the solution to the problem of multiple confessions in Corinth. This interpretation goes something like so: when all the parties in Corinth cease their divisive self-declarations and confess only 'I belong to Christ', then the Christian community of Corinth will be of the same mind and the same judgment. Further, when a Christian community stands in a proper relation to Christ, then the community will be free of internal communal strife. Therefore a community that experiences internal strife is not, as a whole, in a proper relation to Christ.

Conzelmann weakens the strong sense of division between the four credos as 'slogans' that represent a divisive faction in the Corinthian Christian community. He suggests that the larger Christian community is 'composed' of different smaller groups, noting that 'The word *schisma* (translated in 1.10 "that there be no dissensions among you") ... implies in itself merely a neutral statement of the existence of divisions.'[2] So, Con-

---

1.　The 'shared discourse' might be a common confession, or a creedal theological formulation, or a liturgy, or a ritual, or a canon of texts, or an 'interpretation' of the canon.

2.　Conzelmann, *1 Corinthians*, p. 31. 'These are not cases of personal quarrels but of differences in the *attitude* of the individual to the community. The word *hekastos*,

zelmann maintains that while a significant portion of the community had split into parties, the larger community was not dissolved by the time of Paul's correspondence.[3] The differences between the parties are not so great as to constitute mutually exclusive systems of doctrine that are in contention in Corinth. For Conzelmann, the community continues to enjoy social integrity because everyone in the Corinthian Christian community declares in the end the *traditional creed*: 'I (belong) to Christ'. Those who declare an allegiance to Paul, Apollos or Cephas could all agree that their 'principle allegiance' is to Christ.[4] So, for Conzelmann, Paul 'can discuss the party system comprehensively, without entering into differences between groups, because the community still exists as a whole and *all the groups recognize the traditional creed*'.[5]

Differing with Conzelmann's contention that the differences between the three social groups expressed by the first three slogans were secondary to the primacy of the fourth slogan ('I belong to Christ') and therefore not mutually exclusive, Robert Funk contends that Paul nowhere attempts to directly refute the various theological doctrines of the Corinthian factions, but asserts the word of the cross over against all theology.[6] Taking his cue from Ernst Käsemann, Funk contends that the confessions of allegiance to Paul, Apollos and Cephas are *theological* alliances, which he associates

"each", must not of course be pressed to the effect that every single member has associated himself with one of the groups mentioned.' Thus, on his terms, it would be a mistake 'to render *schisma* as "breach" and *katartizō* as "repair"' (my emphasis). Conzelmann, *1 Corinthians*, pp. 32-33.

3.   'It does not mean the existence of different systems of doctrine. Paul indeed hopes that unity will be restored as a result of his exhortation. The split into groups has not yet led to the dissolution of the community; they celebrate the Lord's Supper together (11.17ff), and Paul can address his letter to the whole community.' Conzelmann, *1 Corinthians*, p. 32.

4.   Inclusive interpreters have employed the saying 'I belong to Christ' to further the incorporation and tolerance of peoples of diverse cultures and races. If Christ is single, if Christ is the true center of the church, then all who 'belong' to Christ are 'one'. Those who 'belong' to Christ form a society with a center. The essential relation is between each individual to the center, to Christ. But what about the relation of individuals to one another? In the inclusive Christian tradition, which employs the slogan, the proper response to the diversity and differentiation among individual Christians is to be one of tolerance. Beyond the primary relation of the individual to Christ, all other relations are secondary.

5.   Conzelmann, *1 Corinthians*, p. 34. My emphasis.

6.   Robert W. Funk, *Language, Hermeneutics and Word of God* (New York: Harper & Row, 1966), p. 275.

with the characterization in v. 17 of eloquent wisdom (*sophia logou*). For Funk, the difference between the first three confessions is that they are theological, whereas the fourth confession is 'the word of the cross', which Funk assumes is *not* a theological proposition. Thus the word of the cross ('I belong to Christ'), taken to be a nontheological confession, enjoys an exclusive status relative to the three competing *theological* confessions. Funk's Paul is a critic of theology.

Despite subtle and not-so-subtle differences, traditional interpreters (Conzelmann and Funk, for that matter) assume that there is a division between the fourth and final quoted statement from the preceding three declarations. Various assessments of the division range from the contention that the first three are heretical claims that must be abandoned, and that those who made such claims must assent to the fourth and final confessional proposition, to the contention that the first three slogans represent subgroups in the community who would also make the fourth and final confession. Those who hold this division between the first three and the fourth credo all maintain that the status of the fourth and final proposition 'I belong to Christ' is an appropriate Christian credo or slogan. The association of vv. 10 and 12e is assessed to be a scriptural warrant for the predominance of creedal propositions in Christian social thought and practice.

Critical biblical scholars have been hesitant to differentiate the fourth credo from the previous set of three. Many historical-critical readers affirm 'there actually was a group at Corinth that rallied around the name of Christ in opposition to those who rallied around the names of Paul, Cephas and Apollos'.[7] Influenced by Baur's Hegelian formalism, many assessed that the 'Christ party' was a group of Judaizers or Christian Jews. Others identified the 'Christ party' with Corinthian 'enthusiasts', pneumatic Gnostics. Still others identified the fourth credo as a rhetorical flourish declared by Paul to counter and conclude the series of three divisive credos.

I argue that the division commonly made between the first three confessional statements and the final confessional statement is inadequate. Secondly, I reject the conclusion that the fourth and final slogan 'I belong to Christ' is assessed by Paul to be an appropriate proposition of Christian conviction. I concur with Collins when he notes that there is 'no indication in the letter that there were three or four distinct factions *in the community*

---

7.   Raymond F. Collins, *First Corinthians* (Sacra Pagina Series, VII; Collegeville, MN: Liturgical Press, 1999), p. 72.

at Corinth, each with its own theological point of view, behavioral pattern, and putative authority'.[8] But I disagree with Collins's contention that Paul's argument appears to be addressed to the community as a whole and that Paul nowhere directly addresses the factions associated with the slogans. Thirdly, I argue that Paul directly and forthrightly calls the final slogan into question. In fact, I will argue that the focus of Paul's critique in the passage from vv. 10-13 is the self-declaration 'I belong to Christ'. And finally, I argue that those who are identified in 1.26-31 as being of 'noble birth' (whom those of common, if not scandalous, ancestry in Corinth bring to nothing) and the declaration 'I belong to Christ' are references to the same contentious faction. But I also argue that the faction that declared 'I belong to Christ' is not a group in Corinth!

The Question of Belonging

egō men eimi Paulou, egō de Apollō, egō de Kēpha, egō de Christou.
I belong to Paul, I to Apollo, I to Cephas, I to Christ.

There is no clear division evident between the first three and the fourth proclamations in the text of 1 Cor. 1.12 (quoted above). If there is a clear grammatical differentiation between any of the four phrases, it is between the first and the last three. The first phrase is an independent, complete sentence: *egō men eimi Paulou*, 'I belong to Paul'. The subsequent phrases are grammatically incomplete without the transitiveness of the verb (*eimi*) from the first phrase to the subsequent phrases. In fact, the four are strung together by the practice of carrying the verb from the first phrase to the second, third and fourth. If the fourth and final self-identification were to be differentiated from the preceding phrases, then would we expect there to be some indication, some differentiation, between the third and the fourth phrases? For example, the author might have emphasized the fourth self-declaration by an emphatic claim, like *egō men eimi Christou*. Or, as Collins has suggested, 'one might have expected Paul to have employed a stronger adversative "but" (*alla*), but he does not'.[9]

It is also important to note that the second, third and fourth phrases include the particle *de* as the middle term between the subject and the object of each of the sets of self-identification. Fan argued that the particle *de* is a negative conjunctive which marks an opposing or adversative

8. Collins, *First Corinthians*, p. 73.
9. Collins, *First Corinthians*, p. 72.

force, especially in letters. Hurd contends that Paul employs the particle *de* several times at just those turning points in 1 Corinthians that take on an adversarial posture.[10] In 11.3, when Paul begins to quote from the letter to him in which he represents the position of a Corinthian faction with which he will take issue, he inserts the particle *de* to mark to the reader his opposition. I argued that the particle *de* marked Paul's opposition to the contention that God is the head (source and ruler) of Christ, Christ is the head (source and ruler) of man, and man is the head (source and ruler) of woman. At 11.11-12 Paul offered a counter position in which man and women were cooriginating and codepending on one another. The causal/political hierarchy quoted at 11.3 was so at odds with Paul's own thinking that he explicitly marked their adversarial character from their introduction at 11.2, as well as again and again at each of the source/ruler sets.

It is my judgment that Paul is responsible for the inclusion of the negative particle *de* in the second position of the second, third and fourth self-declarations in 1.12. The purpose of so marking the quotations is to tip off the Corinthian reader that Paul will take issue with each and every one of those quotations. Paul's marking his critical assessment of the last three quoted phrases does not suggest that the fourth and last phrase is to be differentiated from those that precede it.

Mitchell is convincing when she argues that the common practice among critical biblical scholars of contending 'that the phrases in 1.12 mirror common formulae of political self-identification in antiquity'[11] is unsubstantiated.[12] The formula, reports Mitchell, composed of the personal pronoun + *eimi* (or eclipsed) + genitive of a proper name, is nowhere to be found as an ancient *political* slogan.

> In ancient political parlance one did refer to 'the people of someone' (*ēmeris tinos*) or 'the people around someone' (*oi peri tina*), but neither of these nominal phrases is a political slogan. As much as these phrases rightly point to the dependency of a follower upon a leader, that is all they can show. They do not supply formal parallels to Paul's statement in 1 Cor. 1.12.[13]

---

10. In *A Post-Patriarchal Christology*, I pointed out that the particle *de* occurs four times in 11.2 and 3, as well as in vv. 5, 6, 12a, 15 and 16.

11. Margaret Mitchell, *Paul and the Rhetoric of Reconciliation* (Louisville, KY: Westminster / John Knox Press), p. 83.

12. Mitchell, *Paul*, pp. 83-86.

13. Mitchell, *Paul*, p. 84.

Mitchell continues, 'The absence of this formula in our extant historical writings, a considerable corpus of material, is significant, and casts doubt on the view that these share a common *form* of political sloganeering.'[14] She concludes, 'That Paul interprets to the Corinthians the "slogans" as self-pronouncements, not of self-determined politicos, but of children and slaves' is shown definitely in 3.1-4, 6.19-20 and especially 7.23. Mitchell's point is that the formula is not part of the *political* rhetoric of identification but is employed in or with reference to *domestic* identification. The formula conveys both that one 'belongs' to a particular household and/or family, and that the one who makes the self-declaration is inferior in rank or status to the named person in the household and/or family order. So, with respect to 1 Corinthians, Mitchell concludes that the assumption by many biblical interpreters that the formula was a secular political slogan that was employed by members of the Corinthian community to convey their religious political alignments with Paul, Apollos and Cephas is inadequate.

Given Mitchell's convincing argument, I suggest that we consider the following translations of the four phrases of self-declaration:

'I am a slave to Paul', 'I am (a slave) to Apollos', 'I am (a slave) to Cephas', 'I am (a slave) to Christ'.

Or

'I am a child of Paul', 'I am (a child) of Apollos', 'I am (a child) of Cephas', 'I am (a child) of Christ'.

Or more generally

'I am of the household of Paul', 'I am (of the household) of Apollos', 'I am (of the household) of Cephas', 'I am (of the household) of Christ'.

Or more particularly

'I am of the family of Paul', 'I am (of the family) of Apollos', 'I am (of the family) of Cephas', 'I am (of the family) of Christ'.

If we keep to the traditional assessment of the four quotations which assesses that the first three self-declarations are unacceptable declarations and that the final self-declaration is appropriate, then those in Corinth who profess that they were a slave, or child, or member of the household or family of Paul, Apollos or Cephas are understood to be making divisive declarations, in response to which Paul asserts that the proper self-decla-

14. Mitchell, *Paul*, p. 88.

ration is 'I am a slave, or child, or member of the household or family of Christ'. In concert with the common, established assessment of the status of the four verses, Mitchell assumes that the final self-pronouncement is offered by Paul as a proper formula that serves to resolve the division within the Corinthian community.

But if there is no trace of a Greco-Roman political slogan constructed in the formula of a personal pronoun plus *eimi* (or eclipsed) and genitive of a proper name for a faction in Corinth to imitate, as Mitchell claims, then we might raise the queries: 'How would making such *domestic* claims benefit the person or persons making the self-identification with Paul, Apollos, Cephas or Christ?' 'Who would benefit *politically* from being a family member or domestic servant/slave of one of the named persons?' 'How would making such *domestic* assertions contribute to the schism of the community?' 'Who would want to formulate their associations in these ways?' And, finally, 'Who would benefit from such *domestic* rhetoric in emergent Christian communities?'

Let me state that I do not assess that the immediate source of the formula (personal pronoun + *eimi* [or eclipsed] + genitive of a proper name) was a faction in which individuals declared themselves belonging as slaves, or children or as members of the household or family of Paul, Apollos or Cephas. Instead, I argue that the source of the formula was a faction that is quoted by Paul as having asserted, 'I belong to Christ'.

Questioning the Authority of Belonging

The first negative rhetorical question in 1 Cor. 1.13 reads: *memeristai ho Christos?* The root of *memeristai, merizō,* conveys the sense of 'to divide' as in 'to separate'. But *merizō* differs from the English term 'divide' in a number of significant ways. If I *divide* two people in a fight, I separate them from one another. However, if I *divide* my meal with my children, it is true that I 'separate' the food as a unit into 'portions', but I also 'distribute' the meal between my offspring, with each receiving an 'allocation' or 'share' of the 'divided' whole. Whether the term *divides* means exclusively 'to separate' or both 'to separate and to distribute' is often context-dependent. Likewise, *merizō* conveys a spectrum of meanings, such as 'to divide, distribute, split up the amount, make a division; assign a part, allot, allocate, bestow'; and even 'to sever' or 'to cast off', depending on the context.[15]

15. Liddell-Scott, *Lexicon*, p. 1103.

The term *merizō* occurs a total of 14 times in the New Testament. In the RSV, *merizō* is translated twice as 'apportion', twice as 'assign', and ten times as 'divide'. At Rom. 12.3 ('each according to the measure of faith which God has assigned him') and 1 Cor. 7.17 ('Only let every one lead the life which the Lord has assigned to him, and in which God has called him'), *merizō* is translated as 'to assign', as in something having been allocated or accredited to one by the Lord or God. At 2 Cor. 12.13 ('But we will not boast beyond limit, but will keep to the limits God has apportioned us, to reach even to you') and in the contested Epistle Heb. 7.2 ('and to him Abraham apportioned a tenth part of everything'), *merizō* conveys a sense of distribution, dealing out, apportioning of something to someone, and clearly not the limited sense of division as simple separation. Six of the ten instances in which *merizō* is translated 'divide' in the RSV occur in the parallels at Mt. 12.25-26 and Mk 3.24-26, in which the sense of 'divide' is clearly evident. However, even in these instances *merizō* conveys the sense of *distribution*, in that a house or kingdom that is *divided* against itself is a house or kingdom that has been broken into components; the assets and commitments have been *distributed* out, and are now in competition or conflict with one another. In such instances, the assets of the formerly complete house or kingdom have been distributed and are now turned against one another.[16] At Mk 6.41 ('he divided the two fish among them all') and Lk. 12.13 ('bid my brother divide the inheritance'), *merizō* conveys a clear sense of distribution or allocation in conjunction with division.[17]

The two remaining instances in which *merizō* is translated as 'divide' occur in 1 Cor. 1.13; 7.34. At 1 Cor. 7.33-34 ([33]'but the married man is anxious about worldly affairs, how to please his wife, [34]and his interests are divided') the anxious married man's interests are not simply separate but *distributed* between worldly affairs and the Lord.

Of the fourteen times *merizō* appears in the New Testament, five of the appearances occur in undisputed Pauline Epistles, and of those five occurrences, three are in 1 Corinthians, one in 2 Corinthians and one in Romans. In every instance in the Pauline corpus (including the contested

---

16. Mt. 12.25 'Every kingdom divided against itself'   Mk 3.24 'If a kingdom is divided against itself'
    Mt. 12.25 'house divided against itself will stand'   Mk. 3.25 'And if a house is divided against itself'
    Mt. 12.26 'Satan … is divided against himself'   Mk. 3.26 'If Satan … is divided, he cannot stand'

17. A more forthright sense of simple division as separation without distribution assigning or apportioning is better conveyed by the terms *diadidō* or *diamerizō*, or *diaireō* or *schēzō*.

Epistle to the Hebrews, but not 1 Cor. 1.13a, which we have yet to consider), and in every instance in the non-Pauline texts in the New Testament *merizō* conveys the sense of apportioning, allocating, assigning or bestowing in the division.[18] And yet, in the RSV, the only time these nuances of meaning are not suggested in translation is with respect to 1 Cor. 1.13a.

I think translators have been quick, maybe too quick, to accept a strong sense of to divide without distribution in translation of *memeristai* because of the common practice of translating *schismata* at v. 10 as 'divisions'. *schizō* commonly means 'to split, divide, separate, tear apart, tear off', with *schisma* meaning 'split, division, dissension, schism'.[19] *schizō* conveys a sense of to divide *without* a sense of distribution. While the choice to translate both *schismata* and *memeristai* in terms of 'division' and 'divide' provides the English translation with an enhanced sense of phonetic consistency based on the root 'div-', I judge that such a selection fails to elucidate the conceptual nuances that *merizō* may convey in this particular situation. So, I argue that such a limited rendering of *merizō* at 1 Cor. 1.13a as 'divide' or 'separate' without the accompanying sense of 'distribute' is inadequate.

Returning to the three negative rhetorical questions in v. 13, it is clear that the second and third questions elicit negative responses, which confront and critique the schisms within the Corinthian community that counter Paul's appeal for them to be of one mind and one judgment. However, as it is commonly interpreted, the question at v. 13a, 'Has Christ been divided?' would elicit an affirmative answer that *confirms* the problem of division in Corinth. 'Yes, the factions have divided Christ/the community'. So, on the common reading, the question at v. 13a and the answer

18. As regards Corinthians, *merizō* is used at 1 Cor. 1.13 (RSV selects the unfortunate translation 'Is Christ divided?'); 7.17 ('Only let every one lead the life which the Lord has assigned to him, and in which God has called him'); 7.33-34 ([33]but the married man is anxious about worldly affairs, how to please his wife, [34]and his interests are divided'); and 2 Cor. 12.13 ('But we will not boast beyond limit, but will keep to the limits God has apportioned us, to reach even to you'). In each instance there is a sense of division, but the division entails as well the distribution, dealing-out, assigning, apportioning of something to someone, and clearly not the sense of division conveyed by the terms *diadidō* or *diamerizō*, or *diaireō* or *schēzō*. The other Pauline epistle of interest here would be Rom. 12.3, where the sense is of assigning, and the pseudo-Pauline or contested epistle Heb. 7.2 ('and to him Abraham apportioned a tenth part of everything').

19. *schismē* means 'crack' or 'fissure'.

elicited neither confront nor critique the divisions in Corinth in a manner similar to the second and third negative rhetorical questions at v. 13b, c. Instead, the question as commonly translated ('Has Christ been divided?') simply confirms that there are divisions in the community, and that Christ has been divided by others.

Given that *merizō* conveys a variety of meanings associated with the sense of division with distribution, I suggest we consider the following options for translating *memeristai ho Christos?*

Has Christ been allocated?
Has Christ been distributed?
Has Christ been bestowed?
Has Christ been assigned?
Has Christ been portioned out?

While the customary English translation ('Has Christ been divided?') and the common interpretation of the question assume that something inappropriate has been done to the Christian community (which Paul conceives as the body of Christ) by those who declare their belonging to Paul, Apollos and Cephas, the relation of the first negative rhetorical question to the first three pronouncements of identification in v. 12 becomes difficult to understand when we take into account the range and nuances of meaning that the verb *merizō* suggests. How would belonging to Paul, Apollos or Cephas have allocated, distributed, assigned or portioned out Christ? And why would the sharing and distribution of 'Christ' be something with which Paul would take issue?

The common interpretive practice assumes that the verb *memeristai* is passive, and that Christ has been divided by others, by those who profess their 'belonging' to Paul, Apollos or Cephas, instead of by those who make proper confession: 'I belong to Christ.' The question at v. 13a is taken to be rhetorical and metaphorical. 'Has Christ been divided?' queries whether the body of Christ, the community, *has been divided by others.*

One of the difficulties I have with the common reading of the text is the presumption that the subject (Christ) is passive. The passive reading ('has been divided') of the verb (*memeristai)* works well with the common interpretation that assesses that what is at issue was the 'division' of Christ as community. However, the passive translation of *memeristai* does not work well with the sense of 'division' *with distribution or allocation.* Given Paul's characterization of the community in vv. 10-12, Christ's community in Corinth has been divided by various factions, each for their own purposes and gains. So, to read the verb *memeristai* in the passive voice,

'Has Christ been divided or allocated?' the reader would most likely read
the rhetorical question as eliciting a positive response: 'Yes, Christ has
been divided and distributed by those who make the various declarations of belonging.' But so translated and understood, the first rhetorical
question in v. 13 would be out of line with the two following *negative*
rhetorical questions.

While the grammatical practices that marked the middle voice were
fading from Greek texts by the beginning of the Christian era, nevertheless
the middle voice was expressed periphrastically primarily through the
passive voice. I demonstrated the usefulness of translating some passive or
middle voice verbs as middle voice periphrastic constructions (particularly
with regards to the reconciliation fragment of 2 Cor. 5.19).

There is only one other instance in which the term *memeristai*, a third
person singular, passive or middle voice perfect, occurs in the New
Testament besides 1 Cor. 1.13a. In 1 Corinthians 7 we read:

> [32]Now I want you to be free from anxieties. The unmarried man is anxious
> about the affairs of the Lord, how to please the Lord; [33]but the married man
> is anxious about worldly affairs, how to please his wife, [34]and his interests
> are divided [*memeristai*]. And the unmarried woman or girl is anxious
> about the affairs of the Lord, how to be holy in body and spirit; but the
> married woman is anxious about worldly affairs, how to please her
> husband. [35]I say this for your own benefit, not to lay any restraint upon you,
> but to promote good order and to secure your undivided devotion to the
> Lord (1 Cor. 7.32-35).

The division and distribution of the married man's interests are the
cause of his anxiety. The division and distribution of the married man's
interests is assumed in most interpretations of 1 Cor. 7.32-35 to be caused
by the competing 'demands' of the world and his wife. Yet this interpretation is incomplete (rather than simply inadequate) if we take into account
that it is the married man himself who divides his own interests between
his wife and the Lord. The concerns of the world and the Lord are not
pressing external demands upon a passive believer. Instead, the anxiety is
the product of the husband's own desires to please both his wife and the
Lord. *The married man divides himself.* He is both agent dividing and that
which is divided.

I contend that *memeristai* at 7.34a is not in the passive voice but is in
the middle voice periphrastically constructed. The subject is both the agent
who acts and the object acted upon. If that which was divided were not
self-divided and self-distributed, there would be no cause for Paul's

conclusion at v. 35 that 'I say this for your own benefit, not to lay any restraint upon you, but to promote good order and *to secure your un-divided devotion* to the Lord'. In order to avoid the divided or distracted devotions of married life, Paul advises those who are not so divided to remain in the state—as unmarried—that they are in so that they may be devoted without self-reservation or self-divided devotions to the Lord. The unmarried believer may secure his or her own 'un-divided/un-distributed' devotion to the Lord.

If the verb *memeristai* is a perfect periphrastically constructed middle voice, then (given the customary translation of *merizō* as 'to divide') the question at v. 13a would read 'Has Christ *divided* himself?' Like the married man or woman who divides himself or herself between the Lord and the world, Christ is both the *agent* who divides and the *object* that is divided. The assumed answer to this question expected by the author and consistent with Paul's conception of Christ as the one who reconciles opponents and opposites would be no! For Paul, Christ does not divide himself. The divisions of the Corinthian Christian community are not the work of Christ. Playing upon the person/body/community metaphors that are played out in the text, Christ the person has not divided his communal body. Thus, assuming that the first of the rhetorical questions of v. 13 is a perfect middle voice periphrastic construction, then all three questions invoke negative replies which confront and critique the division of the community.

[13]Has Christ divided himself?	No.
Was Paul crucified for you?	No.
Or were you baptized in the name of Paul?	No.

But *merizō* conveys more than simply 'to divide', for the division may also entail a 'distribution'. So, seeing the verb form as a perfect periphrastically constructed middle voice verb which means 'to divide' *and* 'to distribute', I suggest the following translations of *memeristai ho Christos*:

Has Christ allocated himself?
Has Christ distributed himself?
Has Christ bestowed himself?
Has Christ assigned himself?
Has Christ portioned himself out?

But which self-declaration of belonging does the negative rhetorical question at v. 13a call into question?

Before we answer the query, recall our discussion of the habit of many who divide the self-declarations of belonging and of domestic association into two sets: (i) Paul, Apollos or Cephas and (ii) Christ. But I argued that there are no grammatical reasons and no textual evidence for assessing that the four sayings should be divided into two sets composed of (i) the first three sayings and (ii) the fourth.

When we take into consideration that the self-declarations made in v. 12 are pronouncements of domestic association, and we take into account that *merizō* means 'to divide' *and* 'to distribute', as well as the significance of *memeristai* as a middle voice periphrastically constructed verb, then I argue that Paul's negative rhetorical question at v. 13a is a critique not of the 'domestic divisions' of the Corinthian Christian community into various factions centered on Paul, Apollos or Cephas. Rather, Paul's negative rhetorical question at v. 13a directly critiques the fourth and final statement at v. 12e:

> 'I belong to Christ.' Has Christ allocated himself?

Given Mitchell's interpretation of the slogans as domestic associations, it is my contention that those who make the domestic claim 'I belong to Christ' established their own authority among other Christians as representatives of the Lord's household. As regards the fourth declaration in v. 12, 'I belong to Christ', the one who belongs to and represents Christ presumably does so at the pleasure and request of the head of the house. The senior family member or disciple of the household of Christ does not take such authority from the head of the house and then establish their authority as the new head of the household. Those who declare 'I belong to Christ' receive their *allocation* from Christ on whose behalf they serve.

Now, if servitude is implied in the self-identifications that 'I belong to Christ', then we should not forget that an obedient servant who enjoys the favor of the head of the household may serve as a representative of the householder. It is an odd, paradoxical move in the rhetoric of servitude, which is nonetheless frequent, whereby the one who claims to be merely in obedient service to a superior also represents the superior to others in the absence of the superior. The servant is the presence of the absent Lord. And so the one who is the obedient servant of Christ, who is an immediate inferior to Christ, may nevertheless be a superior to all others in Christ's absence. To be an inferior yet representative of the head of the household is to enjoy the power and authority of the householder in his absence.

The inferior who was selected by the head of the household to exclusively represent the absent lord enjoys a power and authority in the household and on behalf of the lord to represent the household which is the same as or similar to the power that the head of the household would enjoy if present. To 'belong' to the Lord, to be an 'obedient brother' or 'disciple', to be the representative 'member' of the household of Christ 'selected' by Christ himself to head the household in his absence is to have connections in very high places.

Paul's periphrastically constructed middle voice question at v. 13a directly and forthrightly critiques the assumed presumption by members of the Lord's household that Christ himself allocated his authority to a member or members of his family and/or disciples. If Christ allocated himself to specific members of his household, then those of authority in the household would enjoy an *exclusive distribution* from the Lord. The negative rhetorical question at v. 13a is Paul's critical reply that confronts the contentious boast and political aspirations of those who declare that they 'belong' to Christ. The first negative rhetorical question calls the fourth 'saying' into question, in much the same way that the second and third negative rhetorical questions call the first 'saying' into question. Paul's periphrastically constructed middle voice negative question at v. 13a critiques the presumption that there are a few, or at least one, who contend, 'I belong to Christ'. And that one, or few, are questioned by Paul regarding the assumption that they received an allocation from the Lord.

Earlier we considered Paul's critique of those who assumed social authority by appeals to their wisdom, power and genealogy. I argued that Paul's critique proceeded in such a way that each of the privileged identifications were called into question, with the conclusion that the strife that generated the hierarchies was brought to nothing, and with its cessation the differentiations collapsed, making a privileged identification impossible. Identity decomposed into a dependency upon difference, and the socio-theological structures ceased to generate a theocratic hierarchy. *No one represented the presence of God.*

Also, I mentioned and then skirted the issue regarding to whom Paul was referring by the characterization that some were wise, authoritative and of noble birth. I noted that his critique of the wise and authoritative who should be 'shamed' by the foolish and weak of Corinth, while direct, did not convey the force or extreme critique issued against those who counted themselves of noble birth. Those of noble birth, who counted themselves or were counted by others as 'something' were brought to nothing, Paul contended, by those who were of common or scandalous birth.

Greek *eugeneis* in 1 Cor. 1.26 is commonly rendered 'of noble birth', and translators assume that its root, *genos*, means 'family', as in one's natural family, into which one is born. When the root is combined with the prefix *eu-* (meaning 'well' or 'good'), the yield is the 'good or noble family'. Of course, *genos* conveys a variety of related meanings which play out the sense of origin, like the contemporary English terms 'generate', 'genealogy' and 'generation'. The range of meanings conveyed by *genos* includes 'descent, race, stock, kin, birth and origin'.[20] Thus *eugeneis* suggests a range of meanings from 'good, reputable or honorable family', to 'being of nobility', to 'having good or important ancestors'.

Paul contends that in opposition to the *eugeneis* are the *agenēs* who are chosen by God to bring those of 'noble birth' to nothing. The negative prefix *a-* is assumed by translators to negate the common meaning of *genos* as birth and origin, race and stock. Those who are *agenēs* have no origin, no race or no family. Yet, given the differences played out between *agenēs* and *eugeneis* in the text, I contend that Paul does not suggest that the Corinthians have no origin, race or family. Rather, *agenēs* denotes that the Corinthians stand in opposition—an intense differentiation—to *eugeneis*. The *agenēs* have origins, race and family, but what the *agenēs* lack is *eu-geneis*, 'nobility'. The Corinthians are from ignoble or insignificant families. Thus, the negative prefix of *a-genēs* negates the prefix of *eugeneis*, and not the root *genos*. The *eugeneis* are brought to nothing by the *a/eugeneis*.

But who are the *eugeneis*? Influenced by the demographics of Rome-Corinth, it is fashionable since the latter half of the twentieth century to assume that relative to the ruling classes of Roman society, the population of Rome-Corinth, assembled from the ghetto of the city of Rome and freed slaves from various Roman cities to repopulate the defeated Greek city Corinth, was *agenēs*, 'of scandalous pedigree'. Therefore 'noble birth' in the letter was assessed as designating the nobility of Roman society. It is

---

20. *genos* often means: I. race, stock, kin. A *genei uios* is one's 'own' son, as opposed to an adopted son. And in genitive *genous eivai tinos* means to be of his *race*. One who is *engutata genous* is the next of kin. And *ai kata genos basileiai* are *hereditary* monarchies. II. *Offspring*, even of a *single descendant;* collectively, *offspring*, posterity. III. Generally, *race*, of beings, b. clan, house, family, c. tribe, d. caste, e. of animals, breed, and 2. Age, generation, hence age, time of life. IV. Sex, gender. V. Class, sort, kind, (in the animal kingdom, the modern Classes, such as birds, fishes, and so in the vegetable kingdom, b. genus, c. a species of plant, and later crops, produce, materials, in kind). 4. *ta genos*, the elements (Liddell-Scott, *Lexicon*, p. 344).

the common folk in the Corinthian congregation who bring those from distinguished families in the congregation to nothing.

While demographic study is interesting and useful on this topic, this association fails to address the theocratic privileges assumed by those of noble birth. Those *eugeneis*, of noble birth, are presented as presuming privileged access to God. Further, no mention is ever made in the early chapters of the letter that the *eugeneis* are members of the Corinthian congregation. Rather, the Corinthians are all assumed to be *agenēs*.

In more traditional interpretations, the designation of 'noble birth' in these few verses has been interpreted as Paul's critique of the Jews. As the elect, the Jews are a noble race who presumably enjoy the presence of God. The Gentiles of Rome-Corinth, who are *agenēs*, bring the Jews who are *eugeneis* to nothing. On this reading, God selects the Gentiles to replace the Jews as God's elect.

Of course, one issue is the criterion that differentiates between noble and common, between noble and insignificant family. Apparently, those of 'noble birth' assume—or it is assumed by others that they have—a special relationship with God. Thus those who are designated *eugeneis* are presumed to enjoy sacred privilege.

The interpretation that presumes that the *eugeneis* are the Jews has an advantage over the demographically informed interpretation to the extent (but only to the extent) that sacred privilege is considered to be a deter-mining characteristic in the assessment of what is 'good', valued' or 'noble' in the designation *eugeneis*. But the identification of the Jews as the *eugeneis* is too universal a generalization. So, I suggest that we proceed by questioning not which 'race' is *eugeneis* but—more precisely—which family associated with emergent or inchoate Christianity might be so desig-nated a noble family, and which would convey that the family is noble because the family has sacred associations or kin.

I argue that *eugeneis* does not simply designate 'the household of Christ'. Rather, *eugeneis* is a specific reference to those who are kin to Jesus, namely James, the brother of the Lord, who is the head of 'the household of Christ'.

To be *eugeneis* is taken to mean that one is from a good, reputable, honorable family, or of nobility, having good or important ancestors. Sib-lings would enjoy the same status as *eugeneis*. Good birth, good *genesis* on rare occasions refers to those of the same generation who, having been carried and birthed by the same mother, are in a very specific sense of a noble generation.

The reference to 'noble birth' is not a reference to a noble ethnic group. Nor is it directed at the 'nobility' of Roman society. Rather, Paul's critiques are aimed at the family of Jesus who assert their noble birth and presume that such kinship warrants their theocratic authority and power. The designation of *eugeneis* plays out the significance of the sibling relationship of Jesus and James, the Lord and the Lord's younger brother, the savior and the next-born.

We noted in our study of the self-declarations at 1 Cor. 1.12 that the formula is not a political slogan but a claim of domestic association. Thus I contend that the fourth self-declaration of domestic association, 'I (belong) to Christ', is a more general reference to the household of the Lord. Disciples and servants who 'belong' to the household might make the declaration. And the self-declaration 'I belong to Christ' might be a declaration of kinship. However, the designation *eugeneis* at the end of the chapter is a more exclusive designation referring to the Lord's kin within the household.

The *agenēs* of Corinth, who are counted as nothing, bring those who are *eugeneis*, who are *something*, to nothing. Throughout the first chapter of the first Epistle to the Corinthians, Paul pursues a sustained critique of the household of the Lord. I argue that there is a progression in the first chapter. At the beginning of the chapter those who declare that they 'belong to Christ' are characterized by Paul as quarrelsome and divisive. But it is at the end of the chapter that Paul identifies with whom in the household of the Lord he is most at odds. The claim in v. 12, 'I belong to Christ', could be made generally by any member of the household of Christ, including his mother and siblings, as well as other extended family members closely aligned with the household, the chosen disciples and even servants. But the identity of those of 'noble birth' is a more restricted reference to the Lord's family.

The complex interplay of kinship, authority, sacred privilege and critique characteristic of 1 Cor. 1.26-31 are played out in the early chapters of another letter written by Paul during the couple of years he lived in Ephesus. In the first chapter of the Epistle to the Galatians, Paul recounts going up to Jerusalem to visit Cephas (Peter) and seeing James the Lord's brother. He quickly comments, 'In what I am writing to you, before God, I do not lie!' He recounts that he returned to Jerusalem 14 years later with Barnabas and Titus. He presented the gospel before those of repute. In the conflict over Titus's not being circumcised, Paul then proceeds to level his critique:

⁶And from those who were reputed to be something (what they were makes no difference to me; God shows no partiality)—those, I say, who were of repute added nothing to me, ⁷but on the contrary, when they saw that I had been entrusted with the gospel to the uncircumcised, just as Peter had been entrusted with the gospel to the circumcised ⁸(for he who worked through Peter for the mission to the circumcised worked through me also for the Gentiles), ⁹and when they perceived the grace that was given to me, James and Cephas and John, who were reputed to be pillars, gave to me and Barnabas the right hand of fellowship that we should go to the Gentiles and they to the circumcised; ¹⁰only they would have us remember the poor, which very thing I was eager to do (Gal. 2.6-10).

Those who were reputed to be *something*—either the pillars or some or at least one among the pillars—were reputed to be *something*, to enjoy divine partiality. But, counters Paul, those who were reputed to be *something* added nothing to him because God shows no partiality. The pillars were themselves *nothing*. They lacked *something*. They were empty of that *something* that would have set them apart as enjoying God's selection. Like the conclusion at the end of the first chapter of 1 Corinthians, no human flesh may boast of having some special relationship to God. No flesh may boast of standing in the presence of God.

I argue that those who were *reputed to be something* at Jerusalem according to the Epistle to the Galatians, and those who were *reputed to be something* according to the 1 Corinthians, are the same person or persons. The self-evaluation or their privileged evaluation by others as *something* was unfounded according to Paul, for those who are of noble birth—who are reputed to be *something*—are brought to nothing! The scandalous, the common, the uncircumcised of Corinth, are elected by God to bring those who are reputed to be *something* by virtue of their noble birth to nothing! All claims to partiality are unfounded. God shows no partiality, not even to the brother of the Lord!

One of the primary purposes of Paul's letters to the Corinthians and the Galatians is to persuade the Corinthians and the Galatians not to engage, or to cease engaging or to reject those who do engage, in using wisdom, authority and natural family connections to establish the authority of those who belong to Christ.

The conclusion that Paul seeks to put forward so as to influence his reader, 'that no human being might boast in the presence of God', may have less to do with those who claim wisdom and power per se and more to do with the theocratic claims of the family of Jesus, who may have believed themselves to be in closer relationship than others to God. Then the low and despicable of Corinth (by worldly standards) is a reference neither to the status of the Corinthians relative to Roman or Greco-Roman social/cultural/political standards nor to 'the Gentiles' relative to 'the Jews' as God's chosen. It is a reference to the *worldly standards of value* presumed by the household in general and the family in particular. We should not think that Paul assumes the differentiation between 'the church' and 'the world' as it has commonly become interpretive practice when characterizing social arrangements. In this case, 'the worldly standards' referred to in 1 Cor. 1.26-28 are the worldly standards of the *household* and *family of Jesus*. The 'household of the Lord' is an all-too-worldly institution in which authority is determined by that all-too-common *worldly standard* of kinship and household rank. Paul's declaration of having a revelation only of Christ crucified rather than having known Christ in the flesh, often inadequately labeled to be a 'spiritualization', may be better understood as a rhetorical device that devalues the worldly, flesh-and-blood justifications of the Lord's household and family. Paul can not successfully argue for the authority of his ministry of reconciliation so long as the worldly standard holds sway.

As we noted earlier, the term most commonly associated with Christian communities and institutions in the Germanic languages is 'church', cf. *Kirche* (German), *kirk* (Scottish), *kirke* (Danish). These modern designations are believed to be related to Greek *kuriakon*, meaning 'that which belongs to the Lord'. The root *kurios* conveys a range of meanings: from persons having power or authority over another to the declaration that the person so designated has supreme authority. It can refer to some claim being 'valid' as opposed to *akurios*, 'invalid'. Of times, it can mean 'ordained'; it can mean 'legitimate'; or it can refer to 'proper' or 'real' goodness. The Greek *o kurios* , 'the Lord', commonly designated the power and authority of gods or deified rulers (especially in the East). *kurizuō* is 'to be lord and master of, to gain possession of, to seize, to be dominant' or, as a passive, 'to be dominated, to be possessed'.[21]

The church are those persons who confess that they belong to the Lord, that Jesus the Christ has power and authority over those who submit to him. The similarities of the phrases 'belonging to the Lord' and 'belonging to Christ' are striking, so much more so given that in the LXX, *Christos* and *kurios* are both offered in translation for *Adonai*. Both *christos* and *kurios* convey in the LXX a person of legitimate power and authority. And,

21. Liddell-Scott, *Lexicon*, p. 1013.

likewise, to belong to 'the Lord' or to belong to 'the Christ' meant that, since the power and authority of the Lord/Christ is legitimate, one's submission to the Lord/Christ was also appropriate.

The distinction between the description that one 'belongs to the Lord' and a profession that one 'belongs in the Lord' differentiates kinship and/or household relations from a credo that declares a relation *like* kinship or household belonging. I will argue later that the interpretation of the fourth self-declaration as a credo is a later historical activity of biblical hermeneutics. But the descriptive self-declaration of belonging to Christ quoted by Paul at 1 Cor. 1.12 was a description of household membership.

A group that professed that it 'belonged' to the Lord/Christ asserted that others in the community submitted to the power and authority of the Lord/Christ. However, those who belong to the Lord/Christ also served the Lord/Christ as representatives in the world.

Paul contends that God selects the foolish, weak and scandalous, those who are assessed by 'the church' as outside of God's presence, in order to bring 'the church' to nothing, to nullify the theocracy. No one enjoys the presence of God. God shows no partiality. Theocracy is an economy of authority based upon the scarcity of sacred presence and an abundance of sacred absence. Those who claim to enjoy the good fortune of sacred presentation are privileged over those to whom the sacred does not visit. Paul's critique is that God is partial to no one. No one 'represents' God.

The task of Paul's negations of theocratic privileges attempts to bring theocracy to an end. Paul was not seeking to reform 'the church', the household of the Lord, or to reform the political structures within the household in which Peter (the first among those selected to join the household as a disciple) and James the Lord's own brother exercised significant authority. For Peter and James in their own way signified, referred to and represented Jesus. Instead, Paul called the church, the household and the salvation that it offered *into question*, countering the presumptions of church/family/household privilege.

Paul was not seeking to broaden or to extend the privileges of family connections to those who were previously excluded. Paul was not seeking to extend family privileges and God's partiality out beyond the confines of the church. Rather, Paul was seeking to deconstruct the church, to disestablish the theocracy and hierarchy of privileged 'belonging'.

Salvation for Paul was not the privilege of being allowed into the household of the Lord. Instead, for Paul, the church and its privileges are extremely critiqued, disallowed, decomposed and deconstructed. *For Paul,* the work of salvation was to deconstruct the various means by which some sought their own privilege in a theocracy, in order that the gospel to the Gentiles and the gospel to the circumcised might decompose their differentiation and bring them into holy reconciliation, devoid of theocratic hierarchy and sacred privilege.

Thus Paul was not seeking to reform or destroy the church. It is not that the foolish, weak and of common birth bring the church to ruin. The Roman legions under Titus would accomplish that in the destruction of Jerusalem in 69/70 CE. Instead, in the early to mid-fifties CE Paul was seeking to disestablish *the church's* theocratic claims and to bring *the church* to 'no-thing'.

If the self-pronouncement 'I belong to Christ' (in Mitchell's interpretation) declares one's relationship to Christ as a member of Christ's household, as members of his natural family or as a servant or disciple in Christ's household, then the statement 'I belong to Christ' was an assertion of a power relation. The purpose of the identification 'I belong to Christ' was to establish the privilege of those who could make the claim in competition with any other rivals.

If the identification with Christ is the focus of Paul's critical rhetorical query in v. 13a, then the profession 'I belong to Christ' is not presented by Paul as the means for *overcoming* social fragmentation. Instead, contrary to the common interpretation, the saying 'I belong to Christ' is presented by Paul as *causing* social stratification and schism.

In an economy of self-declarations, the contention that 'I belong to Christ' trumps all differing self-declarations. Anyone who might be a member of Christ's household would enjoy a considerable degree of authority and power among non-household members in the larger Christian community. And anyone who served as the representative of Christ, to whom authority had been allocated by Christ himself, would enjoy the status of 'belonging' to Christ as a duly appointed representative of the Lord to all others. Further, to declare one's noble generation as a sibling of the Lord in a community that understood itself to be the extended family of Jesus would establish both communal integrity and political stratification. Within emergent Christian societies the act of identification with Christ and the collateral implication that others in the community 'did not belong to Christ' would have been a powerful rhetorical tool to differentiate and stratify between those who 'belong to Christ's household' and those who do not. To be among those who belonged would enhance one's status in such a Christian hierarchical social arrangement. Thus, among contending groups, those who could convincingly assert their being members of the family or household of Christ might easily trump the authority of their competition within Christian communities. Paul's first negative rhetorical query at v. 13a critiques the declaration 'I belong to Christ' immediately, seeking to nullify the use of such 'identification' in the economy of power in the Corinthian Christian community.

Paul critiques the socio-religious convictions of those who identify themselves as members of Christ's family or household and who in belonging to Christ receive some allocation or distribution or assignment or appropriation of authority and power to *represent* him among the followers of the Lord. It is these inferences (that those who claim 'I belong to Christ' enjoy an allocation or distribution or assignment or appropriation of the authority and power of Christ) that Paul's first negative rhetorical question queries. 'Has Christ distributed himself?' calls into question the possibility of an allocation between the one that makes the declaration of self-identification and a sacred *distribution*. The negative rhetorical question at v. 13a calls into question the assumption that Christ divided and distributed his authority or sanctity.

Paul's critique is not all that concerned with the slogans regarding Paul, or Apollos or Cephas. In fact, I do not think Paul is concerned much at all about the identifications with Apollos and Cephas. Instead, the focus of Paul's critique was the faction that made the fourth and final declaration of self-identification with Christ.[22] Those who profess 'I belong to Christ' were party to the divisiveness in the Corinthian Christian community. Paul addresses his critiques to those who identify themselves as members of the household of Christ, who assume their superior status within the church as being of 'noble birth' and who believe they enjoy an exclusive sacred connection with the Lord.

In the decades following the events of Jesus' crucifixion and resurrection, two members of the Lord's household came to exercise authority in the church. James, the younger brother of the Lord, and Pete, a disciple selected by the Lord, were forthrightly and in a very narrow sense members of the Lord's household. James, Peter and the other chosen disciples were the *church*. They *belonged to the Lord*. And any one of them would have declared, 'I belong to Christ.'

Certainly, being the blood brother of the Lord enhanced the authority of James in the Church in Jerusalem. James the brother of the Lord could

22. It is possible that the first three slogans were exaggerations or caricatures of factional self-declarations *fashioned by* Paul, and not quotations of factions in Corinth.

emphatically claim, 'I belong to Christ', meaning, 'I am a family member of the household of the Lord.' The claim to familial relations with the designated person as a superior (that is, an older brother who is the head of the family) could be made with little or no religious, political or theological interpretation by James. However, for James the brother of the Lord to make the self-declaration 'I belong to Christ' would carry with it enormous religious, political and theological implications within the Christian community.

Given that there are reports in the letter that a contingent did travel to Corinth from the Church of Jerusalem as representatives of the disciples and James the brother of the Lord, they may have declared that they were the representatives of Christ because they 'belonged to Christ', meaning they were the representatives of 'James, the head of the *church* in Jerusalem who was the brother of—who quite literally *belonged* to—Christ'. Such a declaration would suggest that the group from Jerusalem was in service to James the brother of the Lord and so employed an association to the household of Christ to warrant the legitimacy of their convictions and authority.

If a group in the Corinthian Christian community aligned themselves with James the brother of Christ, then I think it possible that such persons in Corinth might repeat the declaration 'I belong to Christ' and mean that they were aligned with the church, the household of the Lord. Such a repetition could accomplish a number of things. Those who aligned themselves with James through his envoys from Jerusalem might be seeking solidarity with James who enjoyed 'family' connections with the Lord. For members in Corinth to possess or claim to possess such connections, that they 'belong to the house of Christ', that they belong as servants to the household of James who is the brother of the Lord, could possibly bring with it benefits in the form of enhanced status as members of 'the church' within the Corinthian community.

The apostles could also have declared that they 'belong to Christ' to the extent that they are members of Christ's self-constructed household, his family of followers whom he gathered to himself. Persons in the Corinthian congregation may have declared that they 'belong' to Christ because they accept the authority and teachings of the disciples who 'belong' to Christ.

Now given what we know about the convictions of James and Peter, and the conflicts Paul is reported to have had with them, not everyone in the Corinthian Christian community could or would have wanted to make the self-declaration 'I belong to Christ' and mean by it that they are in solidarity with James the brother of the Lord and/or Peter the Lord's disciple. James maintained that there are clear ritual and ethical boundaries that mark off the household of the Lord—'the church'—from the world. And only those in Corinth who could fulfill the requirements could be admitted, while those who could not or would not did not belong to Christ and therefore were beyond 'the church'.

It is significant to recall that Paul enjoyed no connection with the person of Jesus or his historical ministry. Those who were members of Jesus' family and his chosen disciples enjoyed considerable influence and authority among Christians everywhere in the decades after the crucifixion. So we must remember that in these conflicts and confrontations, Paul is the 'johnny-come-lately', without the power and authority that came with discipleship or family connections. Clearly, to have belonged to Christ, to have been a member of his immediate family, as in the case of James the brother, or a member of the extended family, as in the case of Peter, may have been perceived as a necessary but not sufficient requirement to be a leader of the Lord's household, the church, in Jerusalem. We should not forget that in the decades between the crucifixion and the destruction of Jerusalem in 69/70 CE there appears to have been a succession of leadership of the household of the Lord in Jerusalem that passed from Jesus to James to Simeon, all blood relatives. Each of these leaders could have used a formula like 'I belong to Christ' and have meant by it that they were family members of the household of Christ, as brother or cousin, to warrant or support their authority. In the church, the succession of leadership was not apostolic but dynastic.

In the traditional interpretations of 1 Cor. 1.10-13 the divergent 'sayings' that dissent from correct confession are presented as quarrelsome acts which divide the community.

> [11]For it has been reported to my by Chlóe's people that there is quarreling among you, my brethren. [12]What I mean is that each one of you says, 'I belong to Paul', 'I to Apollos', or 'I to Cephas...' (1 Cor. 1.11-12).

The appeals 'that all of you agree', 'that there be no dissensions among you' and 'that you be united in the same mind and in the same judgment' are assumed to be calls for *church* unity through the *repetition* of the same statement of self-declaration. 'Dis-unity' in the social 'body' of the Corinthian Christian community is expressed by and is possibly the outcome of a multiplicity of confessions. Such a multiplicity of confessions that divide the community can be overcome by the assent of a single creed common to all. When all repeat the same confession ('I belong to Christ'), differences yield homogeneity. When all say the same thing, solidarity is achieved. Communal unity or division is understood to be a matter of prepositional singularity or multiplicity.

Such readings emphasize the importance of shared propositions or the mimesis of creeds to provide social integrity. If a proposition becomes a creed and the 'saying' of a creed becomes a religious rite of entry or proper social arrangement within the community, then any diversity in prepositional convictions or slogans threaten the integrity of the community. Communal unity is the outcome of mimetic confession.

However, by my analysis, 'I belong to Christ' was a descriptive claim by those who belonged to the household of the Lord. I judge that 'I belong to Christ' was not offered by the household of Jesus as a 'creed' which would bring diverse groups into social unity. The claim to represent Christ as members of his household, including members of the Lord's natural family and disciples, was not a claim to be shared or distributed. One of the purposes of the assertion was to differentiate between those who belonged to the *church* from those who did not, and to distinguish between legitimate and illegitimate leaders. The contention that 'they' were members of the household of the Lord was employed to win an argument and silence an opposition. In this case, the self-declaration of the Lord's household would serve to counter and silence Paul. As members of Christ's household and his representatives, the leaders of the *church* in Jerusalem sought to establish and maintain their authority, to determine who was accepted and who was rejected in the *church*.

We must also consider the possibility that the phrasing 'I belong to Christ' was itself an exaggeration by Paul of the significance of the natural relationship between the brothers. Such an exaggeration could have served Paul's own agenda quite well, as Paul sought to undermine or at least to contain the influence of the Jerusalem *church* under the leadership of James and the disciples among the Christian communities in Paul's missionary sphere of influence.

By reading the statement 'I belong to Christ' at v. 12e as a quotation that is immediately critiqued by the negative rhetorical question of v. 13a, I suggest an interpretation that resonates with Paul's other critical responses to those who seek to establish their rank and privilege in Corinth, and his ongoing, often toxic, confrontations with the leaders in the church of Jerusalem, particularly James the brother of the Lord and Peter. Thus, contrary to the customary interpretations that assess the first three slogans to be expressive of heretical heteronyms in the Corinthian community, the reading I offer suggests that Paul critiques those who identify themselves as 'belonging to Christ'.

'I belong to Christ' is questionable for Paul for a number of other reasons which we have yet to explore. For someone to assert their *identity* with Christ and to assess that such identification entitled them to power and authority was evaluated by Paul as a contentious boast that hampered, if not violated, salvation as reconciliation or 'at-onement'. Further, his vision of the community as an *ecclesia*, a gathering of differences in the body of Christ (expressed in imagery such as the clothing or baptizing of differences in Christ) presupposed that no one enjoyed authority in the community as the representative of Christ.

The declaration 'I belong to Christ' meant that in a sacred economy the person shares in the distribution of the sacred. Thus the self-profession 'I belong to Christ' suggests that Christ is divided and distributed out to each one who legitimately says, 'I belong to Christ.' 'I belong to Christ' establishes an economy whereby the sacred is allocated, distributed, bestowed from Christ to the individual making the self-declaration.

No doubt the profession 'I belong to Christ' later came to be a contagious and successful declaration. But the declaration as quoted by Paul in the first chapter of 1 Corinthians was not a confession of faith. 'I belong to Christ' was not a credo. In fact, I suspect that given the broad appeal and success of the profession with Christians, the interpreters who followed assumed that the making of self-declarations was a proper religious act for Christians to make, found the confession to be an appropriate declaration by Christians and so did not find the self-identification with Christ quoted at 1 Cor. 1.12 to be a contentious boast. So began the hermeneutical practice of appealing to the fragment 'I belong to Christ' as a text to warrant Christian creedal formulation.

On this later point it is interesting to consider the Gospel of Mark, written by a one-time associate (and possible relative) of Paul's. In the Gospel of Mark, the disciples and the family of Jesus are not portrayed in favorable lights. With respect to his family, there is one instance where the mother and siblings of the Lord are presented as believing their son and brother is possessed by an unclean spirit. So they came to the door of the house he was visiting to take him away—because he had an unclean spirit. He was possessed—and mad.

> [31]And his mother and his brothers came; and standing outside they sent to him and called him. [32]And a crowd was sitting about him; and they

said to him, 'your mother and your brothers are outside, asking for you'.
[33]And he replied, 'Who are my mother and brothers?' [34]And looking
around on those who sat about him, he said, 'Here are my mother and my
brothers! [35]Whoever does the will of God is my brother, and sister, and
mother' (Mk 3.31-35).

It is certainly pertinent to our present discussion to consider that in the
Gospel of Mark, written about a decade after the Corinthian Epistles, the
author has Jesus *disowning* his brothers. Then, after disowning his natural
family, Jesus names his followers who hear and do the will of God as his
true family. This is a powerful political move. The true family of the Lord,
the true mother, brothers and sisters of the Lord, are not his natural family
but those who, according to Mark's Jesus, do God's will. And if we read
this narrative in Mark in the context in which the leadership of the Jerusalem church is dynastic, and Mark is aligned with those in Christianity
who do not enjoy the authority that comes with such sacred family connections, then Mark's portrayal of Jesus disowning his own family would
strongly suggest that the dynastic character of power and authority in the
Jerusalem church is illegitimate and that the convictions of the Jerusalem
church that were in competition with Mark's conviction were not sanctioned by the Lord. In other words, Mark's Gospel is subversive in that it
contains a strong political-religious critique of possibly the most powerful
leaders of the time in Christian institutions.

I am not making an assessment on whether Mark's portrayal of Jesus'
return to his hometown at Mark 3 is historically accurate. What I am
saying is that such a portrayal may be influenced by the political circumstances at the time of the authorship, and that it would have been a powerful propaganda tool for those who were not aligned with the leadership of
the church in Jerusalem.

But the Gospel of Mark had not been written when the Epistles to the
Corinthians were composed. I recall these features of Mark's Gospel to
illustrate that a political struggle that was being carried out among competing Christian groups and authors in the decades immediately after
the crucifixion of Jesus is evident in a number of documents in a brief,
two-decade period. And so I suggest that the reader pay attention to the
possible propaganda uses of Paul, Mark and James in their struggles in the
volatile Christian communities.

The contention 'I belong to Christ' was a claim by those who belonged,
who were the *church*, to their theocratic authority. And if my argument
that James the brother of the Lord and/or the disciples in the *church* in

Jerusalem made the claim 'I belong to Christ', then the purpose for making such a claim—according to Paul—was a means to authorize the church conviction that all who would 'follow' Christ must accept the authority of the church and must keep or enact the rites of purification as defended by the Lord's brother. Interpreters have commonly agreed that Paul was a critic of the keeping of such rites by Gentile Christians, but have not questioned the status for Paul of the self-declaration to belong to Christ, because within subsequent communities that identified themselves as the church (as those who belong to or follow the Lord) it was assumed that such confessions were appropriate for believers. Later, 'orthodox' church readers of the text could identify with the slogan 'I belong to Christ'. The rhetoric of the later, orthodox church as the household or family of God has become so woven into the very structure, the symbolism, the convictions, the language and behavior of Christian communal institutions that the institutionalized reader, meaning those of us who read the text in accord with the hermeneutical habits of Christendom, are hardly able (if at all) to entertain the possibility that Paul could be a critic of the conception of Christian community as 'church', as the 'family' of the Lord. Paul was a critic of this practice of communal conception in the first decades following the resurrection of Jesus. Paul was a critic of the dynastic 'church', which is a redundancy. Only the household of the Lord is 'the church'. Paul was a critic of the family of the Lord and the exclusionary conception of Christian community as the sacred family, the sacred 'church'.

And so the verse fragment 'I belong to Christ', expressive of orthodox Christian convictions, was plucked from the text and canonized as a scriptural justification for the establishment of theocratic authority. Clearly, the verse fragment enjoys considerable interpretive vitality and plasticity, as the quotation came to enjoy the status as a scriptural, archaic prototype of a proper Christian creed. Individual Christians would have had little difficulty declaring their allegiance to Christ. No one would have doubted the appropriateness of a Christian making a self-declaration of belonging to Christ, of belonging to the Lord, or being a member of the sacred family—a family composed of peoples who often shared no genetic, or even ethnic or historical, connections with the Lord, or even with one another. And so, a verse fragment that so easily and obviously became part of the habit of Christianity was not questioned as to its source or status in the text from which it was drawn. For who would have thought that the declaration 'I belong to Christ' or 'I belong to the Lord' would have been questioned by Paul as a boastful and divisive act?

To read 1 Cor. 1.10-13 as an argument that critiques the slogan 'I belong to Christ' rather than defends it is to read the text against the established habits of interpretation. The rhetoric of self-identification with Christ was no doubt contagious and successful among subsequent Christians. Interpreters and translators, assuming that self-identification and mimetic pronouncements were appropriate religious expressions or acts, read the creed as non-political.

Suppose the self-declaration 'I belong to Christ' is immediately critiqued and rejected at v. 13a, and the 'slogan' is a focus, if not the instigating incident, of a boastful, contentious claim to which Paul replies. Suppose also that we accept Mitchell's interpretation of the formula that the declaration 'to belong' means that one is a member of the household. Then the quotation of the slogan 'to belong' to the household of Christ and the immediate and forceful critique by Paul of the contemptuous use of one's claim to be related to Christ ushers us quickly to a controversy that permeates much of the Pauline corpus, and the emergent Christian communities between the crucifixion of Jesus and the destruction of Jerusalem.

> I appeal to you, brethren, by the name of our Lord Jesus Christ, that all of you agree and that there be no dissensions among you, but that you be united in the same mind and the same judgment (1 Cor. 1.10).

Mitchell contends that 1 Cor. 1.10 is the thesis statement of a series of arguments that address social discord and call for concord.[23] It is Mitchell's assessment that 1 Cor. 1.10a contains technical language derived from political oratory and treatises concerning political unity. 'In this verse Paul urges the Corinthians to end their factions and become restored as a unified political community by using *stock phrases* [my emphasis] from Greco-Roman antiquity for dealing with just this issue.'[24] While I agree with Mitchell that v. 10 contains technical language, I argue that the verse, especially the second clause of the verse, employs technical terminology which does not support her general claim that Paul employed 'stock phrases from Greco-Roman antiquity', or her more specific contention that Paul's appeal employed *homonoia* rhetoric in order to maintain 'order'. (In other words, I do not think that Paul was concerned with 'order' in the way that Mitchell presents the topic. My major problem with Mitchell's

23. Mitchell, *Paul*, p. 66.
24. Mitchell, *Paul*, pp. 65-66.

interpretation is that she assumes as a 'given' the traditional reading of the text.) While her interpretation is forceful and insightful, her argument is with the traditional interpretations of the Epistle that were employed to serve *homonoia* political agendas. I argue that there are many reasons for not accepting the traditional interpretation of the text, so I conclude that Mitchell's thesis is flawed to the extent that she accepts as 'given' the standard hermeneutical practices. I will return later to Mitchell's thesis when I argue that Paul's appeal for 'unity' among the Corinthian Christian community is not an appeal for *homonoia*.

The practice has been to assume that the saying at v. 13e, 'I belong to Christ', was offered as the means to fulfill the appeals 'to agree and to overcome dissensions' and 'to be united in the same mind and the same judgment'. It is an established habit of interpretation to assume that to be in agreement and to be in the same mind and judgment meant to say the same creed and make the same identification: 'I belong to Christ.' However, given our close reading of the text and my argument that the first negative rhetorical question is a critique of the fourth self-declaration, the appeal to be united in the same mind and the same judgment and the statement 'I belong to Christ' are no longer associates. Instead, the saying 'I belong to Christ' is the prime example in the immediate text of a boastful conviction employed for contentious political purposes among Christians.

So how are we to understand Paul's appeal for the Corinthians 'to agree' and 'to be united in the same mind and the same judgment' if he is not proposing a 'creed'? How are we to understand the appeal by Paul for the Corinthians not to have 'dissensions' or 'divisions' among themselves? What sense of social order, if any, does Paul seek to institute that is non-creedal and non-dynastic? Or is Paul a social anarchist?

The term *schismata* suggests a separation. The stem *schisis* means 'cleavage' or 'parting'. *schismē* names the cleft or division of hoofs, or leaves, or the rent in a garment. But *schismē* also names the division of opinion, the ploughing of the ground, or the vulva. In other words, the term is a descriptive one that does not carry evaluative connotations of the separation, cleavage, parting, cleft, division, rent, ploughing or opening. The verb *schizō* means 'to split, to cleave, to rend asunder'; generally, 'to part, to separate, to divide, to rent or to tear (as in a garment)'.[25] So, in one sense, the use of the term *schismata* simply describes the fact that there are

25. Liddell-Scott, *Lexicon*, p. 1746.

divisions, splits, partings, openings, rents within the community.

The common practice of translating *schismata* as 'dissensions' assumes that there was an earlier unity from which there is now a division, and that the diverse group or groups have dissented from that with which they should have remained in unity and to which they should have assented. Traditionally, interpreters believed that what the factions were said to dissent from or fail to assent to was the 'creed'. A return to the 'creed' was presented as the means for overcoming division and for establishing theocratic unity. As such, the other three sayings were taken to be 'creeds' or identifications that were 'deviations' or 'dissensions' from the authentic 'creed'.

However, given the status of the fourth saying as a boastful slogan that is a cause for the contentious division of the Corinthian community, I judge that the tradition of translating *schismata* as 'dissensions' is inadequate. Further, I do not think that a simple descriptive, neutral translation is adequate, given that the divisions in Corinth are, according to Paul, influenced by the political ambition of at least one group to assert its power and privilege within the community. Paul's appeal 'that there be no *schismata* among you' is an appeal for the factions, and particularly the faction that contends 'I belong to Christ', to cease its 'contentious strivings'. So Paul is not appealing for an end to differentiation, but an end to the *contentious struggle* by one group to subordinate all others. I suggest that we translate the appeal:

> that all of you agree and that there be no contention [*schismata*] among you.

This assessment that the Corinthian community is embattled in an internal struggle for power is evident:

> For it has been reported to my by Chlóe's people that there is quarreling among you, my brethren (1 Cor. 1.11).

Traditionally, as we saw earlier, the first three sayings have been identified as expressive of the quarreling among the Corinthians. The reason commonly inferred by Christian readers for this quarreling was the outcome of *credo* nonconformity. Thus, on a traditional reading, 'saying' the correct formula, making proper pronouncements of self-declaration, was believed to be a means for ensuring correct social concord. Given the common preponderance of creedal interpretations in service to theocracy, the opposition has been presented as between those who were creedal-conformist and those who were nonconformist, between orthodoxy and heresy. But the coherence, the weave of the fabric of the creedal hermeneutic, never took into account the fact that Paul immediately critiques the fourth self-declaration. So I judge that the translation of *schismata* as 'dissension' suggesting deviation from the proper 'creed' to be inadequate.

The sayings—all them, but particularly the fourth—are presented as expressions of the quarreling that is dividing the community. The fault lies in the religious contentiousness of those who seek their own advantage in the community, and especially in those who claim that their particular group enjoys an exclusive and special relation with Christ as members of the Lord's household.

The common practice, as we have seen, has been to correlate the appeals to be in the same 'mind' and in the same 'judgment' with the saying 'I belong to Christ'. Often the term 'mind' conveys a strong sense of 'identity'. To be of the same mind would be for everyone to have the same thought, to be the same, to be one. Thus, given the habit of reading the text as a defense of a creed, the appeal to the Corinthians to be of the same mind is understood as an appeal for all to say the same phrase, to mentally engage in making a single proposition of identity that would yield a united community. Such a community would share the same thoughts, repeat the same sayings and be of the same mind. And so, differences—different concepts, different convictions, different words and different minds—threaten social integrity and theocratic connection. Thus understood, assent to and repetition of the same credo promises much.

Given the highly intellectualized sense of 'mind' that was influenced by Greek academic philosophy, the appeals to be of the same mind and the same judgment have often been understood to be calls for an assent to a single proposition, an intellectual object, idea or stated belief. The creedal hermeneutical practice has been to assume that the Corinthians were of 'many' minds and judgments expressed in the multiple 'creeds' quoted in v. 12b. Assent to a common saying meant that the community was of the 'same' mind and judgment, and the many would thus enjoy social integrity. And, given the content of the saying and its assumed legitimacy, those who declare 'I belong to Christ' would also enjoy the benefits of the theocratic connection.

Conclusion

At the beginning of this chapter I noted that the interpretive practice has been to string together 1 Cor. 1.10 and verse fragment 12e, and to construct from the association a warrant for the predominance of creedal propositions in Christian thought and practice. However, I argued that Paul does not differentiate the verse fragment 12e from the proceeding three sayings, and that with the negative rhetorical question at v. 13a, the confession 'I (belong) to Christ' was critiqued and rejected by Paul. In fact, I read the fourth saying to be an expression of those who are contentious within the community and not the means for the resolution of such division. Paul's appeal for unity in the same disposition and the same accord was not an appeal for all to assent to a proposition or to repeat the same credo, as his appeal to unity has been commonly taken to mean.

The credo hermeneutic must so manipulate the reading of the text—concealing some and overemphasizing other aspects of the text—in order to render a coherent credo interpretation. But the construction of the credo reading fails in the sense that the integrity of the structure fails. The various pieces and connections fail to work, and the interpretation fails to perform. On close reading, the credo interpretation of these few verses begins to fall to pieces, the relations fail to hold (the internal relations between verses fail to work in ways that support the credo hermeneutic, and the relations between the hermeneutic and the material text become problematic). The 'grammar' of the hermeneutic is found wanting.

For those accustomed to and committed to *credological* readings of the text, the possibility that the text is a critique of their habit of reading and understanding, a critique of their system of religious convictions, valuation and practice, will strike them as in*cred*ible. If the text does not serve credo-theocratic purposes, they might retort, 'What good is it?' The assumption is that if you do not know what you believe, if you lack a creed, then you are an 'unbeliever', sacrilegious. I argue that what has been commonly taken to be a declaration of a credo-identification was a declaration of dynastic-identification: the credo is 'de-creeded'.

Paul's critique of those who declared 'I belong to Christ' was not a critique of credo-identification but was his critique of the theocratic presumptions of the identity and authority of the *church*.

So how are we to understand the appeals to social unity, and the sameness of 'mind' (*noi*)[26] and 'judgment' (*gnōmē*), given these complications?

26. Gerhard Kittel, *Theological Dictionary of the New Testament* (trans. and ed. Geoffrey W. Bromiley; Grand Rapids, MI: Eerdmans, 1964–76), IV, pp. 951-60. In Greek philosophy and religion, *nous* (dative *noi*) became more theoretically oriented, as 'reason' or 'spirit'. In Anaxagoras *nous* is the cosmic reason that orders the universe and links perception and creativity. For Plato, *nous* rules the world, so it controls moral action. With truth, it is the product of the marriage of humanity with pure being.

Except for three instances (Lk. 24.45; Rev. 13.18; 17.9), *nous* is used almost exclusively by Paul in the New Testament. There are four inter-related meanings of *nous* in the Pauline Epistles according to the *Theological Dictionary of the New Testament*. The most common use of the term conveys the sense of 'disposition', in keeping with the usual meaning in the Apocrypha. I suspect that modern readers are so biased by the Cartesian dualism of body–mind that it is difficult to employ the English term 'mind' and its equivalents and understand by their use much else than that which is in distinction to the body, as in the nonphysical, subvocal, deliberative self.

With respect to *gnōmē*, the English term 'judgment' often carries the sense of objective assessment, and so fails to convey the nuances or complexities that *gnōmē* carries in Greek, including 'will', 'sentiment', 'accord' or 'resolve'.[27] While I risk being too brief in explaining my deliberations on this matter, I suggest that we translate the last two phrases of 1 Cor. 1.10c thus: 'But that you be united *in the same disposition and the same accord.*'

Clearly, my choices for translating *noi* and *gnōmē* as 'disposition' and 'accord' are influenced by my judgment to translate *schismata* as 'contention' and to continue a hermeneutic that plays out themes of social affection and disaffection. The people to whom Paul addresses his letters are divided into groups that are not *disposed* towards one another, and this lack of *accord* between those who are in *contention* with one another stands in opposition to a unity for which Paul makes an appeal.

Aristotle sees in *nous* our characteristic *energeia*. Theoretical *nous* is the power of logical thought, and practical *nous* sets goals for the will. The *nous* is immortal and comes into the body from outside (*TDNT*, IV, pp. 954-55).

Nous is imprecise in the New Testament, although never equated with *pneuma* or *psychē*. It first means 'mind' or 'disposition' in the sense of inner orientation or moral attitude. In 1 Cor. 14.14-15 *nous* produces intelligible words and clear thought. It also means 'thought', 'judgment' or 'resolve'.

27. *TDNT*, I, pp. 717-18.

Chapter 3

A/*Eugeneis*

Theocracy is established upon the claim that someone or some group enjoys the benefits that come from being selected by God to administer divine rule in the mortal world. In selecting a few out of the many to privilege, an economy of power and authority is constructed which is based upon the scarcity of sacred presence in a world of abundant sacred absence or desecration. Those who enjoy the good fortune of sacred selection and presentation are privileged over those whom the sacred has not visited.

In the early chapters of 1 Corinthians, Paul offers an extreme critique of the *church*. The occasion for Paul's confrontation with and critique of the *church* was the divisive consequences of the claims to privilege made by and about members of the Lord's household upon the Roman-Corinthian Christian community. In the beginning of the first chapter Paul confronts the claims that those who belong to the Lord were privileged by and received an allocation from the Lord. But the critique of the authority claims of the household of the Lord at 1 Cor. 1.12-13 was mild when compared with Paul's critique of the theocratic claims of the Lord's dynasty at the end of the first chapter.

While Paul marks out for criticism the wise, powerful and those of noble birth in the early verses of the paragraph, in the concluding verses the theocratic claim to authority made by the *eugeneis* of the Lord are the target of Paul's extreme critique. In opposition to the authority of the dynasty of the Lord, Paul appeals to a Jewish theological conviction that no flesh is to be confused with God, and that no one human being is privileged over another by God. Thus, if we read those verses with that conclusion in mind, the coherence of the radical critique becomes evident. In opposition to the family of the Lord (*eugeneis*), God chooses their 'other' (*ageneis*) to bring those of 'noble birth' in the Lord's family to nothing. The hierarchy of the *church* collapses. Sacred privilege is emptied.

In 1 Cor. 1.26-27, Paul plays upon the dyadic configuration of the *church*'s theocratic valuation. The first term is assessed to enjoy the privileging selection and presence of God. The second term in each dyadic set is the other or opposite of the first and so lacks the association with sacred selection and presence that the first term enjoys. Those who are wise, powerful and of noble birth assess that they enjoy legitimate theocratic authority.

Wise	Foolish
Powerful	Weak
Noble birth	Scandalous birth
God's presence	God's absence

But Paul contends that God selects those who are divested by the theocratic legitimization of the wise, powerful and those of noble birth for the purpose of nullifying those who are privileged. So Paul proceeds to note that, in each case, when opposites are understood as being united and dependent, the opposition and the political hierarchies collapse. The integrity of the construct is not brought to a conclusion but is rather deconstructed.

I argue that Paul's critique serves to empty all theocratic identifications. The making of identification is understood by Paul as a construction that is not founded but is instead the product of social differentiation. The wise are wise in opposition to those who are not wise. So the wise are dependent upon the degrading designation that their other is not wise in order to enjoy the privileged designation as wise. The designation that some are 'wise' *already*, *always* assumes that there are those who are unwise, foolish. Without the opposition one cannot make the designation that one is 'wise'. The identification that one is wise enjoys no reference. The wise and the foolish enjoy no 'significance'. To be wise, as to be foolish, is an empty designation. Paul's critique proceeds by stating that God has 'chosen' the weak, foolish and ignoble to 'shame' the powerful, wise and noble. God's having chosen those who are commonly assessed to lack sacred preference serves to reverse the structure of theocratic valuation. God has 'chosen' the 'un-chosen' to bring to nothing those who previously were reputed to be the 'privileged chosen'. What is shameful is that the very designations that established the theocratic privilege of the wise, powerful and noble become designations that divest the wise, powerful and noble in the event of radical theocratic re-evaluation. What is 'shameful' is not the degradation of those who are privileged upon God's volatile, willful re-evaluation. Rather, what is judged to be shameful is that those who enjoy privilege are dependent upon their opponents, their opposites, for their privileged, investing designation. What Paul takes to be shameful is that the wise, powerful and noble are dependent upon the divesting designations 'foolish', 'weak' and 'lowly' in their claims of theocratic privilege. Without a theocratic economy, there is no privilege. That the household of the Lord benefits at the cost of others, and that in the name of God the dynasty privileges itself at the expense of others, is egregious.

It is important to note that Paul does not seek to exalt those chosen by God to counter the wise, powerful and of noble birth. Contrary to modern theologies of liberation in which the oppressed enjoy an elevated status as being more pure, or as having wisdom or knowledge, Paul's valuation of the lowly is such that they are lowly only in relation to the loftiness of those who apparently enjoy privilege. Paul's conception of opposition is quite formal. Paul assumes that each of the identities is the product of oppositional differentiation and strife, and, as such, the lowly are themselves nullified as lowly in the bringing of those who are counted as something to nothing. Thus Paul does not seek to re-establish theocratic authority by rejecting the dynasty of the Lord through an appeal that claims that the foolish, weak and ignoble are the true church.

Paul's contention that God brings the wise, powerful and those of noble birth to nothing by selection of the foolish, weak and lowly is not a simple reversal but a dialectical inversion that does not leave the opposing identities unmarked. Rather, all the identities are in play and come to dissolution.[1] God privileges no flesh.

In opposition to the dynastic theocracy in which power and authority are assessed according to one's position in the household of the Lord, Paul offers an extreme atheocratic critique of the dynasty. Sacred presence is absent from all flesh, including the 'flesh' and blood of the Lord. No one enjoys the privilege of representing Christ, neither his disciples nor even his younger brother. Theocracy is negated. The *church* is empty.

Now, I have no way of knowing whether the theocratic elite of the *church* (the household of the Lord) were shamed by Paul's critique. It seems unlikely, given what is known about James the Lord's brother and the *church*, that the dynasty of the Lord concerned themselves all that much with Paul's assessments. But then, Paul's critiques were not addressed to the *church* but to the *ecclesia* at Rome-Corinth and Galatia. It

---

1. Mark C. Taylor, *Erring: A Postmodern A/theology* (Chicago: University of Chicago Press, 1984), p. 10.

is unlikely that the dynasty ever read the letters to the Corinthians or the Galatians, although they may have heard about the letters second hand. Rather, it is aim of the rhetoric of Paul in reply to the situation in the *ecclesia* at Rome-Corinth and Galatia that the elite of the *church* should be shamed and that the dynasty should come to nothing. But these comments were for the eyes and ears of the Corinthians and the Galatians.

The 'call' of the Corinthians, Paul's conception of the purpose of the Corinthian *ecclesia*, was not to upset the distribution of power and authority whereby one group replaces or displaces another in a Christian theocratic hierarchy. The call of the Corinthians is to decompose the formative structures of power and authority of the *church* as the means by which the household of the Lord is deposed. Thus the weak, foolish and common do not come to enjoy a reverse of fortune, they do not come to rule a new church, a nondynastic household of God's chosen; instead, they serve in the deconstruction of theistic designation and theocracy. Paul assesses that all claims to be in the presence of God are boastful, and that those who boast forget their own status as mere human flesh in which a dependent relation with another generates all identification. Thus the boastful claim by the *church* that they enjoy identification with Christ is *not* generated because some one is 'the same' as the Lord, of the same generation, from the same womb or selected by the Lord to be a disciple. The privileged enjoy their privilege at the expense of those who were divested in the theocratic enterprise of the *church*.

Paul's critique of the theocracy of the *church* rests upon the assumption that the veracity of any identification with God is untenable, and that all identifications are the product of strife. Since God shows no partiality and no one enjoys identification with God, those who seek to warrant their authority by an appeal to sacred identification do so without sanction and for their own advantage.

I have argued that Paul began his critique of the household of the Lord in the early verses of 1 Corinthians, and went on in the final verses of the first chapter to press an extreme critique of the theocratic pretenses of the 'family' of the Lord. In light of the thesis I have proferred, the allusions to 'false brothers' in 1 Cor. 5.11, 2 Cor. 11.26 and Gal. 2.4 may well be other instances at which Paul identified one who was not a 'true brother' even though the individual was the Lord's 'blood brother'.[2]

While it is not the purpose of this study to engage in an analysis of

---

2.   Martyn, *Galatians*, p. 14.

Paul's conception of the church and his various methods of justification, it is nevertheless clear that Paul's appeals to revelation as opposed to the wisdom of men or worldly power are Paul's means of making room for himself in emergent Christian social institutions in which those who possess wisdom and the worldly power of having lived with Jesus enjoy established authority. Paul knows only Christ crucified, whereas James and the disciples knew Jesus in the flesh. Paul knows only Christ crucified and declares that Christ crucified and resurrected is superior to the Lord who was present to James and the disciples. So Paul declares his superiority because he was selected by the crucified Lord in a revelation. Paul's methods of justification serve to devalue the assumptions of his superiors to his own advantage all the while he is declaring that no one should seek their own advantage. But the advantage that Paul seeks is not 'theocratic'. Paul does not seek to establish a 'hierarchy' (the rule of priests or religious designates) in which he would rule as God's chosen. The declaration by Paul that he knows only Christ crucified is a heuristic device to counter the authority of the *church* for the purpose of overcoming the *church*'s authority to stratify and exclude.

I join with Elliott in his critique of Judge, Theissen and Meeks who argue that many of the problems addressed in the letters to the Corinthians arose from social stratification within the Corinthian *ecclesia*. Their contention that Paul established the *ecclesia* with a few individuals of modest means ('not many...wise, powerful, well-born') and that Apollos baptized a number of higher-status Corinthians ('I planted, Apollos watered') rests on scant textual evidence. But I find Elliott's contention that the resulting congregation was a combination of 'Paul's people' and 'Apollos's people' and then, in parenthesis, 'and perhaps a few others who belonged to neither contingent: those "of Cephas" and those "of Christ"...' nevertheless continues the social stratification within the Roman-Corinthian *ecclesia* hypothesis that he takes issue with.[3] I argue that the hypothesis that the conflict in the Roman-Corinth *ecclesia* is more or less the result of, or influenced by, stratification in the larger Roman-Corinthian society is an attempt to resolve interpretive difficulties born of an inadequate assessment of the structure and purpose of the text.

It is my contention that Paul's 'challenge to the ideology of privilege'[4] was not first and foremost, or even secondly, an engagement with Roman

3.   Neil Elliott, *Liberating Paul: The Justice of God and the Politics of the Apostle* (Maryknoll, NY: Orbis Books, 1994), p. 205.
4.   Elliott, *Liberating Paul*, p. 205.

socio-economic stratifications replicated in the *ecclesia* at Rome-Corinth. Paul's engagement in 1 Corinthians, as with his letter to the Galatians, is with the *church*'s ideology of privilege. And this ideology of privilege does not replicate the socio-economic stratifications internal to Roman society but is influenced in good measure by imperial occupation and the ideologies and utopian desires of Judean ethnic and national sovereignty.

Painter maintains in *Just James* that there was no evidence to confirm James or the party of James in the strife addressed in 1 Cor. 1.10-12 and 3.3–4.21.[5] At best, contends Painter, 'when Paul encountered opposition from the circumcision mission in the diasporas, it was associated with Peter, although there might be influence of James in the background'. Clearly I disagree with Painter on this point. James is not mentioned by name, but the pronouncement of household belonging to the Lord and the unambiguous designation of those who by virtue of their noble birth presume sacred privilege is strong evidence that Paul perceived that the Lord's brother's influence contributed in a significant way to the divisiveness of the Corinthian congregation.

5.   John Painter, *Just James: The Brother of Jesus in History and Tradition* (Columbia, SC: University of South Carolina Press, 1997), p. 78.

Chapter 4

CHRIST CRUCIFIED AND THE EMPTINESS OF THEOCRACY

The quoted 'sayings' introduced in 1 Cor. 1.12 ('I belong to Paul', 'I to Apollos', 'I to Cephas' or 'I to Christ') are repeated in the second chapter when Paul replies to the boastful claims of those who believe themselves to be *spiritual*. At 1 Cor. 1.26 Paul notes that among his audience in Corinth not many were wise according to worldly standards, not many powerful, not many of noble birth. But there is a reversal of fortune that comes with the gospel, if only as a device to negate theocratic privilege. For God selected what is foolish in the world to shame the wise, and the weak in the world to shame the strong, and the low and despised in the world, even things that are not, to bring to nothing things that are, for the purpose that 'no human being might boast in the presence of God' (1 Cor. 1.29). So who is to boast in the presence of God? No one. Instead, 'let him who boasts boast in the Lord'. And so Paul proceeds, having critiqued those who seek their own advantage, to present himself as someone who is lowly.

> [1]When I came to you, brethren, I did not come proclaiming to you the mysteries/testimony of God in lofty words or wisdom. [2]For I decided to know nothing among you except Jesus Christ and him crucified; [3]And I was with you in weakness and in much fear and trembling; [4]and my speech and my message were not in plausible words of wisdom, but in demonstration of the Spirit and power, [5]that your faith might not rest in the wisdom of men but in the power of God (1 Cor. 2.1-5).

The purpose of Paul's rhetorical strategy may be to rely upon the re-versals, which he has formulated and deployed in the immediately pro-ceeding verses, to improve or at least protect his status among the Corinthians. He did not come proclaiming to the Corinthians in lofty words or wisdom 'the *testimony* of God' or, as it is phrased in a significant number of manuscripts, 'the *mystery* of God'. Paul makes no self-glorify-ing claims of eloquence, reminding the Corinthian readers that he came to

Corinth in weakness and in much fear and trembling, with speech and a message that were implausible, so that the faith of the Corinthians would rest upon the power of God rather than human wisdom.

Unlike James the Lord's brother and the Lord's disciples, Paul can make no claims to knowing Jesus. Paul associates his weakness, his lack of worldly knowledge, his not belonging to Christ, with the weaknesses, foolishness and ignoble families of the Corinthians to whom the letters are addressed. Paul seeks in this way to influence those to whom the letters are addressed by associating himself with the Corinthians, and by differentiating himself and the Corinthians from the *church*. Instead of the private, secretive knowledge of the *church*, instead of the wisdom of men, Paul seeks to persuade the Corinthians to establish their faith upon the power of God. So, opposed to the *church*, Paul resolved not to know anything except Jesus Christ, which he quickly qualifies lest the reader mistakenly concludes that, like the *church*, Paul is founding his authority upon some worldly association. For Paul contends that he was resolved not to know anything except the *crucified* Jesus Christ. The *church* may have known the *worldly* Jesus Christ before he was crucified, but Paul knows only the *crucified* Jesus Christ. The *church* may have worldly knowledge of the Lord, but Paul's knowledge of the Lord is unworldly and revelatory. The wisdom of the *church*, which Paul does not possess, is declared by Paul to stand in opposition to the power of God. The *faith* of the Corinthians, who are characterized as foolish, weak and ignoble, should not be dependent upon those who are wise, powerful and of noble birth. The faith of the Corinthians should be dependent not upon the worldly power of the *church* but upon the power of God revealed in the crucified Lord.

Thus, given that he does not have the *church*'s means of authority, Paul cannot establish the authority of his ministry and his person by appeal to a worldly relationship with the Lord. Paul reverses the economy of authority and makes his own weakness, his lack of relationship, the means to establish his own authority. He turns the tables so that the alleged strength of his critics as members of the Lord's household becomes their disadvantage among the Corinthians. The contention that Paul's association with the crucified Christ is superior to those associated with the non- or precrucified Christ is Paul's attempt to subvert the authority of the *church*, the household of the Lord.

Is 'Christ crucified' Paul's pragmatic and prophetic proclamation that offers a critique of those whose 'household' rhetoric is a means for establishing their own superiority at the subordination of others? In opposition to such knowledge (worldly, household knowledge), Paul knows nothing. Drawing upon the concluding comments of the first chapter of the letter, Paul's knowing nothing—except for the crucified Christ, the one humiliated and executed—plays out the critical theme that that which is nothing brings to nothing those who are *something*. Paul's declaration that he knows nothing—except that which is lowly, including the crucified Christ—empties all such theocratic proclamations.

The transition from what preceded 1 Cor. 2.6-15 is clear.

> [6]Yet, among the mature we do impart wisdom, although it is not a wisdom of this age or of the rulers of this age, who are doomed to pass away. [7]But we impart a secret and hidden wisdom of God, which God decreed before the ages for our glorification. [8]None of the rulers of this age understood this; for if they had, they would not have crucified the Lord of glory. [9]But, as it is written,
>
> What no eye has seen, nor ear heard, nor the heart of man conceived, what God has prepared for those who love him,
>
> [10]God has revealed to us through the spirit. For the spirit searches everything, even the depths of God. [11]For what person knows a man's thoughts except the spirit of the man which is in him? So also no one comprehends the thoughts of God except the spirit of God. [12]Now we have received not the spirit of the world, but the spirit which is from God, that we might understand the gifts bestowed on us by God. [13]And we impart this in words not taught by human wisdom but taught by the spirit, interpreting spiritual truths to those who possess the spirit (interpreting spiritual truths in spiritual language).
>
> [14]The unspiritual man does not receive the gifts of the spirit of God, for they are folly to him, and he is not able to understand them because they are spiritually discerned. [15]The spiritual man judges all things, but is himself to be judged by no one (1 Cor. 2.6-15).

Evident in the Greek manuscripts but finding little expression in the English translations is the particle *de*, appearing in the second position in the first and second clauses of v. 6, which suggests the possibility that Paul is quoting not just from another source but from material with which he is in disagreement. The RSV translates the verse, '*Yet* among the mature we do impart wisdom, although it is not a wisdom of this age or of the rulers of this age, who are doomed to pass away.' But who are the subjects that assume that they have a wisdom to impart to the mature? And what does it mean to suggest that those who accept the wisdom you offer are mature and those who do not are immature?

Let me see if I have the common interpretation straight. Paul declares that those who are wise according to worldly standards are brought to shame by the foolish in Corinth and are critiqued by Paul for having been boastful. Paul then declares that he did not come proclaiming to the Corinthians—whom, in being foolish, God chose as his instrument to bring the wise to shame—the mystery of God in lofty words or wisdom. Like the foolish Corinthians, Paul too is foolish. His foolishness is further clarified by his contention that he knows nothing except for the crucified Jesus Christ. Paul's lack of wisdom provides the Corinthians with a basis of faith resting not on the wisdom of men but in the power of God. Would Paul then proceed by asserting that, in spite of all that has just been written, he actually does impart a wisdom that is superior, a wisdom that is different from the wisdom of the age and the rulers of the age—all of whom are doomed to pass away? And note v. 7, where it is declared that 'we' impart a secret (*mustēriō*) and hidden wisdom of God. Does this reverse the contention by Paul in the first person in 1 Cor. 2.1 when he declares that he did not proclaim to the Corinthians the secret (*mustērion*) of God in lofty words or wisdom?

Those who declare their possession of the secret and hidden wisdom of God contend that their wisdom is not human wisdom but wisdom taught by the spirit, and so only those who possess the spirit can understand what is taught by the spirit. Beginning with v. 7 the text begins a process of declaring the exclusivity of those selected by God to possess the spirit that grants wisdom. The elucidation of the scarcity of the spirit develops till it concludes with a final political declaration of the theocratic power of the spiritual man in a nonspiritual world (v. 15): 'The spiritual man judges all things, but is himself to be judged by no one.' God gave a select few the spirit, and the spirit given by God revealed to those few the secret and hidden wisdom of God. Those who possess the spirit have the luxury of an unrivaled means to knowledge of everything, including the depths of God. Their ability to comprehend apparently knows no limit. To possess the spirit is to enjoy complete and total knowledge.

In this spiritual economy only those who possess the spirit can acquire, transmit, receive and interpret knowledge of the cosmos and God. Those who possess the spirit enjoy unrivaled authority regarding matters of cosmology and theology. No dissension will be tolerated! Those who are spiritual know everything. The unspiritual know nothing. Those who have all-inclusive and superior knowledge also have the power to judge all others, although they themselves are not to be judged by those who have not received the spirit. The spirit is the spirit of knowledge, and knowledge is power.

To the authoritarian contention that those who possess the spirit are to judge all things but are not to be judged by others, Paul immediately raises a negative rhetorical question which confronts and critiques their assumed power by calling into question—and therefore making evident—their anthropological and theological assumptions (v. 16):

> For who has known the mind of the Lord so as to instruct him?

Quoting from Isa. 40.13, Paul employs the rich themes of radical negation to cut to the very heart of the boastful assumptions of those who maintain that they, mere humans, stand in the likeness of God.[1] Paul's negative rhetorical question at v. 16, drawn from Isaiah, makes the point that those who claim to be spiritual are making self-serving political claims. What they are about is not knowledge of God, for such knowledge is not possible. Rather, their claims to the spirit/power of God to judge and instruct everyone else is nothing more than a crude grab for power.

The claims to the spirit are claims to spiritual *power* or *authority*, and that power rests on the assumption that the difference between God and humanity is overcome by those few who possess the spirit, who possess the power of God. Those who receive the gift of the spiritual power of God are no longer merely human, they are closer to God than others: they are *like* God, in that they have been chosen by God to possess the spirit and so enjoy the power of God's knowledge.

Paul's negative rhetorical question at 1 Cor. 2.16a turns the advantage of claiming spiritual knowledge and power into a disadvantage. The issue raised by Paul is not about the *political* relation between those who identify themselves as spiritual and others as nonspiritual, but between those who claim to possess the spirit and the Lord. Since those who claim to possess the spirit also claim to know the Lord, then, given the political power to judge and instruct that comes with the spirit, Paul questions whether they are also to judge and have power over the Lord. Are those who claim to possess God's spirit to exercise authority over the Lord?

Another way to understand the text is to note the difference between the claim of the spiritual who know God and Paul's query as to their

---

1.   Isa. 40.12-19. See especially, vv. 13, 14 and 17:

[13]Who has directed the Spirit of the Lord, or as his counselor has instructed him?

[14]Whom did he consult for his enlightenment, and who taught him the path of justice, and taught him knowledge, and showed him the way of understanding?

[17]All the nations are as nothing before him, they are accounted by him as less than nothing and emptiness.

knowledge/power *over the Lord*. Paul's reply in 1 Cor. 2.16–3.4 nowhere addresses the topic of God, but rather raises questions as to the implications of the claim to knowledge and power of the spiritual group with respect to 'the Lord' and 'Christ'. Likewise, the spiritual faction as quoted nowhere mentions 'the Lord' or 'Christ'. Their claim to possess the spirit is strictly a theological claim that substantiates their theocratic power. Theological knowledge yields theocratic power; knowledge of God yields the power to represent God, and to have the power of God in relation to community.

> [16] 'For who has known the mind of the Lord so as to instruct him?' But we have the mind of Christ.
> [3.1]But I, brethren, could not address you as spiritual men, but as men of the flesh, as babies in Christ. [2]I fed you with milk, not solid food; for you were not ready for it; and even yet you are not ready, [3]for you are still of the flesh. For while there is jealousy and strife among you, are you not of the flesh, and behaving like ordinary men? [4]For when one says, 'I belong to Paul,' and another, 'I belong to Apollos,' are you not merely men? (1 Cor. 2.16–3.4).

Paul does not find those who declare themselves to be spiritual to be spiritual at all, but men of the flesh—in fact, no more than babes in Christ. If we are to take Paul's critical deployment of 'flesh' as an indication, then we may presume that the bifurcation of 'spiritual' and 'flesh' was a fundamental differentiation and stratification in the spiritual economy. The flesh stands in counter-distinction to the spirit and is inferior to the spirit. The spirit is from God but the flesh is not. Paul's assessment that he could not address them as spiritual men but as men of the flesh reverses their self-assessment *within the economy of their own political and spiritual convictions*. Paul's assessment is a degradation of those who claim to be spiritual. By turning their own words against them, Paul employs the distinctions by which they enhanced their own prestige at the degradation and humiliation of others in order to humiliate and degrade those who said that they possessed the spirit of God. In fact, Paul asserts that those who count themselves spiritual are not only 'men' of the flesh: they are 'nursing babes' who are utterly dependent on their care-givers for milk, since they cannot consume solid food. Paul's assessment that the spiritual are of the flesh and that they are in fact infantile human flesh is meant to be stinging and derogatory. A nursing baby is inferior, vulnerable and the most dependent of all human flesh. The spiritualists are presented by Paul as infants who understand nothing or very little (given the low valuation of young children in that day and society). Their speech is comprehended by no one. Paul continues the degradation of the spiritualist by declaring that those who count themselves spiritual are obsessed with jealousy and contentious strivings, which are motivated by desires of the *flesh*. Those who claim to possess the spirit of God that knows all things, even the depths of God, and so assess themselves to be superior to everyone who does not possess the spirit, are represented by Paul to be no different from ordinary persons. And in fact, those who claim to possess the spirit, who claim to enjoy theo-cosmic knowledge, are 'less' than the ordinary because they are driven by grand, contentious desires. He concludes that those who make claims of possessing the spirit and 'belonging' to a sacred person are themselves no more than boastful humans who make contentious claims for their own advantage.

It is presumed that a presentation is a creation, something original, whereas a representation is a copy or extension or sign that does not claim its own originality or self-originating power or authority. Instead, the representation is authentic only to the extent to which the representation 're-presents' a presence that is other than the representation. And the power and authority of a representation depends upon the authority of the referent. A beginning of critical thought is said to be the critique of simple representation. The contention that 'x' is a representation of another is itself a presentation that presents 'x' *as* another. Such a critique of representation, while much in vogue among intellectuals, is a dangerous enterprise when the representations are said to represent 'God' with power and authority, particularly violent power and political authority. To critique representation in a theocracy is to call into question the legitimacy of supreme authority.

When 'theocratic' representation is critiqued as illegitimate, and the claims to representation are assessed to be no more than a presentation that claims representation, then theocratic authority is less inchoate, less veiled. The structures and practices of representation faultier, and the transcendent significance of 'theocratic' authority resolves clearly into power arrangements. Authority becomes more immediate and less symbolic, much the way the force of an empire asserts itself without symbolic 'representation'. The 'authority' of an empire whose force is immediate and brutal does not enjoy significance to conquered peoples. The use of signs and claims of representation appear flat and manipulative to those who, not sharing the significance, are identified for subjugation by those seeking domination.

In opposition to the dynastic theocracy in which power and authority are assessed according to one's station in the household of the Lord, Paul offered an extreme a/theocratic critique that asserted sacred absence to all flesh. No one represents Christ. Therefore no one enjoys the privileges of representing Christ. Theocracy is negated. The *church* is empty.

In 1 Cor. 1.26-27, Paul lays out the dyadic configuration of the *church*'s theocratic valuation. The first term in each set is invested with theocratic value, is assessed to enjoy the privileging selection and presence of God. The second term in each dyadic set is the 'other' of the first, lacking the association with sacred selection and presence that the first term enjoys, and so does not enjoy the theocratic privileges that come with sacred representation.

Wise	Foolish
Powerful	Weak
Noble birth	Scandalous birth
God's presence	God's absence

Into this dyadic structure Paul contends that it is God's intent to employ the second divested term to nullify the theocratic economy. And so Paul proceeds to note that, in each case, when opposites are understood as being united, the system of opposition and the political hierarchies that such structures serve collapse. The integrity of the construct is not brought to a conclusion but deconstructs of its own accord.

Theocracy is founded upon a transcendent 'presence' that, in selecting a few out of the many to privilege, creates an economy based upon the scarcity of sacred presence in a world of abundant sacred absence. God privileges those who enjoy the good fortune of sacred presentation over those whom God has not visited with good fortune.

I argue that Paul's critique is a radical attempt to empty all theocratic identifications, in fact to deconstruct the making of identification so that identity is understood as a construction in the process of social differentiation. The wise are wise in opposition to those who are not wise. So the wise are dependent upon the degrading designation that their other is not wise in order to enjoy the privileged designation as wise. The designation that some are 'wise' *already*, *always* assumes that there are those who are unwise, foolish. Without the opposition the designation that one is 'wise' is empty. The identification that one is wise enjoys no reference for wisdom; it is not an essence, a self-sufficient entity, a state, or sacred association.

God has 'chosen' the previously 'un-chosen' to bring to nothing those who previously were reputed to be the privileged 'chosen'. God's having chosen those who are commonly assessed to lack sacred preference serves to reverse the structure of theocratic valuation. What is shameful is that the very designations that established the theocratic privilege of the wise, powerful and noble become designations that divest the wise, powerful and noble in the event of radical theocratic re-evaluation. What is 'shameful' is not the degradation of those who are privileged upon God's volatile, willful re-evaluation. Rather, the shame that comes to the wise, powerful and noble is that they have always been dependent upon their opponents, their opposites, in order to enjoy their investing, hierarchical designation. What Paul takes to be shameful for the wise, powerful and noble is that the structure of the theocratic economy and their privileged identifications have no sacred reference and designate no 'other' presence—sacred or otherwise.

The 'call' of the Corinthians, Paul's conception of the purpose of the Corinthian *ecclesia*, was not to upset the distribution of power and authority whereby one group replaces or displaces another in a Christian theocratic hierarchy. The call of the Corinthians is to deconstruct the structures of power and authority of the *church*. Thus the weak, foolish and common do not come to enjoy a reverse of fortune, for they do not come to rule a new church, a nondynastic household of God's chosen, but serve in the deconstruction of theistic designation that disallows theocracy. Paul assesses that all claims to be in the presence of God are boastful, and that those who boast forget their own status as mere human flesh in which all identification is generated by a dependent relation with another person. Thus, the boastful claim by the *church* that they enjoy identification with Christ is *not* generated because someone is the same as Christ, of the same generation, from the same womb or selected by Christ to be a disciple. For Paul, the disestablishment of theistic identification and the collapse of theocratic hierarchy is a moment of salvation. The privileged enjoy their privilege at the expense of those who were divested in the theocratic enterprise of the *church*. Those who are foolish, weak and of common birth have been chosen by God not to become wise, powerful or noble— but to bring the wise, powerful and noble 'to nothing'. Salvation is the collapse of the *church* when no one can boast of their being in the presence of God.

An *a*/theocratic reading of the Corinthian and Galatian epistles will invert established meaning and subvert what has heretofore been deemed to enjoy established sacred authority in Christendom. But the inversion and subversion of established theocratic authority is not the outcome of a critical or dismissive interpretation of the epistles. Rather, *a*/theocracy is woven into the very themes and textures of the epistles which come to invert and subvert the very authority and authorizes which sanction and maintain the epistles as scripture. *A*/theocracy can be understood in terms of a radical *ecclesiology* that prepares the way for reinterpreting the notion of the a/t-oning body of Christ beyond the conception of 'community'.

Part II

DE/SECRATION

INTRODUCTION

Traditionally, interpreters have read the following passage as Paul's intro-duction to the theme that 'the church' is the sacred temple of God.

[16]Do you not know that you are God's temple and that God's spirit dwells in you? [17]If anyone destroys God's temple, God will destroy him. For God's temple is holy, and that temple you are (1 Cor. 3.16-17).

This 'introduction' is then associated with 2 Cor. 6.14–7.1, which is customarily assessed to be Paul's further or mature elaboration of what he means by the claim that the Christian community is the temple of God and that it is the responsibility of those who would be the *sacred* temple to seek perfection.

However, in our study of 1 Cor. 3.16-17 I argued that Paul was *not* making the claim that Christians are the temple of God. Instead, I argued that Paul quoted and critiqued the boastful contention made by some that they possessed the spirit that gave them knowledge, even knowledge about the mysteries of God. And further, those who claimed to possess the spirit presumed a privilege to judge those without the spirit, while those with the spirit were to be judged by no one else. Paul's critical reply to these claims included his assessment that those who claimed to possess the spirit behaved like ordinary flesh, jealously seeking their own advantage. In fact, they behaved like babies.

Immediately following Paul's quotation and his reply to the convictions of those claiming to possess the spirit of God, Paul introduces the claim made by a faction that they are God's temple. At the time we focused our attention on Paul's critique of the boastfulness of those who believed themselves to enjoy a special connection to the sacred. Traditionally, inter-preters have assumed that Paul was making the claim at 1 Cor. 3.16-17 that Christians are the temple of God and have assumed that Paul eluci-dates at 2 Cor. 6.14–7.1 what he means by the claim that the Christian community is the temple of God and the responsibility of those who would be the *sacred* temple to seek perfection. However, I argued that Paul was *not* making the claim that Christians are the temple of God in 1 Cor. 3.16-

17 but was quoting those who made the claim in order to critique the claim as deceptive and to judge those who made the identification as self-destructive.

In Part II we shall consider the pre-eminent presentation of the Christian community as 'the sacred temple' in the Pauline corpus. I argue that 2 Cor. 6.14–7.1, like 1 Cor. 3.16-17, is a quotation by Paul from other sources which he includes in his reply in order to directly and forthrightly critique.

The extended text at 2 Cor. 6.14–7.1 has a notorious history. It has been called upon, and continues to be called upon, to warrant a wide range of exclusionary practices in Christian communities. For instance, the opening verse and its echo a few lines later have been employed to forbid the marriage of Christians and non-Christians, or to differentiate between 'sacred matrimony in the church' and a secular marriage, or to justify the annulment of a marriage between a member and a nonmember of the 'church'. In other instances, the text has been employed to warrant the disciplining and sometimes expulsion of believers from the church who associate with 'contaminated' unbelievers. In American church history, a verse of the text as translated in the King James Version of the Bible became a slogan and rallying cry for the exodus of Holiness/Pentecostals in the 'come out-ism' movement from the Methodist Church in the 1890s. The Methodists were judged by the faction to have forsaken their call to seek sacred perfection.

And of course, one of the more notorious uses of the text was to justify the expulsion of Jews or other non-Christian peoples, as well as Christians judged to be unorthodox, as desecrations of Christian society. Given the harshness of the 'defilement' discourse and the fantastic promise of theonomy, the text has been employed to support a range of violent measures against persons judged to be defilements. In some instances, those who were judged to compromise the sanctity of the Christian state were sanctioned and excluded from access to locations and services. And in the most horrific instances, those assessed as contaminates of sacred Christian society have been 'cleansed' from that society through acts of execution and extermination.

Chapter 5

TENSIONS IN THE *TEXTUS*, CONFLICTS IN THE CORPUS

Introduction

The coherence of 2 Cor. 6.11–7.3 has been a matter of debate for the past century. Furnish notes that 'Most commentators agree that the intervening material (6.14–7.1) is, to at least some extent, *disruptive*.'[1] Moffatt, meanwhile, characterized the material as standing 'like an erratic boulder' which drastically disrupts the flow of the text.[2] The reasons for such characterizations are quite clear to a critical reader. Verses 6.11-13 and 7.2-3, which bracket 6.14–7.1, are a defense and a plea to the Corinthians, or a faction therein, to open themselves to Paul's ministry of reconciliation.

> [11]Our mouths are open to you, Corinthians, our hearts are wide. [12]You are not cramped by us; you are cramped, rather, in your feelings. [13]In reply—I am speaking to children—widen (2 Cor. 6.11-13).

> [2]Provide us room! No one did we wrong, no one did we corrupt, no one did we defraud. [3]I do not say this to condemn you, because I have stated before that you are in our hearts to die together and to live together (2 Cor. 7.2-3).

Yet in the midst of these verses stands a piece (6.14–7.1) that is diametrically opposed to reconciling openness and inclusion.

> [14]Do not mismate yourselves with unbelievers. For what have righteousness and lawlessness in common, or what partnership has light with darkness? [15]What concord has Christ with Beliar, or what share has a believer with an unbeliever? [16]What agreement has the temple of God with idols? For we are the temple of the living God; as God said, 'I will live in them and move among them, and I will be their God, and they shall be my people. [17]Therefore, come out from them, and be separated from them, says the Lord, and

---

1.   Victor Paul Furnish, *II Corinthians* (The Anchor Bible; translated with Introduction, Notes and Commentary; Garden City, NY: Doubleday, 1984), p. 368.

2.   James Moffatt, *An Introduction to the Literature of the New Testament* (New York: Charles Scribner's Sons, 3rd rev. edn, 1929), p. 125.

touch nothing unclean; and I will welcome you, [18]and I will be a father to you, and you shall be my sons and daughters, says the Lord Almighty' (2 Cor. 6.14-18).

As regards the content of 6.14–7.1, critical readers have been more or less content to concentrate their attention on noting the discrepancies between the rejected unions listed in vv. 14-16 and claims made elsewhere in the Pauline corpus accepting such unions.

What Fellowship has Light with Darkness?
The rejection of the *koinonia*, commonly translated 'partnership' or 'fellow-ship', of light and darkness in v. 14c stands in opposition to what Paul has stated a few chapters earlier, where light comes from archaic darkness.

> For it is the God who said, 'Let light shine out of darkness', who has shone in our hearts to give the light of the knowledge of the glory of God in the face of Christ (2 Cor. 4.6).

Do Not be Mismated with Unbelievers
It is commonly pointed out that v. 14a advances that the union of believers and unbelievers in marriage is *heterozygein*, 'mismating' or 'misyoking'. But this stands in stark contradiction to a passage in 1 Corinthians where Paul advises believers not to divorce their unbelieving mate.

> [12]To the rest I say, not the Lord, that if any brother has a wife who is an unbeliever, and she consents to live with him, he should not divorce her. [13]If any woman has a husband who is an unbeliever, and he consents to live with her, she should not divorce him. [14]For the unbelieving husband is consecrated through his wife, and the unbelieving wife is consecrated through her husband. Otherwise, your children would be unclean, but as it is they are holy (1 Cor. 7.12-14).

Note that in 1 Corinthians 7 the unbelieving spouses are 'consecrated' by virtue of being mated to the believer, and the children of the union of the believer and the unbeliever are 'holy'. In 1 Corinthians 7 the holy is contagious, whereas in 2 Cor. 6.14–7.1 it is the profane that is contagious. In the former, any relation between the holy and the unholy occasions a contagious holy transformation of the unholy. In the latter, any relation the sacred has with the profane is an accommodation that tarnishes purity and sanctity. While I do not intend to rehearse the full details of this manner of critique, it is clear that individual claims made in 2 Cor. 6.14-16b sharply digress from, even contradict, similar kinds of claim made elsewhere in the Epistles. The noting of such obvious contradictions has dominated much of the critical analysis of the texts by those defending the judgment that 2 Cor. 6.14–7.1 is an interpolation.

I will argue that vv. 14-16a are a critique of Paul's ministry of reconciliation. This 'Critique of Reconciliation' (vv. 14-16b) opposes more than the individual sets of unities. The 'Critique of Reconciliation' is a critique and rejection of Paul's ministry and thought—in particular, Paul's assumption that the holy brings coherence or unity to opposites.

Traditional Responses

Textual Coherence, Corpus Integrity

Traditional interpreters assume that in 2 Cor. 6.14–7.1 Paul is warning the Corinthians against compromising with the world. A common strategy is to assert that 6.14–7.1 was placed after Paul's discussion of the reconciliation fragment and the defense of his ministry of reconciliation in order for the apostle to clarify the limits of reconciliation. Thus, 6.14–7.1 provides a much-needed limit to the scope of an overzealous notion of reconciliation. True, God was reconciling the world to God's self in Christ but, in keeping with orthodox ecclesiastical interpretations, the reconciliation does not entail that the entire world is or can be one with God. Given the traditional reading, it would be mistaken to conclude that, with reconciliation, the differences between God and the world, or God and the devil, or believers and unbelievers, are to be overcome. *The reconciliation in Christ is not inclusive of all differences.*

Traditional readers brush off the charge that the verses in question are incoherent as regards (if not in positive contradiction with) the immediate verses and the larger conception of the ministry of reconciliation. Traditional readers contend that the verses that frame Paul's admonition should be read as a call for the Corinthians to be *open to Paul's authority.*

> [11]Our mouths are open to you, Corinthians, our hearts are wide. [12]You are not cramped by us; you are cramped, rather, in your feelings. [13]As a response in kind—I am speaking to children—widen (2 Cor. 6.11-13).

> [2]Provide us room! No one did we wrong, no one did we corrupt, no one did we defraud. [3]I do not say this in condemnation, because I have stated before that you are in our hearts to die together and to live together (2 Cor. 7.2-3).

The appeals to openness are read as calling for the Corinthians not to resist Paul's admonition and authority. Thus it is assumed and assessed that the text is integral in the local text, coherent with the general corpus of Pauline epistles, and authoritatively Pauline.

Interpretive Plays, Interpretive Problems

The Textual Integrity of 2 Cor. 6.11–7.3 and the Origins of 2 Cor. 6.14–7.1
A variety of interpolation hypotheses have been proposed to explain the incoherence of 2 Cor. 6.14–7.1 relative to the local text and the Pauline corpus. The 'minimal interpolation' hypothesis holds that the text is incoherent in its local context but may cohere elsewhere in the exchange, or possibly with some texts of the exchange that were not included by the editors in the canonical collection of the Paul-Corinthian correspondence. The 'radical interpolation' hypothesis agrees with the minimal interpolation hypothesis that the verses are incoherent with respect to their placement at 6.13/7.2 but differs from the minimal hypothesis by further assessing that conceptually and linguistically the text is incoherent with regards to 1 Corinthians, 2 Corinthians and indeed the Pauline corpus.

Thus the interpolation hypotheses offer speculative models that seek to provide causal explanations for the specific and/or general incoherence of the verses. Both the minimal and radical interpolation hypotheses assume that the verses are misplaced, but differ as to the origin of the verses in question and the extent of the incoherence.

With the minimal interpolation hypothesis, it is concluded that 6.14–7.1 is coherent with the thought of Paul as evident in the Pauline corpus in general but incoherent in its canonical location between 6.13/7.2. The hypothetical editor, as opposed to the author, misplaced or misjudged the appropriateness of placing the Pauline material at 6.13/7.2. However, I judge that such a hypothesis proposes a hypothetical editor who was incompetent, for only an incompetent editor would have inserted 6.14–7.1 between a set of verses with which it would be so strikingly at odds. Thus, according to the interpolation hypothesis, some hypothetical, incompetent editor causes our critical textual problems. Or maybe there was a committee of incompetent editors who were persuaded by some incompetent suggestion to so place the Pauline verses. Who knows, hypothetically speaking?

The radical interpolation hypothesis holds that 6.14–7.1 is non-Pauline or even anti-Pauline material inserted by a hypothetical editor or editors. Assuming the material is non-Pauline, it might be the case that the hypothetical editor thought that the material actually supported Paul's arguments, and chose to break the text at 6.13 and 7.2 in order to insert these supportive verses. However, given the extent to which the verses disrupt the flow of the text, the hypothetical editor proposed by the radical interpolation hypothesis is as incompetent as the hypothetical editor proposed by the minimal interpolation hypothesis. Both might be hypothetically well intentioned—that is, they sought to insert material that they judged to be supportive of the text's thesis—but their editorial skills suggest that they were nevertheless intellectually and linguistically incompetent for the task.

Now, if we conclude with Betz and company that the text is anti-Pauline in origin and was inserted by a later editor (or editors), then not only is the hypothetical editor(s) incompetent but dishonest. Seeking an advantage, the editor(s) sought to garner authority for a set of socio-religious convictions by inserting the exclusivistic, patriarchal, theocratic text into the Pauline corpus. Like the hypothetical editors proposed in the minimal interpolation hypothesis, the radical interpolation hypothesis proposes an incompetent hypothetical editor who, seeking to advance his or her convictions, breaks the text and inscribes the verses *at just the right place*[3]— where the verses conspicuously run counter to the flow of the text in which they are inserted. In my judgment Betz and company, who propose a radical interpolation hypothesis, propose a radically incompetent, as well as dishonest, hypothetical editor.

If we follow this hypothesis, we may find ourselves engaged in a paranoid speculation. A hypothetical editor or group of editors, while preparing the Corinthian manuscripts for reproduction and circulation, tampered with the content in order to further their own socio-religious agenda. Thus, in a conspiracy to manipulate those who value the texts (the Corinthian Church? Gentile Christians?), they mutilated the text in an attempted forgery and defrauded the author.

Complications

In response to the interpolation hypothesis, Furnish writes:

> Indeed, since an accidental intrusion of 6.14–7.1 into its present location is highly unlikely, and since there is no textual evidence that 2 Cor. ever existed without the passage, all interpolation theories must suppose that the material was added deliberately at this position at the time the Corinthian correspondence was assembled for general circulation. But then the question becomes why the passage was placed just here, even if it was a genuine Pauline fragment. For those who regard the fragment as non-Pauline in origin, the question is rather more difficult; for those who describe it as anti-Pauline, the problem is *almost insurmountable.*

3.   To be read ironically.

> What evidence there is would seem to be best satisfied by the hypothesis that the passage is of non-Pauline composition, but was incorporated by the apostle himself as he wrote this letter.
>
> This passage therefore remains an enigma within 2 Cor., neither its origin nor its place in the context being entirely clear. It may be integral to the context, but—if it has only been cited by Paul and not actually composed by him—it remains only marginally Pauline.[4]

Furnish concludes his comment on the text:

> And even if it is both integral to the context and of Pauline composition, it remains a secondary appeal, subordinate to the primary one which is introduced in 6.11-13 and then resumed and concluded in 7.2-3.[5]

In other words, argues Furnish, 6.14–7.1 is cited as a *secondary* appeal in support of the *primary* argument which is presented at 6.11-13 and concluded at 7.2-3. The assumption is that if the piece belongs in its location, then it must positively support the general argument.

The Question of Textual Coherence

What troubles me about Furnish's judgment that 6.14–7.1 is a secondary appeal is that he fails to show how the secondary appeal 'supports', weakly or strongly, the primary argument. In fact, I suspect that his qualification that the text is a secondary appeal is simply a way of conceding that no reasonable interpretation has been put forth so far that positively connects the text as a *support* to the primary argument. For, when all is said and done, Furnish concludes, 'This passage therefore, remains an *enigma* within 2 Corinthians, neither its origin nor its place in the context being entirely clear.'[6] In other words, the verses in question are judged to 'support' the argument, but no one seems to know how the verses actually do 'support' the argument.

---

4. Furnish, *II Corinthians*, p. 383 (my emphasis). Furnish notes that Klinzing suggests that the material is perhaps drawn from Christian baptismal parenesis into the text (George Klinzing, *Die Umdeutung des Kultus in der Qumrangemeinde und im Neuen Testament* [Göttingen: Vandenhoeck & Ruprecht, 1971], pp. 179-82). But, Furnish convincingly points out, 'if this were the case, would not one expect more adaptation and specific application of the material than seems to have taken place?' (p. 383). Furnish points out that 'the Christ hymn of Phil. 2.6-11 is not just inserted into the letter, but carefully integrated into the argument...' whereas the text at 6.14–7.1 is not well integrated.

5. Furnish, *II Corinthians*, p. 383.

6. Furnish, *II Corinthians*, p. 383 (my emphasis).

While Furnish is in a quandary over the apparent lack of coherence between the verses in their canonical location and the ways the content of the verses differ, even blatantly contradicting positions and convictions voiced by Paul in other texts, Furnish clearly sees and presents the dilemma. He concurs with those who hold the minimal interpolation hypothesis that the verses are from a non-Pauline source, but rejects the radical interpolation hypothesis that they were included by later, corrupting editors. Furnish concludes that the verses were 'cited' by Paul. As we will see, I think Furnish is correct as to his assessment that Paul 'cited' the verses! But Furnish goes on—mistakenly, I judge—to contend that while the passage 'is only *marginally* Pauline', because it was not 'carefully *integrated* into the argument', the verses were *somehow* cited by Paul in *support* of his argument.[7]

Patte judges the common hermeneutical practice of reading the text as an argument is wrong. He contends that such a reading of the text assumes that everything in the text is incorporated specifically to support Paul's argument. The judgment that 6.14–7.1 'does not seem to fit into the overall argument' identifies something of the difficulty.[8] The alleged incoherence of the text is the product of readers who attempt to discern the 'logical flow of the argument'. Patte continues:

> the overall coherence and unity ... are those of a discourse addressed by an author, Paul, to certain readers, the Corinthians, with the hope to achieve some kind of effect upon the readers, and this through the overall organization of the discourse and its figurativization.

The assumption that the text is an argument, and therefore must conform to logical argumentation, is wrong, argues Patte. In opposition to such an assumption, Patte offers an analysis of the metaphorical ways of thinking that are expressive of a text rich in metaphor.[9]

While I disagree with Patte's metaphorical interpretation of the text, his critique of those who assume that the text (6.11–7.3) is an argument is partially helpful. The strength of Patte's position is his assumption that the text was written to be read by a particular audience and that the text was not written to be read by that audience as a logical argument in which every aspect of the presentation was to be read as a premise in a

7.   Furnish, *II Corinthians*, p. 383 (my emphasis).

8.   Daniel Patte, *Paul's Faith and the Power of the Gospel: A Structural Introduction to the Pauline Letters* (Philadelphia: Fortress Press, 1983), p. 24.

9.   Patte, *Paul's Faith*, p. 39.

developing argument which drew a conclusion. Thus I concur that any interpretation that does not take the assumed readers into account is flawed. Yet, contrary to Patte, I will argue that both the larger text (6.11–7.3) and the shorter passage (6.14–7.1) *are* argumentative. I will argue that the larger text is a complex argument that includes a quoted, com-posite argument (that is, the shorter passage) which is counter to the general argument of the larger text.

I find that the customary categories of 'origin' and 'place' may limit the discussion of the disjunctive pieces of 6.11–7.3. The assumption has been that if the text in question is not the work of the author, if the author is not its 'origin', then an argument must be made to show how the author em-ployed the 'nonoriginal' work *in support of* the author's thesis or cause. It is the assumption that 'other', 'nonoriginal' texts are employed by authors of biblical texts only to *support* their thesis.

Furnish's conclusion (that those who judge 6.14–7.1 as anti-Pauline are faced with an almost insurmountable problem) assumes an overtly simple understanding of textual integrity (or conceptual coherence, for that matter). This simple understanding of textual integrity fails to note that the texts in question are *epistles*. The judgment that the verses provide enig-matic 'support' for the passage in which they are included assumes an understanding of textual 'coherence' that is not openly addressed in the secondary material on the text. The integrity of an epistle need not duplicate the integrity of an orthodox theological treatise or a propo-sitional argument. I will return to this topic below.

The Textus *of a Reply*

I concur with those who hold that 2 Cor. 6.14–7.1 stands in opposition to Pauline convictions. However, I do not assume that the passage is a simple text. I will argue that 6.14–7.1 forms a 'composite text'. The first part of the composite text (vv. 14-16b) is a critique of Paul's ministry of re-conciliation. The second (vv. 16b-18) is the presentation of an alternative communal vision that appeals to a theonomic patriarchal promise. The critique of the reconciliation of opposites and the quotation of a theonomic patriarchal promise are employed to justify the third part of the text (7.1), which is an appeal for communal self-purification through the exclusion or purging of those who violate communal sanctity.

Thus I agree with Betz and company, who argue that 6.14–7.1 contains anti-Pauline convictions. But they are only partially correct. The claim that

6.14–7.1 is anti-Pauline fails to critically discern the complexity of the quoted verses and to distinguish between 'anti-Pauline' and 'non-Pauline' material and convictions. To say that the material is anti-Pauline is to assert that the material is in a significant sense a direct critique of the work, convictions and/or thought of Paul. I will argue that vv. 14-16a are a direct and detailed critique of Paul's convictions expressed in the ministry of reconciliation. But vv. 16c-18 are not anti-Pauline. They are from a non-Pauline text employed in the complex argument of 6.14–7.1 to *warrant* the direct critique of Paul's ministry of reconciliation at vv. 14-16a and the appeal for communal self-purification at 7.1. I assume that vv. 16c-18 carry some sense of authority for those who deploy the verses in the extended argument (6.14–7.1) of the passage. Thus the origin of vv. 16c-18 are non-Pauline (but not anti-Pauline), although they are employed by the author(s) of 6.14–7.1 in their direct anti-Pauline critique of the ministry of reconciliation.

Verse 7.1 is the conclusion that unites the exclusivistic, theonomic convictions with ritual purity—reiterating the opposition to Paul's ministry of reconciliation and the at-oning community that he envisions. The passage (6.14–7.1) is thus composed of material that is cited from an authoritative source (vv. 16b-18) that is deployed to serve as a critique of reconciliation (vv. 14-16a, 7.1). In terms of source criticism, the passage is composed of both anti- and non-Pauline material. Nevertheless, the non-Pauline material is employed by the authors of 6.14–7.1 to warrant a direct, anti-Pauline critique.

Counter to Betz and others, I reject the radical interpolation hypothesis that the verses in question were inserted by a later editor. Instead, I argue that the text is a compound argument against Paul's convictions that Paul quotes from the Corinthian letter to him in his letter back to the Corinthians. I have presented my defense for reading the Corinthian correspondence as a reply elsewhere.[10] I have demonstrated the usefulness of such a hermeneutical strategy with respect to 1 Cor. 7, 8.1-9, 10.31–11.16 and 14.34-36. I offer the following exegesis as a continuation of that enterprise.

So what is the status of the verses in question? What purpose do they serve in the context?

I argue that 6.14–7.1 does not support the argument of 6.11-13 and 7.2-3. Instead, 6.14–7.1 is counter to Paul's position. The verses are quoted by

---

10. See Part II, 'The Language of Difference in the Pauline *Textus*', especially Chapter 6, 'Hermeneutical *Textus*', in Odell-Scott, *A Post-Patriarchal Christology*, pp. 123-40.

Paul to stand in counterpoint. But, contrary to Furnish and company, the verses are not marginally related to the topic at hand. Instead, they are at the center. They are the focus. They are the *targets*. They are the focus and the target of the verses that frame the discussion at 6.11-13 and 7.2-3, because Paul quite clearly sees that the theonomic that is being proposed in vv. 16b-18 and the communal policies that such a vision yields (in vv. 14-16a and 7.1) stand in direct opposition to *his* ministry and the baptismal, salvific, ecclesiastical and reconciling convictions that he has proclaimed.

I will argue that 6.14–7.1 is a quotation from a letter to Paul expressing the opinions of a faction within the Corinthian congregation. I will also argue that 6.11–7.3 forms a coherent text.

But the question will be raised, 'What is the purpose of Paul's inclusion of the piece which stands in stark opposition to his ministry of reconciliation?' My answers will come at the end of this study. However, to put it briefly and in broad strokes, the inclusion of the nonsupportive argument demonstrates the exclusivity of the faction of which Paul is critical. Second, Paul's reply provides an opportunity for him to demonstrate the 'inclusive' capacity of the ministry of reconciliation to at-one with 'others' who stand in stark opposition to his convictions and ministry. Thus the 'inclusion' of the 'exclusionist' serves as a demonstration of the radical gathering of difference, the at-onement in Christ. I will argue that Paul's strategy is to call into question the exclusionary conviction of his opponents in order that all might be reconciled to one another. Third, I will argue that Paul's reply in 7.2 is expressive of Paul's deconstructive method of argumentation, whereby he empties the identifications with the sacred and asserts that those who seek their own advantage fashion distinctions to their own advantage.

Unlike all previous interpreters who identify 6.14–7.1 as anti-Pauline, I reject the radical interpolation hypothesis that a later hypothetical editor inserted the text in question. Instead, I argue that 6.14–7.1 is a compound argument against Paul's thought, which Paul quotes from the Corinthian letter to him in his letter back to the Corinthians.

The critique of reconciliation is itself a reply to Paul and to which he replies. The texture is convoluted, reversing, and doubling back on reverses. This is no flat *textus*. It is an intimate, striking, intense exchange between adversaries who know one another's positions well. This exchange goes to the heart of the discussion.

Furnish began his commentary with the observation that:

> Here [2 Cor.] one sees the Apostle Paul in spirited and sometimes anguish-
> ing dialogue with his congregation in Corinth, with a group of rival apostles
> who have intruded themselves into the congregation there, and even with
> himself.[11]

That Paul is engaged in such a convoluted dialogue—with the congregation in Corinth, with each rival faction within the congregation and with
himself—is more expressive of the texture of the text than the simple
assumption that the text is more or less a coherent presentation and that
everything in the text serves in a simple, straightforward, unsophisticated
manner to support a thesis.

Contra Furnish and the great company of scholars who contend that
6.14–7.1 offers positive support for Paul's argument, I argue that Paul
quoted those verses precisely in order to call into question the self-righteous, exclusionary convictions of those who assert and/or ascend to this
theocratic vision. In other words, 6.11–7.3 is a complex *textus* that bandies
replies in a tight exchange between adversaries.

In my work on 1 Cor. 14.34-36, I argued that Paul quoted from a letter
addressed to him from the congregation in Corinth which proposed that
women should keep silence in the churches (vv. 34-35) to which Paul
replied in v. 36 with a two-fold negative query which rejected the presumptions to male privilege.[12] Paul's use of material drawn from persons
and positions with whom he disagreed are often incorporated into his
letters not as supports to his own positions but to provide clarity for what
it is he directly and forthrightly critiques.

---

11. Furnish, *II Corinthians*, p. 3.
12. See Odell-Scott, 'Let The Women Speak in Church', pp. 90-93; 'In Defense of
an Egalitarian Interpretation', pp. 100-103; *A Post-Patriarchal Christology*, Chapter 8
'Replying the Gender Hierarchy', pp. 163-95.

Chapter 6

A SACRED CRITIQUE OF RECONCILIATION

Desecrating Unions

[14a]Do not mismate yourselves with unbelievers.[1]
[14b]For what have righteousness and lawlessness in common, or
[14c]What partnership has light with darkness?
[15a]What concord has Christ with Beliar, or
[15b]What share has a believer with an unbeliever?
[16a]And what agreement has God's temple with idols?
[16b]For we are the temple of the living God (2 Cor. 6.14-16).

The text begins with an admonition addressed to the assumed readers (believers): do not mismate yourselves with unbelievers. Translated 'mismate', *heterozygein* in v. 14a is a compound of *heterōs* and *zygon*. *heteros* may convey little more than the simple description that things are 'of a different kind' or 'diverse'. If a difference between the two is inflated, *heteros* may in some cases convey the judgment that things are more than different: relative to one another, 'unusual' or 'strange'. Infrequently, *heteros* may denote a difference that deviates from 'what should be'.[2]

It is assumed in the biblical hermeneutical corpus that the latter,

---

1. The verb *me ginethe* is a second person plural, present middle/passive (negative) imperative of *gignomai*. If the verb is translated as a passive, then the verse would read, 'Do not be mismated…' (RSV), whereas a middle-voice translation would render the verse 'Do not mismate yourselves…' I have selected the middle-voice translation for a number of reasons. First, I assume that the admonition is directed at believers who may mate *themselves* with unbelievers. If the verb is passive, then it is assumed that the believers are passive agents who are being mated with unbelievers. If they are passive, can they choose not to be mismated? Second, I read 2 Cor. 6.14–7.1 to be an argument by Paul's opponents calling for communal *self*-isolation and *self*-purification. A middle-voice translation of *ginesthe* suggests that the imperative is an admonition for believers to not mate them*selves* with unbelievers, thus continuing the self-reflexive activity of self-determination.
2. Liddell-Scott, *Lexicon*, p. 702.

infrequent moral sense of *heteros* is implied in v. 14a. The unity of believers and unbelievers is 'different from what should be'. In other words, the unity of these opposites is morally and possibly ontologically wrong.

The two standard English translations of *hetero-zygein* are 'mismated' and 'misyoked'. The 'yoke' interpretation is preferred by many translators, given the common use of *zygon* in Greek texts to name the yoke of a plough or carriage. A yoke is not used to harness one animal but is a tool for harnessing two animals together. Animals that are yoked are paired to work side by side, rather than in line. Thus yoke has come to metaphorically convey a close pair, equals or that which unites a pair. Given that the yoke is that part of a machine that harnesses (controls, manages) the labor (power, energy) of a pair of animals, yoke also conveys a sense of burden, even enslavement. Thus *zygon* may convey a sense of subjugation. 'Do not be *enslaved* with an unbeliever.' Such a reading would suggest that a unity of believers and unbelievers 'subjugates' the believer to the unbeliever. And, given the identification at v. 16b, the subjugation of believers by unbelievers would encompass the subjugation of the sacred to the profane, light to darkness, God to idols. In other words, a unity of opposites will violate not only those believers seeking sacred perfection in the local community, but such a unity will violate the sanctity of God.

While neither *heterozygein* nor its cognates occur elsewhere in the New Testament, the adjective *heterozygōs* is employed in the LXX at Lev. 19.19: 'You shall not let your cattle breed with one of a *different kind (heterozygō).*' However, *heterozygein* is not used in LXX Deut. 22.10: 'You shall not plow with an ox and an ass together.'

If we judge that v. 14a is a play upon LXX Lev. 19.19, then the 'yoking' interpretation may not express the bond of unity that 'mating' suggests, or express the connection between the admonition against the 'mismating' of believers and unbelievers with the various Levitican codes of ritual purity that forbid the mating of different animals, the mixing of different fibers in cloth or the sowing of different seed in the same field. Thus, if the admonition against the unity of believers and unbelievers is influenced by LXX Lev. 19.19, then it is the *mating* of believers and unbelievers, and not simply the 'yoking' of believers and unbelievers, that violates propriety as set forth in the Torah. This differs from the predominantly Greek conception of *hetero-zygon* as the improper yoking of different animals or animals of different strengths.[3]

3.   Liddell-Scott, *Lexicon*, p. 701. *Hetero-zugeō* draw unequally.

The admonition against the mismating of believers and unbelievers is followed by five negative rhetorical questions that demonstrate by example (rather than as premises in an argument) that a unity of opposites is self-evidently incoherent and improper. I contend that vv. 14b-16a provide a sustained direct critique of a unity of opposites, hammering away at the various sets with negative rhetorical questions.

> [14b]For what have righteousness and lawlessness in common, or
> [14c]What partnership has light with darkness?
> [15a]What concord has Christ with Beliar, or
> [15b]What share has a believer with an unbeliever?
> [16a]And what agreement has God's temple with idols? (2 Cor. 6.14b-16a)

Righteousness and lawlessness have *nothing* in common. There is *no* partnership between light and darkness. Christ is in 'dis-cord', not in 'con-cord', with Beliar (the Devil). Believers are to have no share with an unbeliever. And God's temple cannot be in agreement with idols.

Each of the rhetorical questions negates the proposed unity of the terms in each opposing set.

Righteousness	Lawlessness
Light	Darkness
Christ	Beliar
Believers	Unbelievers
God's temple	Idols

The unity of each dyad is presented in such a manner as to call into question any possible unity between the opposites. The unity of opposites is rejected as self-evidently incoherent and improper.

However, the binary sets must be proposed in the text in order for the unity of opposites to be rejected and the privilege of the first term over the second in each rhetorical set established. Thus the matrix of opposition is necessary for the hierarchical evaluation to proceed. Without the presentation of the sets of conflicting opposites, the procedure of developing the privilege of righteousness, light, Christ, believers and God relative to lawlessness, darkness, Beliar, unbelievers and idols could not be generated. Nor could the association of those who stand in opposition to the desecrated be established. In other words, the presentation of the conflicting oppositional sets is the occasion, the context, in which the privilege and sanctity of righteousness, light, Christ, believers and God's temple occur. Negation of conflicting opposites makes sacred identity possible.

heterozygein is a complex negation. Believers are not to be mated, connected or yoked with unbelievers. What constitutes a misconnection is any unity drawn between conflicting opposites. Believers are properly in unity or association with believers. Unbelievers properly unite or associate with unbelievers. Proper unity is between things that are in some significant sense the same. The differences of identity are proper and are to be maintained. Kinds should be connected with their own kind. The unity of believers and unbelievers, the unity of differences, is a mismatch (although the criteria for the identities and also the distinctions between believers and unbelievers are never clarified in the text).

Those who share the same convictions in a significant sense may be said to be alike. It is assumed that 'community' and, in this case, 'sacred community' are homogeneous. In order to dwell together with God, the community must be of one mind, one opinion. Everyone in a sacred community shares the same beliefs, are believers of the same convictions. To be otherwise, to include those who differ, who do not share the same convictions, is to violate sacred community.

The critique at vv. 14-16b asserts the privilege of homogeneity over more complex relations and identities. A sacred connection is simple, a play of sameness and identity. To introduce difference in the sacred play of positive simple connections, let alone introduce opposites into a homogeneous network, is to disconnect the reproductive play of identity. Such complexity is seen as violating the integrity and coherence of homogeneity. The logic of identity cannot admit difference except as an illogical intrusion that disrupts and disturbs the coherence. In the end, such disruptions, such disturbances, threaten the theo-social coherence and court the destruction that comes with theo-social division. To admit differences into a sacred community, to allow for associations with those who stand outside or in opposition to the sacred community, violates the theo-social logic of identity. The admittance of such differences into the sacred community shifts the division between the sacred and profane. The boundary between the sacred and the profane shifts away from the border between the sacred community and the profane world towards an emergent border between the community that desires to be sacred and God.

God and sacred community	/	world
God	/	sacred community and world

Following the admonition against believers mating with unbelievers at v. 14a, the ordering of the five negative rhetorical questions suggests a strategy. I assume that the sequencing of the five negative rhetorical questions is intentional. While it is clear that the questions reiterate all the ways a unity of opposites violates sanctity and propriety, the sequential order of the questions may have served as a device to persuade the Corinthian Christian communities of the strength of the admonition against believers mating with unbelievers.

The move from the admonition against the union of believers and unbelievers to the negative rhetorical question regarding the union of righteousness and lawlessness may have been perceived by some of the assumed readers as moving from a more offensive to a less offensive comment. Many within the congregation might have taken offense at the suggestion that righteousness and lawlessness were improperly united. Clearly, lawlessness and righteousness are not incompatible for those in the community who are non-legalist. Still others might have taken offense at the rejection of the union of light and darkness. The relation of light and darkness is also not questionable among many in the Mediterranean world during this historical period. While the first two sets of opposites questioned in the negative rhetorical queries are being argued against by the writer of the piece, the incoherence or impropriety of their union may not be self-evident to all the assumed readers in Corinth. But with the third negative rhetorical question, 'What concord has Christ with Beliar?' (v. 15a), presumably such a union would violate the sensitivities of most, if not all, in the greater Corinthian Christian church. And likewise negative rhetorical question five, 'And what agreement has God's temple with idols?' (v. 16a) would be received by all as not only a questionable opinion but as blasphemous. Clearly, negative rhetorical questions three and five would be received with resounding conformation.

> What concord has Christ with Beliar?
> *None!*
> And what agreement has God's temple with idols?
> *None!*

The five negative rhetorical questions move from sets of less objectionable oppositional unities (numbers one and two) for a larger audience in the community, to sets of oppositional unity that clearly (if not apparently) violate popular convictions. This move is a forceful rhetorical device, for, tucked away between the two negative rhetorical questions that would enjoy maximum popularity, is inserted the question that repeats the admonition against believers mating with unbelievers.

[15a]What concord has Christ with Beliar?
[15b]What share has a believer with an unbeliever?
[16a]And what agreement has God's temple with idols? (2 Cor. 6.15a-16a)

In this play of negative questions, the move so frames the issue of believers consorting with unbelievers as to render the union of believers and unbelievers to be as incomprehensible and improper as the unions of Christ with the Devil, and God's temple with idols.

Sacred Unity

Not only are we to see the inadequacies or improprieties of the various unions presented and rejected in the five negative rhetorical questions, but we are called to see that the opposition of the various sets discloses as well a more comprehensive, a (shall we say) cosmic, opposition between the sacred and the profane. The first terms listed in each of the sets are properly connected to one another. All of the first terms are on the same side. Righteousness, light, Christ, believers and God's temple form a 'sacred union'. They stand together in opposition to the other side. Lawlessness, night, Beliar, unbelievers and idols are aligned in a 'profane union'. Each side enjoys proper connections.

What began as an assertion against the mating of believers and unbelievers became in the course of the negative query a critique of theo-socio-cosmic importance. The rejection of the union of believers and unbelievers plays out the conviction that a unity of the sacred and the profane violates the integrity, the homogeneity, of the sacred. To unite the sacred with its opposite is to accommodate the profane. For to unite the sacred with a desecration is to nullify the sacred. The sacred is vulnerable to desecration. And while the profane is a powerful contagion, the sacred is not. *Sanctity is non-contagious.* The accommodation of the profane by the sacred violates the integrity of the sacred. Therefore the mating of believers and unbelievers violates the very order of the cosmos, and confuses (blasphemes against?) the absolute difference between the sacred and the profane.

It is clear that the five negative rhetorical questions mimic the unity of opposites in order to call the oneness of such antithetical sets into question. But the five negative rhetorical questions, while they mimic the impropriety of the unity of opposites, do not warrant the admonition against the mating of believers and unbelievers. The five rhetorical questions provide a context in which the admonition of v. 14a, repeated at

v. 15b, is *associated* with other questionable unities. But it is not until v. 16b that a declarative statement is made again. The admonition at v. 14a ('Do not mismate yourselves with unbelievers') and the rejection of the five associations are warranted by the claim at v. 16b, 'For we are the temple of the living God'.

If we move from the admonition at 2 Cor. 6.14a, skipping the five negative rhetorical questions that follow, to v. 16b, then the assumed reader is identified as enjoying sacred communal identity with the author.

[14a]Do not mismate yourselves with unbelievers.
[16b]For *we* are the temple of the living God.

The critique of reconciliation is a well-crafted, self-contained presentation that depends upon v. 16b to warrant the negative rhetorical queries against reconciliation. To see how this is accomplished, note the repetition of 'temple' in v. 16a, b.

[16a]And what agreement has God's *temple* with idols?
[16b]For we are the *temple* of the living God.

Verse 16a assumes that the temple of God must be of such purity that the inclusion of other gods (idols) is self-evidently a violation of the sanctity of God's abode. This is followed at v. 16b with a self-proclaimed identification with the temple: 'We (the believers) are the temple of the living God.' The assumed reader is to see that just as the 'accommodation' of idols in the temple of God is a defilement, so too is the 'union' of believers and unbelievers a defilement.

What connects the non-union of believers and unbelievers with the non-accommodation of idols in the temple of God is the identification of believers as the temple of God. The move from v. 16a ('And what agreement has God's temple with idols?') to v. 16b ('For we are the temple of the living God') equivocates the term 'temple'. The equivocation occurs between two different, though related, concepts: the 'temple' as the site or place of divine habitation and the 'temple' as cult. Of course, the term 'temple' often conveys both senses simultaneously, for the 'temple' is the place where the divine visit or habitat and also the place where the cult habitats. I contend that vv. 16a and 16b each convey the sense of temple as site or as cult. The power of v. 16b is that it unites both the sense of temple as site of divine habitation and temple as cult. To then assert that 'we' the cult *are* the temple is to draw the strongest association between the two meanings of the term. The purpose of the clear distinction followed by the association of these two different senses of the term between vv. 16a and 16b is to draw out the connection that since the 'temple (site) of God' cannot be in agreement with 'idols (sites or shrines)', then the 'temple (cult) of the living God' cannot be in agreement with 'idol worshipers or idol cults'. Therefore believers who are the temple (site? cult? both?) of the living God may not mate with un-believers. Sacred believers are not to be mated with unbelievers. Sacred believers are the temple in whom God dwells. For a believer to dwell with an unbeliever is an accommodation that violates the sanctity of God because God cannot dwell in a desecrated temple.

First, the association of v. 14a with v. 16b suggests that the mating of unbelievers with believers violates or desecrates more than simply the individual believer. The association of v. 14a with v. 16b provides a justi-fication for the non-mating of believers with unbelievers. Believers are the temple (site/cult) of the living God. A believer who is defiled by mating with an unbeliever provides a defiled temple (site/cult) for the living God. And God will not dwell in a place of defilement. Therefore God will not dwell in the temple, the community of believers, if there are believers within the community who are defiled. If believers are the temple of the living God, then a community in which some believers are united with unbelievers would violate the sanctity of God's domicile. Against the unity of opposites, the accommodation of differences, Paul's *ecclesia*, the extended quotation asserts an exclusionary, theologically elitist theonomy.

I concur with Plummer's contention that 'we' in v. 16b is 'very emphatic'.[4]

'*We are* the temple of the living God.' (*ēmeis gar naos theos esmen*)

The emphatic identity that 'we are the temple' might express the radical exclusiveness of the claim, implying 'We are—(*you are not*)—the temple of the living God.'

It is commonly noted that the verse 'We are the temple of the living God' sounds very much like a Pauline slogan. If Paul is being quoted, which I believe is possible, I suspect that the phrase is repeated by the faction back at Paul. Paul may have proclaimed that 'We (all) are the temple of the living God', speaking of the *ecclesia* as the reconciling community. However, the faction's emphatic assertion that '*We are* the temple' may be read as their laying exclusive claim to the status in counterdistinction to Paul's *ecclesia*. For reconciliation, in which various

4.   Alfred Plummer, *A Critical and Exegetical Commentary on the Second Epistle of St. Paul to the Corinthians* (Edinburgh: T. & T. Clark, 1975), p. 208.

oppositions are gathered together into holy community, is, from the vantage point of those seeking sacred identity with God, a desecration. As the temple of God, believers are righteous (law abiding), people of light, in accord with Christ. Sacred believers are not connected with unbelievers, lawlessness, darkness, Beliar or idols. So the critique of reconciliation states that '*We are* the temple of God' in opposition to Paul's ministry of reconciliation and in counterdistinction to the fragment at 5.19 where Christ is the milieu in which God and the world dwell in reconciliation. We, those who seek sacred perfection, are the temple—the place of dwelling—of God in the world.

Second, the claim at v. 16b provides a needed identification to the discussion. The negative rhetorical questions may be affirmed. But an affirmation of the negative rhetorical questions will not identity *who* the believers are. The rejection of the accommodation of idols in the temple of God and the assertion regarding the unity of God and believers/temple is justified by an appeal to the text that follows (vv. 16c-18). As we will see, v. 16b is a transitional verse fragment that connects the 'critique of reconciliation' to the (assumed) authoritative 'divine patriarchal promise'.

Chapter 7

PATRIARCHAL PROMISE

The Temple of God

[16]What agreement has the temple of God with idols?
For we are the temple of the living God;
as God said,
   I will live in them and move among them, and I will be their God, and
   they shall be my people.
[17]Therefore, come out from them, and be separated from them,
Says the Lord,
   And touch nothing unclean; and I will welcome you,
      [18]and I will be a father to you, and you shall be my sons and daughters,
   says the Lord Almighty (2 Cor. 6.16-18).

The promise is presented in the first person singular. It is God who makes
the promise, not an intermediary. And the promise is that when the community of believers has met the conditions, all distance between God and
the believers will be overcome.

   'And I will be their God and they shall be my people.'

   The promised sacred community will be governed not by priests, kings
or other worldly powers that *represent* God. No! The people will be
governed directly by God. What is promised is a *theonomy*. God will live
in and among them without representative. In v. 18 the theonomy is further
clarified. God will not reign as a monarch over God's subjects. Instead, the
people of God will be received as sons and daughters. The theonomy
promised will be a sacred family. In intimate union with God their father,
the people of God will enjoy paradise regained. The 'fall' will be reversed;
the idyllic vision of Eden will be fulfilled. The world will be abandoned.
Temptation will be vanquished. Nothing less than the kingdom of God is
promised.
   Nevertheless, the divine patriarchal theonomic promise is divided in the

text by conditions that must first be met in order for the promise to be fulfilled:

> [16c]as God said,
>> I will live in them and move among them, and I will be their God, and
>> they shall be my people.
> [17]*Therefore, come out from them,*
>> *and be separated from them,*
>> *says the Lord,*
>> *and touch nothing unclean;*
>> *and I will welcome you,*
> [18]and I will be a father to you,
>> and you shall be my sons and daughters,
>> says the Lord Almighty (2 Cor. 6.16c-18).

As is noted in the critical literature, pieces of the promise are extracted from the LXX. Furnish points out that 2 Cor. 6.17 very closely resembles LXX Isaiah 52.11.[1]

Communal self-isolation that promises to yield self-purification is the necessary condition for the fulfillment of the promise and the invocation of the patriarchal theonomy. The meeting of the condition is the responsibility of the community and is not to be accomplished by God.

It is assumed in the promise that God will not or cannot dwell in that which is desecrated. The absence of God from the world is a given because of the world's profanity and God's sanctity. Therefore the people who desire to become God's dwelling place, God's temple, cannot be in the defiling world. To be united or reconciled with defilement is to be desecrated and therefore unsuitable for God.

The people/temple of God becomes suitable for God by differentiating or distancing themselves from the world and all other peoples. In so differentiating themselves, they identify themselves exclusively with God. The people/temple of God distance themselves from the world through communal isolation and communal purification. And by moving *from* the world, they move *closer* to God. It is assumed that God and the world enjoy no association. They stand in opposition. Those who are God's people and who seek to fulfill the promise must also stand in opposition to the world.

A single dualism of 'God' and 'the world' is assumed. The people who seek to 'temple' God must withdraw from the world. If they withdraw from the world, then there is only one direction in which they can be moving, i.e. towards God. Those who would become the temple (site) of

1. Furnish, *II Corinthians*, p. 364.

the living God do so by their act of self-isolation from the world. They establish their identity as God's temple by isolating themselves from all influences that might compromise their sanctity. God *will* dwell in only one people—who are homogeneously sacred. Thus the people/temple would be like God, wholly and holy different from the world.

The difference between God and the world provides the dualistic context in which sanctification is played out. Through communal isolation from the larger social world, the community seeks purification. Since it is assumed that God cannot dwell in the world (the profane), the community seeks to negate the world. And in so negating the world, the community becomes the sacred site of God's dwelling.

In the rites of self-isolation and purification, the community understands itself to be crossing the gulf between the clean and the unclean, withdrawing from the profane world into sacred isolation. The community assumes that the separation between the sacred and the profane is a given that is symbolized spatially in the rites of withdrawal. As such, the self-isolated and self-purified community will accomplish the feat of becoming sacred by self-activity within a static cosmos.

The text thus promises an intimate, exclusive theo-social connection, in which one people alone are the temple of the living God in whom God dwells and among whom he moves like a father. God is God to only one people, and only the chosen people who have sanctified themselves are God's children.

Paradise Postponed

The sacred identity of believers as sons and daughters of God happens, or is disclosed, or is created, at the threshold that marks the differentiation of believers and unbelievers (the *pistoi* and *apistoi*). That threshold is established in the movement of withdrawal. It is the movement of coming out, of withdrawal, that marks the threshold and simultaneously differentiates the outside and the inside. The disclosure of the threshold happens as a move of opposition. The marking of the threshold, the boundary that establishes inside and outside, creates a gap that separates the same from itself in an act of differentiation. To come out is to dissolve integrity. One who leaves or comes out establishes an identity that is defined in terms of negation. In coming out, an assumed sameness is denied. The differentiation between those 'coming out' and those 'staying in' establishes the difference between believers and unbelievers, between the sacred and the profane.

The withdrawal from the world is not an end in itself but is the means of sanctification. Those who are God's people must be disconnected from all who are unclean. To be related to God, to be the sons and daughters of the heavenly father, the people must break all 'relations' with the profane. By isolating themselves from all influences that might contaminate their sanctity, the community becomes sacred. God will dwell in a people who are homogeneously sacred, for the sacred is assumed to be immutable, incorruptible. The inclusion of those who are not sacred, who are unclean, will violate the sanctity of the temple/people and *defer* the promise. Therefore the community that does not attain sanctity, that does not separate itself from all who differ with the sacred, cannot become or delays becoming the temple of God and the sons and daughters of God. Paradise is postponed.

Those who identify themselves as 'believers' by 'coming out' simultaneously differentiate themselves *from* the world and unbelievers. In 'moving out' from the profane world, believers 'move in' or 'move towards' the sacred and thus identify themselves with God. Those who establish their identity with the sacred do so by means of differentiation. In *not* being in the world, in *not* touching anything unclean, believers become sacred. In other words, sacred identity (as the sons and daughters of God) is a negative inscription. Negation is the necessary condition for sacred identity.

Cleansing

> Since we have these promises, beloved, let us cleanse ourselves from every defilement of body and spirit, and make sacredness perfect in the fear of God (2 Cor. 7.1).

The appeal of 2 Cor. 7.1 employs the 'divine patriarchal promise' and the 'critique of reconciliation' to support a plea for a purge of all defilements that contaminate the community. It is assumed that the expulsion of all defilements of flesh and spirit fulfill the promise. However, the appeal at 7.1 differs strikingly from the appeal at 6.17 in the patriarchal promise. In the promise, the appeal is for the company of believers to come out, to separate themselves from cohabitation with the unclean of the world. In the appeal to communal self-purification at 7.1, the process of differentiation is reversed. Instead of the community that desires to fulfill the conditions of the promise 'withdrawing *themselves*' from the defilements of the world, at 7.1 the community that desires sanctity is called to 'withdraw *others*' from themselves. The first is an act of self-isolation. The second is an act of expulsion. In the promise, believers are called to move out of a ritually unclean community, to depart a stationary location and to achieve isolation in divine pilgrimage. In the appeal, believers are called to hold fast and to vanquish the unclean from their midst. Whereas the promise calls for the nomadic search for theonomy, wherein God welcomes the faithful as his sons and daughters for having 'moved out' of the world and 'towards' God, the appeal calls for the defilements to be removed while those seeking purification are stationary. Believers are presented as moving towards God in the promise. In the appeal, the divine is invoked in the evacuation of the unclean.

These differences between the promise and the appeal are glossed by the authors of the composite text in their manipulation of the promise in the appeal for communal self-purification. While the differences between the two are subtle, the reversal is significant. Both promise and appeal play out the interrelated themes of communal self-isolation and self-purification. In both the promise and the appeal, those who are not believers are judged to be contaminates. In both texts, the presence of contaminates in the community of faith delays the fulfillment of theonomic utopia. However, the texts differ, in that it is the failure of believers to 'withdraw themselves' and touch nothing unclean that defers the fulfillment of the promise at 6.17, while at 7.1 it is the failure of believers to 'remove others' who contaminate that defers the promise. In the promise, the community of believers is called to act upon *themselves*, to withdraw themselves further from the profane world. In the appeal, the community of believers is called to act upon *others*, to expel, purge, eliminate or evacuate those within the community who are defilements of body and spirit.

If the promise has not been fulfilled, then in the terms of 6.17 those seeking to be sons and daughters in the patriarchal theonomy must further withdraw from the unclean world. In the appeal to communal self-purification, the solution is to expel those in the community who defile sacred perfection. The reader can see how easily the appeal might be employed to justify the extermination of those contaminates that stubbornly will not leave. Given the fantastic offer made in the promise for the community that fulfills self-purification, a final solution to the problem of contamination would certainly be appealing.

It is suggested by some interpreters that the emphatic claims 'For we are the temple of the living God' (6.16b), and 'Since we have these promises' (7.1a) assert that the faction believes that it has fulfilled the conditions of the promise. They argue that the explicit present voice of the declarative does not suggest that the believers *may* become the temple of God but that they *are* the temple of God. The promise is fulfilled. Thus the introductory frame of the promise at v. 16b does not assume that the satisfaction of the conditions and fulfillment of the promise is in the distant future. If the promise is apocalyptic, then the emphatic assertion at v. 16b suggests that the apocalypse is immediate.

But there are a number of problems with the fulfillment interpretation. It is assumed in the promise that the conditions for becoming the sons and daughters of God have not yet been fulfilled. The community has yet to come out of the world sufficiently. They have not separated themselves from the unclean. They have not abandoned the world. They have yet to attain sanctification. And until such time as these conditions have been satisfied, the promise will not be fulfilled. Like the promise, the appeal assumes that the withdrawal has been incomplete. The believers are not perfect in body and spirit. The defilements have not been removed.

Given these qualifications, I suggest that v. 16b 'For we are the temple of the living God' is not a contention that perfection has been attained. Rather, the verse is a self-identification for a Christian faction that they are the people to whom the promise is *addressed*. I take it that the emphatic assertion of the claim expresses that the faction believes itself to hold *exclusive* claim to being the temple of the living God. There is no other legitimate temple or even possible temple of the living God.

Between v. 16b and the 'patriarchal promise' of vv. 16c-18 there is a shift that discloses a use and manipulation of the promise.

> [16b] For *we are* the temple of the living God...

As stated above, the explicit present tone of the declarative does not suggest that the believers *may* become the temple of God but that they *are* the temple of God. However, the patriarchal theonomic vision is a 'promise'. It is a promise for those who will come (future tense) out and be separate. Then God will receive them as his people. If they touch nothing unclean, the Lord will fulfill the patriarchal promise.

The failure to 'withdraw' and touch nothing unclean defers the fulfillment of the promise. At 2 Cor. 7.1 the inclusion of those who are not seeking sacred perfection defers the promise. The community that does not attain sanctity, that does not separate itself from those who differ, that does not expel those who defile, defers their becoming the temple of God, defers their becoming the sons and daughters of God. Paradise is postponed.

How are we to read the move from the *promise* that God will dwell among his holy people to the emphatic claim that believers already *are* the temple of God? Is it assumed by those who made the argument that they have realized the promise?

The move that covers the gap between vv. 16b and 16c-18, between the promise and its realization, between a possibility and its actuality, is presumptuous. If the promise is a quotation from some authoritative text, or some conviction that enjoys authority, it does not follow that these self-identified 'believers' are the party to whom the promise is addressed. And yet it is assumed by those who employ the promise that it is exclusively addressed to themselves and, further, that the promise can be fulfilled by themselves only. It is presumed by the faction that while they do not as yet fulfill the promise, they hold legitimate title or deed to it. They are the legitimate believers/people/temple/sons and daughters of God. They will fulfill, or are presently fulfilling, the call by God to isolate and purify themselves.

The community that lays exclusive claim to being the temple also levels a judgment against itself. That God does not presently dwell in the temple is an indictment of those who lay claim to being the temple. An explicit assumption in the promise is that God will establish a patriarchal theonomy *when* the people of God have come out of the world. In the appeal the patriarchal theonomic promise *awaits* those who attain sanctity. However, in both the promise and the appeal it is assumed that the patriarchal theonomy has not been established. And the reason given that God has not fulfilled the promise is because the temple/people of God are still defiled. Those who are seeking sacred perfection are seeking that which they have yet to attain. The faction in Corinth that seeks perfection confesses their imperfection in their seeking that which they have not attained. It is this state of affairs that prompts their appeal to withdraw and excommunicate. Those who seek perfection are still, nevertheless, corrupted. However, the confession that the community has failed to accomplish its task of attaining perfection is not a statement about the fallibility of the faction that seeks perfection. The confession is not about some internal conflict within the group. The self-identification of the faction is with God. And that which violates their sacred integrity and enthralls their desire to invoke the patriarchal theonomy are the external defilements that nevertheless infiltrate the 'body' that seeks sacred perfection. Those seeking perfection are consumed by a totalizing fantasy. Seeking to attain an undifferentiated community wherein there are no differences, the community assesses that any violation of its perfection, its sacred wholeness, is wrought by the contamination from outside itself. The community seeking sacred perfection can admit no differences. Differences defile, although differences 'removed' yield perfection. The rite of expulsion promises to be a *total* act that in turn promises to yield an undivided whole, a community that is singular in its sanctity, admitting no imperfection and according no desecration.

What began as an assertion against the mating of believers and unbelievers became in the course of the negative query a critique of cosmic importance. The rejection of the union of believers and unbelievers plays out the conviction that a unity of differences violates the integrity, the homogeneity, of the sacred. To unite the sacred with its opposite is to *accommodate* the profane. But the profane cannot *accommodate* or '*temple*' the sacred. For the sacred to accommodate the profane violates the integrity of the sacred. Therefore the mating of believers and unbelievers violates the very order of the cosmos and confuses (blasphemes?) the absolute difference between the sacred and the profane.

Becoming the Sacred Family of God

One of the reasons I selected to study 2 Cor. 6.14–7.1 following our inquiry into 1 Corinthians 1 was because this text continues to play out the themes of 'belonging', of being a family relation or having a household relation to some sacred person. The slogan 'I belong to Christ' suggests that the person or persons who made the pronouncement believed themselves to be members of the household of Christ and that such belonging was politically significant. In one instance, the identification could have been made by a member of the (let me call it) 'natural' family of Jesus. And with respect to the images and metaphors suggested in a number of Gospels and Epistles, Jesus appears to have called his disciples or followers his family. So I suggested that those who made the claim 'I belong to Christ'—possibly James, the younger brother of the Lord, and/or the disciples—were a focus of Paul's critique.

Now we considered 2 Cor. 6.14–7.1, in which there is a fragment of a text that appears to have been called upon to warrant the conviction and policies of those who seek to establish a purified community of believers. I have named the fragment quoted or closely paraphrased at 6.16-18 the 'patriarchal promise', because in it the Lord promises that if the people 'come out', 'separate' themselves from the world and 'touch nothing un-

clean', God will be their God and they will be God's 'people' or 'household'. And God 'will live and move among them'. Further—and this is the
reason I call the theonomic promise a *patriarchal* promise—the Lord
almighty declares, 'And I will be a father to you, and you shall be my sons
and daughters'. What is promised to those who become perfected is
nothing less than *belonging* to the sacred family of God. God will be their
father and they will be God's sons and daughters.

I am not claiming that the faction that quoted the text at 2 Cor. 6.16-18
in their critique of Paul and those who maintained in 1 Cor. 1.12 that they
'belong' to Christ are the same group. However, what I am suggesting is
that the preoccupations of 'belonging' to the sacred, which are reoccurring
and (dare I say) dominant themes and obsessive desires, are expressed in
both texts. One significant difference between the two fragments is that at
1 Cor. 1.12 it is assumed by those who make the proclamation that they 'in
fact' or 'actually' *belong to*—are members of—the household of Christ.
However, at 2 Cor. 16b-18 it is assumed that the community seeking
sacred perfection *is* the temple of God, although not perfected, not sacred—
yet! If those who 'belong' to God, as in being God's abode, were to attain
the desired perfection, then they would belong to God as children belong
to their father. In other words, a group believes itself to possess the
possibility of becoming the adopted family of the Lord. To belong to the
household of Christ, to be a sibling of the Lord, is an exclusive bond. But
in 2 Cor. 6.14–7.1 the criteria by which one comes to belong to the perfected household of Christ constitute a process of extreme exclusion and
expulsion. The 'sacred' family will be established through acts of division.

This potential to become perfect and to become the family of the Lord
almighty can become a powerful, obsessive desire. The stakes are high.
Those who play, those who envision the possibility as their own attainable
potential, seek to fulfill a grand fantasy that promises to transform at least
their own individual and group identify and status, if not to transform the
very world.

Purity is an Illusionary Phantom

So long as the cult does *not* enjoy the presence of the Lord, so long as the
cult does *not* enjoy the theonomic power of the Lord, then, given the logic
of perfection, the cult has failed to fulfill the necessary purity requirements. This failure could serve to further excite and intensify the phobia.
In the absence of God, the magic of exclusion becomes an obsession. The
community seeking sacred perfection in hopes of attaining patriarchal

theonomic utopia will sacrifice even its own members in the illusion that if it can identify and expel those who defile, then it will fulfill its part of the bargain. Once all defilement is expunged, theophany will occur and the hoped-for theonomy will come to be.

However, the desire of those seeking sacred perfection *is* unattainable. The *church* that seeks to fulfill the promise through withdrawal from unbelievers and the expulsion of defiled believers will yield only the complex array of pleasure and pain associated with such ritual behavior. The promise of patriarchal theonomy will remain an unfulfilled fantasy. It is a powerful phantom, but a phantom nonetheless. Paradise will escape their grasp. But what will be gained, what is graspable, is the violence of classification, isolation and expulsion. The divine will not visit those who seek but fail to attain perfection. God will not adopt these potential sons and daughters. Union with God is a chimera, for the seeking of sacred perfection is an impossible fantasy to actualize. The prize will disappear like phantoms appearing and disappearing in a thick gulf-coast fog. The object of desire, union with the divine, will vanish upon approach. And all that will come from the often hysterical competition and rivalry of those seeking the phantom will be the violence that such seeking inspired.[2]

Mary Douglas in her analysis of pollution contends

> that ideas about separating, purifying, demarcating and punishing transgressors have as their main function to impose system on an inherently untidy experience. It is only by exaggerating the differences between, within and without, above and below, male and female, with and against, that a semblance of order is created.[3]

Separation, classification and cleansing are acts that promise to create unity or order out of ambiguity. In this matrix of purification, *atonement* presupposes the fundamental difference between the sacred and the profane, and offers those willing to keep the symbolic system identification with the sacred.

---

2.   'Their rivalry centers on divinity itself; but behind that divinity there lies only violence. To compete for divinity is to compete for a chimera, because the reality of the divine rests in its transcendental absence. It is not the hysterical rivalry of men that will engender gods—only unanimous violence can accomplish that. Insofar as it is regarded as a prize, it is merely a phantom that will invariably escape man's grasp and turn to violence.' René Girard, *Violence and the Sacred* (trans. Patrick Gregory; Baltimore: The John Hopkins University Press, 1972), p. 144.

3.   Mary Douglas, *Purity and Danger: An Analysis of Concepts of Pollution and Taboo* (New York: Frederick A. Graeger, 1966), p. 4.

The patriarchal theonomic promise serves to coerce those who identify themselves with the 'temple'. The promise of atonement with God in the matrix of purification demands the separation of the sacred and the profane. To lapse, to become defiled through association with unbelievers or association with believers who associate with unbelievers, is to court defilement, to delay (if not negate) the promise of atonement with God. The loss of sacred order yields theological abandonment, de-at/one-ment with God. Transgression of the boundary that divides is at least a danger to the cult's desire to become the site of God's dwelling. But transgressions also threaten the possibility of order (both a sacred cosmos and a related sacred society) and clarity (sacred knowledge). Without these rites of purity/impurity, atonement with the sacred is impossible.

The exclusionary text appeals to the human fantasy of pure identity with the divine and the clean differentiation between the sacred and the profane. In this configuration, metaphors of theo-social virtues and vices provide rites that are believed to draw God and a segment of the social world (a refined sacred community) together.

A community that does not waiver from these fantasies may come to a violent, self-destructive end. The fantasies of withdrawal and exclusion have no built-in means of self-control. Short of the destruction of the community through continual radical withdrawal from the world, or violent disintegration through sacred expulsion, or the abandonment of the fantasies of sacred perfection, the theonomic enterprise may be exchanged for a theocracy. Such an exchange may promise the invocation of a theonomy in the future, but the desire to create a sacred temple for God's dwelling and the expected theophany are deferred for the time being. And, in its place, a theocracy provides the community with a *degree* of sanctification in exchange for social stability. The rites of exclusion, withdrawal and expulsion diminish in frequency. But in the exclusionary text of 2 Cor. 6.14–7.1 no compromise is brooked. No exchange of the theonomy for a theocracy is suggested.

Fulfilling the Promise: Expelling the Defilements

[6.14a]Do not mismate yourselves with unbelievers.

[6.16b]For we are the temple of the living God.

[7.1a, b]Since we have these promises, beloved, let us cleanse ourselves.

In the composite text above, the critique of reconciliation and the appeal for communal self-purification are warranted by the promise. It is assumed that the promise is authoritative and that by association the critique and the appeal enjoy authority. In other words, the promise serves as the host of a contagion ('authority') that is passed on to the critique and the appeal by the tissue of the *textus*.

The promise is framed at the beginning and the end by exclusive, emphatic claims. At 2 Cor. 6.16b and 7.1a, b the promise is 'claimed' by the author of this composite text for the author's community. The divine patriarchal promise is not made to just anyone:

> [6.16b]For *we* are the temple of the living God.
> [7.1a,b]Since *we* have these promises, *beloved, let us…*

Also, both verses serve as joints that accomplish the difficult task of providing coherence between the three pieces that form the composite text. The divine patriarchal promise proposes a possibility. The promise differentiates what God will do (vv. 16c, 17b, 18) when the people 'come out', are 'separated from them…and touch nothing unclean' (v. 17a). To the hypothetical conditions of the promise, v. 16b provides a categorical claim: we are the temple of the living God.

In reverse fashion, the categorical claim at v. 16b provides the needed association to unify the critique of reconciliation and the divine patriarchal promise. As we have seen, the critique of reconciliation is a well-crafted, self-contained presentation. Verse 16b warrants the negative response to the five rhetorical questions by replaying the theme of the temple presented at v. 16a in the last of the rhetorical questions in the critique.

> [16a]And what agreement has God's *temple* with idols?
> [16b]For we are the *temple* of the living God;
> [16c]as God said,
>   I will live in them and move among them…(2 Cor. 16a-c)

The immediate repetition of 'temple' serves to unite the two separate texts through association. The divine patriarchal promise thus comes to warrant the critique of reconciliation through the tissue of repetition.[4] Without v. 16b there is little that connects the critique and the promise. Further, and more important for the faction, without v. 16b there is no claim of *possession* for the promise or explicit identification by the author (or authors) as to where the author stands relative to the cosmic division

---

4. Note that 'temple' is not plural. Thus this is not an argument, as suggested by many, that each person is the temple of God. In this passage, the community of believers is the temple of God.

between the two opposing sides in the critique. 'For *we are the temple of the living God.*' God and idols may stand in opposition, but cultic identification with the sacred is at best an inference in the text prior to the claim. Like v. 16b, 7.1a also lays claim to the promise: 'Since *we have these promises…*'

Verse 1a provides a needed pivot that both joins the promise and the appeal and allows for the manipulation of the promise by the appeal. Without the claim of possession at 7.1a, the appeal for communal self-purification through the expulsion of the defilements would be disconnected from the promise. However, the association of the promise and the appeal is made not through the repetition of a term (like 'temple', as in the case of the critique) but through the 'identification' of the quoted material at vv. 16c-18 as a 'promise' possessed by the cult in the appeal at 7.1a.

The move through the three parts of the texts is clearer. The first part is the critique of 'reconciliation', the 'de-atonement' of believers and unbelievers, righteousness and lawlessness, light and darkness, Christ and Beliar, God's temple and idols. This critique of the 'atoning *ecclesia*' is a call for division. The de-at-onement of opposites, the withdrawal of the people of God from *any* connection with those who are other, is presented as a condition for the fulfillment of the divine patriarchal promise. The theme of simple separation or non-unity of opposites in vv. 14-16 is enhanced in the promise. The people of God are to 'come out' and achieve isolation from the world. And this is followed by an appeal to purge the community of all believers who corrupt the sanctity of the believing community, thereby deferring the establishment of the theonomy, the kingdom of God.

In the critique, the differentiation between believers and unbelievers is an internal/external distinction. Believers are inside. Unbelievers are outside. The critique is aimed at those *in* the community who, by associating with and marrying outsiders, confuse the internal/external distinction. In the critique believers who associate with unbelievers are not judged to be unbelievers. Rather, they are assessed to be believers 'tainted' by their associations. The promise proposes that if the community of faith 'withdraws' from the defilements of the world, if believers withdraw from association with unbelievers, then the promise of the patriarchal theonomy will be fulfilled. But what becomes clear in the appeal is a call for the expulsion not of unbelievers but of believers who, through their association with unbelievers, have become defiled.

In the critique believers and unbelievers are the differentiated social groups (although there is no direct identification in the text as to the criteria for deciding who is a believer and who an unbeliever). In the promise the social differentiation is between those who are members of God's family and those who are not, between those who have 'come out' of the larger social world and those who have 'stayed in'. In significant ways social differentiations in the critique and the promise are presented as already existing. However, in the appeal social differentiation is made in a significantly differently way from these earlier differentiations. In the critique the problem is that the existing differentiations have been blurred. Thus the critique calls for sharper differences between believers and unbelievers. In the promise the differentiation between the people of God and the world is not great enough. So the people are called to 'come out' and further distance themselves from the world. However, in the appeal a new social differentiation is being 'enacted' that reconfigures the social arrangements. In the appeal the social group of 'believers' is divided into two groups: believers who seek sacred perfection and believers who, by virtue of their association with unbelievers, are not seeking sacred perfection.

The division of believers into those seeking sacred perfection and those who are defiled does more than simply sharpen and provide distance between believers and unbelievers by adding a third party to divide the two. The expulsion of those *in* the community who are assessed to be defiled by their association with unbelievers establishes a new definition of sacred community. Unlike the critique and the promise, the appeal does not seek *simply* to sharpen or provide distance between believers and unbelievers. In the appeal social arrangements are now dominated by a radicalized social purification/defilement system. While it is clear that the expelling of those believers who are defiled by their association with unbelievers provides further social distance for those seeking sacred perfection from the contamination of the unbelievers, a remnant faction of the believers is now *radically* sanctified.

The earlier social differentiation between believers/unbelievers is now altered and dominated by the differentiation between those seeking sacred perfection from all others, believers and unbelievers alike. Defilement is no longer defined in the passage as those who are *outside* the community of faith, as is suggested in vv. 14-16. Rather, those who defile are those *within* the community who are not 'seeking sacred perfection'. In other words, the appeal of 7.1 is to purge the community of those believers who violate the sacred integrity of the community. The expulsion of tainted believers will stop the epidemic of defilement from consuming those who seek sacred perfection.

In the economy of human perfection/defilement, corruption is a power-ful contagion that is passed on far too easily, defiling all who come into contact with it. Lacking contagious capability, the sacred is always vulner-able to corrupting contact. In the composite text of 2 Cor. 6.14–7.1, the progression from disassociation from unbelievers who are outside the community to the purging of corrupting believers inside the community is an attempt to attain perfection or sanctification from a potent corruption that is easily passed on and easily contracted.

The promise of a sacred community brings impurity clearly into focus as central to the fulfillment or deferment of the theonomy. Impurity is an active force, a contagion that endangers believers and threatens their hopes and aspirations to become the temple of God. Purification is the necessary condition for divine favor and theistic residency. And if the community of believers were to all become impure, then not only would it be the case that those persons might not participate in the temple or be the sons and daughters of God the father, but God would no longer have a dwelling place on earth.[5] The unclean are presented not merely as being barred from the cult: their continued association would defile the community *seeking* sacred perfection and thus forfeit the satisfaction of the theonomic promise. Such a conception of the contagion of impurity and the theo-nomic significance of seeking sacred purification is rather similar to the community associated with the Dead Sea writings, where the community assessed itself to be God's sacred sanctuary.[6] 'A group claiming to con-stitute a holy community, and comparing itself to the Temple would have to interpret in terms of its sectarian life the Temple's chief characteri-zations, including purity rules, cult and priesthood.'[7] When considered in light of Neusner's analysis of purity, the concept of impurity operative in the exclusionary text is representative of a conception common before the Talmudic law, in that 'purity and impurity constitute a set of highly com-plex relationships' that 'have nothing to do with the physical world'.[8] For in the Talmudic law, 'a great deal depends upon intention and purpose,

---

5.   Thus the conception of impurity in the purification text at 1 Cor. 6.14–7.1 is more in keeping with Baruch A. Levine's conception of impurity (*In the Presence of the Lord* [Leiden: E.J. Brill, 1974]) as an active agent and less like Robertson Smith's conception of impurity as a status.

6.   J. Neusner, *The Idea of Purity in Ancient Judaism* (Leiden: E.J. Brill, 1973), p. 32.

7.   Neusner, *Purity*, p. 33.

8.   Neusner, *Purity*, p. 16.

circumstances and time, as Maimonides asserts'. Purity and impurity are not presented in the exclusionary text as a set of highly complex relations in which intention and purpose, circumstances and time are taken into account. Impurity is assumed to be the given state of the world of which those who would be the temple of God must purify themselves.

Ricoeur contends that the symbolic structure of defilement is neither reflective nor representational; instead it is *acted out*.

> One can catch sight of it in the act of purification and go back from the act that suppresses to the 'thing' suppressed. It is the *rite* that exhibits the symbolism of defilement; and just as the rite suppresses symbolically, defilement infects symbolically.[9]

If the rite exhibits the symbolism of defilement, then the 'rite of expulsion' exhibits the sacred community as an undivided, uncompromised whole, a sacred totality. In the communal ritual of self-purification in which and by which the community expels those who are judged to be impure, the acts of separation and expulsion *establish*; they yield an undivided whole that enjoys totality.

The identity of the 'sacred union' is disclosed, manifested, at the symbolic threshold across which social differentiation is made. In the isolationist withdrawal, identity is substantiated in the movement of 'coming out'. This movement across the threshold differentiates the outside and the inside. The threshold marks an opposition. The move across this marker separates the same from itself in an act of differentiation. 'To come out' is to dissolve the assumed or apparent or previous integrity of the group. One who leaves or comes out of a unity establishes an identity that is defined in terms of negation. As such, a negative relation is the necessary condition for identity.

The theme of identity reoccurs throughout the composite text. The critique of reconciliation was among other things a critique of the identity of opposites. The five negative rhetorical questions capitalize on the assumed absurdity of the identity of opposites. The divine patriarchal promise calls for the isolation of the same with the same and the promise of a familiar identity. The appeal for exclusionary cleansing of all defilement serves to further purify the same, to so isolate what enjoys identity as to admit no difference.

The acceptance of the divine patriarchal promise, the critique of the ministry of reconciliation and the appeal to exclude the corrupt expresses

---

9.   Paul Ricoeur, *The Symbolism of Evil* (New York: Harper & Row, 1967), p. 35.

the *prophetic* appeal for 'justice and righteousness' and the *confession* that there are those within the community who are 'corrupt'. This substructure of meaning permeates all aspects of the sacred community's thinking, actions and convictions. It is the precondition in which or out of which the pious find expression, and in which such piety may be understood as 'proper' or 'right'.

Given their convictions, the Corinthian faction assesses that if Paul's ministry of reconciliation comes to dominate the community, then the entire community will be infected with profane contamination. The taint of impurity will no longer be conveyed to the community up to its borders where those who are desecrations dwell. At the borders the taint may be stopped and those seeking sacred perfection may enjoy quarantine. But with *ecclesia*/reconciliation, the 'taint of impurity' will be brought into the very heart of the temple, driving the sacred out *forever*. And for the community, believing themselves the exclusive channel for the divine into the world, such sacrilegious reconciliation would spell the complete and utter profanity of the world, the utter loss of all sacred intercourse, the utter damnation of the world and everyone.

If the connection between God and humanity is lost, if the believers are not distinct from the unbelievers, are not pure, are not separate from the ungodly, then the promise of paradise is lost. Redemption is vanquished. Paul's ministry of reconciliation occasions a 'sacrificial crisis' for those seeking sacred perfection. If the distinctions between pure and impure are lost, then there are no means by which the people may invoke the presence of God. For God will be invoked and will dwell only in a sacred place.

The purification of those who seek to be sacred, the acceptance of the divine patriarchal promise and the critique of the ministry of reconciliation and its desecrating compromises are enacted in the expulsion of the impure. By negation, sacred order reaffirms itself.

The reconciliation of believers and unbelievers is a violation of the 'sacred'. The exclusionists do not judge Paul and company to be 'unbelievers'. Rather, Paul and company are 'impure' believers, 'tainted' believers, 'desecrated' believers who have carried the contagion of impurity into the community of believers. The boundary between inside and outside, between the sacred and the impure, has become a threshold across which those who belong inside have crossed outside and have returned, bringing the contagion with them across the threshold and into the temple. 'So long as purity and impurity remain distinct, even the worst pollution can be washed away; but once they are allowed to mingle, purification is no longer possible.'[10]

Much is at stake for those seeking sacred perfection. By their continued association with believers who associate with unbelievers, those seeking sacred perfection are stalled, if not arrested, in their pursuit. The contagion of defilement passes from the unbeliever to the believer who associates with unbelievers, and these 'tainted' believers infect believers seeking sacred perfection. The failure to remove from the community those who are not seeking sacred perfection in the fear of God defers the fulfillment of the divine patriarchal promise. And so long as the community does not attain sanctity, does not expel those who defile, the inaction of the community defers their actually becoming the temple of God, defers their becoming the sons and daughters of God. Paradise is *postponed*.

The fear, or rather terror, of those seeking sacred perfection is that if the pure and the impure become reconciled, as Paul wishes, then those who seek sacred perfection will themselves become impure. Purification is no longer possible. Salvation as purification, atonement with the sacred, becomes impossible! For once reconciliation has occurred, those who would be the 'abode' of the sacred are forever tainted and incapable of 're-demption'. Misfortune, evil and suffering will persist because God cannot dwell on earth. Paradise will be not merely postponed but *lost*.

If we take Ricoeur's suggestion and work backwards from the rite of expulsion, we find that it is Paul's ministry of reconciliation that is the threat that must be overcome. Reconciliation courts more than simply the compromising of the sacred with impurity. Oppositional unity courts the sacred abandonment of the desecrated temple. The hope that God will come to rule the world or at least the community and bring an end to evil is dashed. Paul's threat to the total purification of the community is a threat against 'salvation'. Sacred homogeneity promises salvation, while the heterogeneity of Paul's ministry of reconciliation courts suffering, misfortune and damnation. The ministry of reconciliation and the proposal that the *ecclesia* is the gathering of differences in the communal body of Christ/the Lord occasions a sacrificial crisis for the *church*.

Interpolation Revisited

It is my judgment that Furnish's assessment of the present status of the debate over the relation of 2 Cor. 6.14–7.1 in its context as 'almost

10. Girard, *Violence*, p. 38.

insurmountable' is expressive of a tradition and practice of biblical hermeneutics that assumes that authentic biblical texts are textually and conceptually flat, and that texture, deviation, and/or contradictions are signs of interpolation.[11] Yet the argument that 6.14–7.1 is anti-Pauline and that there is no textual evidence that 2 Corinthians ever existed without the passage need not be an 'insurmountable problem'.

The problem of textual coherence is far more complicated. I will argue that the text is coherent. But its structure, as epistolary reply, differs from the structure expected by theological readers, modern and pre-modern alike. The text's coherence is clearly visible, the text hangs together, but only after one has abandoned some of the textual and conceptual assumptions regarding incoherence and intertextuality that dominate much of Christian scholarship. The failure to address the assumptions of what counts as coherence and the positive theological assumption that all intertextual material included in a text must positively support the thesis are expressive of a residue of orthodox Christian theology that has influenced the assumptions of modern critical biblical scholarship regarding the coherence, or expected coherence, of a biblical text.

Paul's Epistolary Reply

To confront is to engage, to reply. The prefix *con-*, meaning 'together', and the stem *front*, meaning 'face' or 'forehead', convey the basic sense of a face-to-face encounter, as in 'to stand or come in front of, to stand or meet facing', in which persons are brought face to face. To confront carries as well a more aggressive sense of face-to-face engagement, as in 'to present a *bold* front, to stand *against, oppose*; to *face an accuser* or as a witness in a trial'.[12] These more aggressive meanings of confrontation convey as well the 'facing' up to one's actions or behavior. In aggressive confrontations, where neither party nor face retreats, or steps to the side, or turns away, the *con*frontation may lead to an *af*front. From Old French *frontier*, 'to affront' is 'to strike on the forehead, to slap in the face'.[13] Thus an affront is an assault made face to face, or to one's face, or in one's face.

While it is clear to me that 2 Cor. 6.14-16b and 7.1 are an *affront* for Paul, given that the critique of reconciliation identifies the unity of oppo-

11. Furnish, *II Corinthians*, p. 383.
12. *OED*, II, pp. 814-15.
13. *OED*, I, p. 162.

sites with anarchy, darkness, the devil, idol worship and so forth, the exclusionary text (the critiques, the theonomic patriarchal promise and the appeal for communal purification) is addressed not to Paul but to those believers who are not associated with unbelievers. Thus while the exclusionary text is demeaning of those who engage in the ministry of reconciliation and/or are gathered in an *ecclesia*, the text is *not* an assault upon or an affront to, or even a confrontation with, Paul and company because the exclusionary text quoted by Paul in this letter to the Corinthians is not addressed to Paul and company (unbelievers or to those believers who associate with unbelievers). In fact, the text does not even name Paul and company. Instead, the text is addressed to those who seek sacred perfection and makes a vague reference to the opponents of those who are to become the family of God by critiquing the convictions of reconciliation as desecrating and absurd. In not facing its opponents, the exclusionary faction slanders its opponents in conversation or correspondence with others.

The exclusionary text seems unconcerned with the 'impact' or 'consequences' of the appeal for communal purification as a means of fulfilling the theonomic patriarchal promise with respect to those believers who will be expelled as defilements. To the extent that the exclusionary text does not address those who are to be excluded, the text fails to confront.

However, Paul's quoting of the text in his reply to the Corinthian Christian community and his framing comments at 6.11-13 and 7.2-4 are addressed directly to the faction and are, as I argue, an *affront*, a strike or critique, directed at the sacred exclusionist. As I will argue, Paul's replies are confrontations that take the slanderous comments made in the exclusionary text as personal and to which he responds directly. In effect, Paul's replies serve to place him between those for whom and with whom the exclusionary text was an exchange and the exclusionists, in whose face he stands, whom he confronts. Paul proceeds to take offense at the exclusionists and assumes that their appeal for communal purification is an affront. I will argue that one of the purposes for the inclusion of the extended quotation in Paul's letter is to make evident to the letter's audience that the exclusionary social vision is an affront, an attack that wrongs, corrupts and defrauds those who are to be purged from the community. By receiving the comments as an affront, whether they were intended as such or not, Paul calls the exclusionary sacred social vision to ethical account.

Framing of the Exclusionists' Strategy

The introductory (2 Cor. 6.11-13) and concluding frames (2 Cor. 7.2-4) differ in a number of ways. The introductory frame responds to charges made by the exclusionary faction that Paul has excluded them, while the concluding frame is a direct response to the implications of the material in the composite exclusionary text. I read the replies at 6.11-13 and 7.2-3 that frame the exclusionary text as a continuation of themes developed in 5.11-19 (that Furnish titles 'the Ministry of Reconciliation') and 5.20–6.10 ('Reconciliation with God').[14] In these sections of the Epistle, Paul appears to respond to the charge made by the same faction in the Corinthian community that they, or their positions or convictions, were excluded by those committed to reconciliation. I contend that 6.11-13 directly addresses this charge and also serves to introduce the exclusionary text, while the concluding frame at 7.2-3 is Paul's confrontation with the convictions presented in the composite text of 6.14–7.1.

The Introductory Frame at 2 Corinthians 6.11-13

[11] Our mouths are open to you, Corinthians, our hearts are wide.

[12] You are not cramped by us; you are cramped, rather, in your feelings.

[13] In reply—I am speaking to children—widen.[15]

Furnish notes that to '"open one's mouth" conforms to a common Hebraic circumlocution for "speaking", in particular the free and candid expression of one's thoughts and feelings (cf. LXX Judges 11.35-36)'.[16] It is commonly assumed that the phrase 'our mouths are open to you' is an expression of 'openness'. But is this adequate? Do the phrases 'our mouth is open to you' and 'our hearts are wide' convey the same signs of affection and openness? Or might 'Our mouths are open to you' express a sense of astonishment? 'Our mouths are open to you (we are astonished), Corinthians, our hearts are wide.'

Such astonishment may be in regard to a judgment made by a faction that Paul and his ministry of reconciliation cramps or restrains (*stenochōreisthe*) or excludes them. Thus the dialogue might look something like this.

Faction to Paul   Your heart is closed to us.
Paul to Faction   Our mouths are open to you, our hearts are wide.

14. Furnish, *II Corinthians*, pp. 305, 338.
15. *tēn de autēn antimisthian, ōs teknois legō, platunthēte kai umeis.*
16. Furnish, *II Corinthians*, p. 360.

Furnish translates v. 12 'You are not cramped by us; you are cramped, rather, in your feelings', noting that *stenochōreisthe* (RSV 'restricted', Furnish 'cramped') has to do with being pressed in, constricted, put under pressure.[17] What we sense in these verses are the subtle yet powerful nuances of relations in which one party relates to the other in manners that are unaffectionate, aloof, withdrawn, distant, detached and judgmental. The use of *stenochōreisthe* is to play the relation to one's own advantage, to withhold full and candid exchange. Such restrictions control the discourse by withdrawing from or excluding the other.

The argument put forth by Paul is that the faction is not 'restricted', 'cramped' or 'repressed' by Paul. Rather, the faction has 'restricted', 'cramped' or 'repressed' themselves. They restrict themselves who seek sacred perfection by 'withdrawal' from or 'expulsion' of contaminating unbelievers or believers who associate with unbelievers. The faction has *not* been excommunicated by Paul, although the exclusionary faction has withdrawn itself, excommunicating itself from the larger reconciling community. The faction to whom this verse is addressed has apparently claimed that Paul's ministry of reconciliation provides 'no place' for them. The ministry of reconciliation fails to incorporate the 'convictions' of the sacred exclusionary faction in so far as the ministry of reconciliation is not open or wide enough to 'tolerate' those who are anticonciliatory.

For Paul, the issue is whether the congregation will enjoy salvation (at-onement) and serve the ministry of reconciliation that gathers radically different people and groups in Christ to form the *ecclesia*. Apparently, Paul has been charged with being 'closed-minded' or 'closed-mouthed' with regards to 'accepting' the exclusionists. If the ministry of reconciliation excludes at least one faction, such an assessment strikes at the validity of Paul's ministry and authority. Paul had earlier written, 'We put no obstacle in anyone's way, so that no fault may be found with our ministry' (2 Cor. 6.3).

Apparently, the faction has charged that Paul's ministry of reconciliation, which seeks to 'accommodate' opposing sets in Christ, is an obstacle that at least hypothetically excludes the sacred exclusionist from full participation at least on their terms in the Corinthian congregation. If those who stand in opposition to the at-oning of opposites in Christ are beyond or are excluded from the ecclesial gathering in Christ, then the ministry of reconciliation is itself inconsistent, if not self-contradictory. Contrary to

17. Furnish, *II Corinthians*, p. 359. The term also occurs in Rom. 2.9, 8.35 and 2 Cor. 4.8.

Paul's stated nonexclusionary social vision, Paul is in fact exclusionary because his ministry of reconciliation excludes those who are against reconciliation.

For the sacred perfectionist, differences are an abomination. God dwells in, lives and moves among a homogeneous people who are not connected with 'others'. And the unity with one's opposite is inconceivable, if not evil. There is no intimate connection between God and the world. Thus God's people, like God, must be sacred and separate from the world. This disconnection, this nonidentity or nonunity of the sacred with the impure, God and the world, must be repeated by the people who would be God's temple, God's family. God's people, like God, must be separated from the world. The nonaccommodation with differences marks the believers as the sacred place, the temple in which God may dwell. By separating themselves from the world, they will be God's dwelling place, the temple.

From the perspective of the exclusionist, Paul's *ecclesia* would be an accommodation with the ungodly, an accommodation with the forces of evil. The exclusionists contend that Paul's *ecclesia* would violate the expectations of God and nullify the theonomic patriarchal promise. In other words, Paul's openness violates the possibility of salvation as purification.

Paul's inclusion of the exclusionary faction in the *ecclesia* could be judged an act of convictional self-contradiction, because such an inclusion may appear to violate the very logic and coherence of Paul's conciliatory social view. If Paul is open to their inclusion, is he also open to their exclusionary social vision?

However, if there are limits to who can be reconciled in Christ, then such salvific limits contradict the authority of the reconciliation fragment and, for that matter, Paul's entire enterprise. If Paul were to conclude, 'Yes, you are correct: there is no place for you in the *ecclesia*, depart', then the ministry of reconciliation is open to charges of inconsistency and self-contradiction. Such exclusion of those who hold non-conciliatory convictions would violate the integrity and authority of Paul's ministry.

Much is at stake. If Paul fails to be conciliated with the exclusionists, does that not entail the violation of the reconciliation of opposites? And if Paul is conciliating with the exclusionists, does he not violate his own reconciliatory convictions?

Paul's introductory reply (6.11-13) addresses the accusation that Paul's ministry of reconciliation is limited, that it cannot include or accommodate its real opposite: the non-conciliatory, sacred exclusionist.

Verse 6.13 is divided by what I judge to be a parenthetical comment.

¹³ In reply (I am speaking to children) widen.

Remove the parenthetical comment, and the verse reads,

¹³ In reply, widen.

Although the opening phrase is commonly translated 'In return', Furnish has suggested that *tēn de autēn antimisthian* be translated 'As a response in kind'. Furnish's translation nicely conveys the sense in which the appeal at v. 13c is a repetition of an appeal by the faction in Corinth. The reader is led to infer that the appeal by Paul at v. 13c for the faction to 'widen' repeats the faction's appeal for Paul to 'widen'. Thus my choice to translate v. 13a 'In reply' should not be read as suggesting that Paul is offering something different in response to what the faction has said. Rather, Paul replies, or repeats, or echoes back the faction's plea to him. Paul's patronizing parenthetical comment at v. 13 ('I speak as to children') may be a judgment against the self-limiting 'affections' of the exclusionists who will not or cannot open themselves to 'others'. Affection is restricted to the familiar. Pleasure is limited to the comfortable. And so does Paul speak as to children who will not try what is different? Paul's defensive responses at 5.3 and 6.11-13 (and 7.2 for that matter) express his frustrations with members of the faction who do not possess or do not know whether they possess the capacity to experience a broader diversity of differentiated affections.

I take the patronizing parenthetical comment 'I speak as to children' (6.13b) to be an addition by Paul in his reply to the faction. Thus I read the verses as expressive of a dialogue.

> Faction: Widen.
> Paul: In reply (I speak to children)
>   'Widen'.

Chapter 8

DE/SECRATION

Introduction

At the concluding frame at 2 Cor. 7.2-3 Paul writes:

> [2]Open to us. No one have we wronged. No one have we corrupted. No one have we defrauded. [3] I do not say this to condemn you.

Furnish translates *chōrēsate ēmas* at the beginning of v. 2 'Provide us room' and interprets the verse to be a plea to the Corinthians to 'take their apostle into their affections as he has taken them into his'.[1] Furnish expresses the common interpretation that the text is about Paul's position and authority in the congregation at Corinth, a position and authority that had diminished because of the missionary and teaching activities of representatives of other apostles, presumably from Jerusalem, and namely, the disciples and James, the brother of Jesus. So the call for the readers 'to widen their hearts' and 'Provide us room' is taken to be a plea for the congregation to accept Paul's apostolate and ministry.

The assumption that the text at 6.11–7.1 is the justification of the authority of its assumed author (Paul) is, I have argued, too simple an act of interpretation, given the complexities of the text and the complex social arrangements and conflicts evident in the letters. The issue in Corinth is not simply whether to accept the authority of Paul, who is assumed by such interpreters to be the authoritative representative of orthodoxy, or that of others who are assessed to be non- or unorthodox. If we read the plea 'Provide us room' as being addressed to *all* Corinthians, and we read 6.14–7.1 as a presentation of a faction that regards itself as the righteous remnant within the Corinthian community, then what we have is a complex conflict in which Paul's plea is directed not at the Corinthians per se but at the sacred perfectionist faction that seeks to expel from the church

---

1.   Furnish, *II Corinthians*, p. 336.

those believers who associate with unbelievers.

The forceful and emphatic claims of v. 2 may be read as Paul's 'defense' against negative judgments assessed by those seeking sacred perfection against those not seeking sacred perfection. And if we move quickly from 6.13 to 7.2, we may entertain the possibility that the defensive claims stated by Paul at 7.2b-d may echo or retrace claims made by the sacred exclusionary faction.

Sacred exclusionists:	Provide us room. No one have we wronged. No one have we corrupted. No one have we defrauded.
Paul:	In reply (I speak as to children) 'Widen'.
	²Provide us room.
	No one have we wronged.
	No one have we corrupted.
	No one have we defrauded.

The three-fold negative reply by Paul to the self-identification of the sacred exclusionists and their desecration of believers who associate with unbelievers has an emphatic repetition that may be glossed over. In Greek, the three phrases read,

oudena ēdikēsamen (no one have we wronged)
oudena ephtheiramen (no one have we corrupted)
oudena epleonektēsamen (no one have we taken advantage of)

The repetitive element of the phrase *oudena*, '*no* one', enjoys emphasis rather than the verbs. The emphatic nuance of the repetition is lost when translators render the phrases, 'We have wronged no one, we have corrupted no one, we have taken advantage of no one.' Such translation assumes (as we shall see) that the three-fold negation is 'defensive' in intent. Nevertheless, given the repetitiveness and what I believe to be an intentional choice of word order, the emphasis lies with the beginning term repeated in each of the phrases.[2]

The sacred exclusionists would certainly have assumed that they have wronged, corrupted or taken advantage of no one. And given the convictions expressed in the divine patriarchal promise and the appeal, the sacred exclusionists would have assessed that those *not* seeking sacred perfection have wronged, corrupted and taken advantage of those believers who are seeking sacred perfection. Paul's reply at 7.2 may be read as simply a self-defense that repeats the claims made by the sacred exclusionary faction back upon them. If this is the case, then Paul's repetition and

2. Furnish, *II Corinthians*, p. 366.

acquisition of the claims of the sacred exclusionary faction precipitate a confrontation between the two parties. If the exclusionary text insinuated that Paul and the company of believers who associate with unbelievers are defilements of flesh and spirit, then, on behalf of those who have been judged to be impure, Paul asserts that the accused have not 'wronged', 'corrupted' or 'taken advantage' of anyone.

While I think that something like this may have precipitated the three-fold emphatic defense at 7.2, I am convinced that there is much more going on with v. 2. The nuances of the three emphatic statements at 7.2 become evident only as we consider the relation of vv. 2 and 3. The second of the three claims at v. 2 will usher us into the complexity of Paul's critical response to the sacred/desecration discourse of the exclusionary text.

As we saw above with the first pass, v. 2 appears to be a simple, emphatic self-defense against the judgments of the sacred exclusionists:

> No one have we wronged.
> No one have we corrupted.
> No one have we defrauded.

But an odd disclaimer follows v. 2:

> I do not say this to condemn you.

The disclaimer at v. 3 complicates the reading of v. 2 because it suggests *through negation* that v. 2 conveys an accusation to which v. 3 is a response or qualification:

> No one have we wronged.
> No one have we corrupted.
> No one have we defrauded.
> I do not say this to condemn you.

Between vv. 2 and 3 is an *implied accusation*:

> No one have we wronged.
> No one have we corrupted.
> No one have we defrauded.
> *(But* you *have.)*
> I do not say this to condemn you.

With the second pass over v. 2 as framed by v. 3, v. 2 reads as more than a self-defense. Verse 2 reads as an accusation. Verse 3a serves no purpose if the three-fold negative response at v. 2 is only a self-defense. If v. 2 was not a critique that might be mistaken for a condemnation, then why the qualification or disclaimer that the verse is not intended to condemn? This maneuvering—reading v. 2 as self-defense, switching to v. 3 with its implication that no condemnation was intended, then going back to read v. 2 as a critique and moving forward again to v. 3—provides a transition that plays upon and fills out the subtle nuances of the text.

I will argue that the three accusations in v. 2 serve to deconstruct the sacred identity of those who seek perfection in hopes of fulfilling the conditions and expectations of the patriarchal promise. As I will argue, Paul's deconstruction of sacred identity is necessary if at-onement between the exclusionists and those vilified as desecrations is to happen in Christ. Reconciliation for Paul is the gathering of different individuals and diverse groups into a nonconflicting social group. Paul's appeal for reconciliation is not an appeal for everyone to 'get along'. The *ecclesia* is not an open community of atomic individuals who are provided with space.

Interpolation Revisited

Those who hold that 2 Cor. 6.14–7.1 is an interpolation have not shown to what the three-fold defense/accusation of 7.2 replies. The verse offers a forceful, emphatic reply:

> No one have we wronged.
> No one have we corrupted.
> No one have we defrauded.

Working backwards from the three-fold defense/accusation we begin to see the incoherence of the interpolation hypothesis. Where in the text is the charge or accusation presented to which Paul replies with the defense that he and company have wronged, corrupted and taken advantage of no one? Those who insist on the interpolation hypothesis have not addressed to what v. 2 replies. Or why would Paul offer such a forceful, explicit reply if not for the forceful, explicit critique leveled against Paul in the exclusionary text? To suggest that Paul's emphatic reply at v. 2 addresses some nonspecific, vague critique implied in the preceding letter or behind the text but not traced in the text strikes me as an inadequate proposal.

The question of textual integrity is complex. I have argued that the tensions in the Corinthian texts disclose the intertextuality of a 'reply' in which quotations and paraphrases from the reports and letters from the Corinthians are incorporated. Incoherence in the text may be traces of quotations, paraphrases and the like. Thus the coherence of the reply may be best described as dialogical. Not all of the verses of the text conform to some simple, monolithic presentation. The exclusionary text of 6.14–7.1 is framed immediately (and by that I mean the last phrase of Paul's reply before the quoted exclusionary quotation and the first phrase of reply following the exclusionary text) by the terms 'Widen' (*platunthēte kai umeis*) and 'Open' (*chōrēsate ēmas*). Those who argue for the radical interpolation hypothesis contend that if one removes what they judge to be the 'corrupting' verses, the text joins together 'nicely'. Expressing this manner of reading, Georgi contends that:

> The segment 6.14–7.1 has been inserted in its present position, the two framing verses 6.13 and 7.2 mated each other very well, but this cannot be said of their relationship to 6.14 or 7.1. 7.2 immediately follows 6.13 with no noticeable influence of the statements between.

It is assumed that the interpolator cut the *textus* of the original letter by Paul and added the offensive text. With the offending text removed, the coherence and integrity of the text is restored. But is it?

Let's look at 6.11-13 and 7.2-3 joined together, as (it is proposed) was the original state of the letter by Paul before the corruption by the later editor(s).

> Our mouths are open to you, Corinthians, our hearts are wide. You are not cramped by us; you are cramped, rather, in your feelings. In reply, I am speaking to children—widen. Open to us. No one have we wronged. No one have we corrupted. No one have we defrauded. I do not say this to condemn you, for I said before that you are in our hearts, to die together and to live together.

I think the two joining verses are too much alike. Georgi contends, 'The two framing verses 6.13 and 7.2 match each other very well.'[3] But I do not think they match at all. Things that are different are said to match; items that are in some opposition are said to match. Two right shoes do not match; nor do two left gloves. The assumption—an assumption that I think is not well thought through by those who argue for the radical inter-polation hypothesis—is that things that are alike enjoy coherence. Verses 6.13 and 7.2 belong together because likes belong together. Repetition is a powerful rhetorical devise. But when repetition is used, it commonly serves to enumerate a point or to re-emphasize a position. But what purpose is served by the repetition at vv. 13 and 2? The contention that the verses properly join together because they are in a significant sense the

---

3.   Dieter Georgi, *The Opponents of Paul in Second Corinthians* (Philadelphia: Fortress Press, 1986), p. 12.

same, that they enjoy identity, does not make textual sense. Those who argue for the radical interpolation hypothesis conceive of an authentic text as enjoying simple coherence. But what they seek is not coherence but identity. Coherence can be complex. I assess that the radical interpolation hypothesis proposes too limited a sense of coherence, and that if you join 6.13 and 7.2 together you get a very strange repetition that does not move the argument forward or develop a theme.

The Desecration

No one have we corrupted (2 Cor. 7.2c).

The root *phtheirō* of the verb *ephtheiramen* ('no one *have we corrupted*') conveys in an active voice 'to destroy, to waste; to corrupt, to bribe; to lure or trap'.[4] The verb was also commonly employed to speak of the perverting and/or seduction of a woman that conveyed in that society 'to spoil' or 'to ruin' a woman. In its more passive voice, *phtheiresthe* was a curse, as in 'May you perish! Ruin take you!' In medical contexts, *phtheiryō* conveyed one being deranged or disordered. And in the LXX *ephthanyē* conveyed what the editors of Liddell-Scott read as the sense of being *morally* corrupted (cf. Gen. 6.11 and Hos. 9.9). I think the qualification of the corruption as 'moral' is an unfortunate translation. The primary text cited is from Genesis 6:

> [11]Now the earth was *corrupt* in God's sight, and the earth was filled with violence. [12]And God saw the earth, and behold, it was *corrupt*; for all flesh had *corrupted* their way upon the earth. [13]And God said to Noah, 'I have determined to make an end of all flesh; for the earth is filled with violence through them; behold, I will destroy them with the earth' (Gen. 6.11-13).

In this passage, the earth is *corrupt* without redemption, save Noah and family. Corruption is presented as more than moral corruption. The earth's corruption is total, complete. The earth is defiled and incapable of being corrected or forgiven and so *must* be destroyed in order to begin renewal. The old totalistic corrupt identity must be replaced by a new totalistic redeemed identity. Of course Noah's family's purity was short-lived, and the old nevertheless came to contaminate the new. But my point is that the sense of corruption is not limited to moral corruption. The corruption of the earth is complete except for Noah, and if corruption succeeds, if Noah succumbs to corruption, then the redemption of the earth will be impossible.

---

4. Liddell-Scott, *Lexicon*, p. 1928.

It is assumed in the exclusionary text that contact with a desecration corrupts, spoils and ruins. Those who contact the defiled also contract the defilement. Any who would seek sanctity are desecrated by contacting those who have contracted the corruption. There exists a matrix of defilement. The source of desecration is the defiled. Defilement desecrates by contact and, moreover, anyone who is caught up in the matrix of defiling associations carries the contagion of desecration. Therefore anyone who is caught up in the matrix of defiling associations is desecrated. One way to avoid being desecrated is to avoid contact with anyone in the matrix of desecration.

However, if v. 2c is read as not so much a defense as an accusation, then the defense ('no one have we corrupted/defiled/ desecrated') also conveys an implied charge: 'but you have corrupted/ defiled/desecrated someone'.

But how might those seeking sacred perfection have defiled another? For those seeking sacred perfection, defilement is caused by defilement. Identification is a chain of signification that repeats itself. Only those identified as defiled can cause defilement. So, assuming that desecration is contagious, we might be led to conclude that those seeking sacred perfection have come into contaminating contact with someone or something that is defiled. But I do not find Paul suggesting that the sacred perfectionists are somehow defiled through contamination. Those seeking perfection are not somehow defiled unbeknown to themselves—and thus defile others through contact, unaware of their own defilement.

As we noted of the exclusionary text, those seeking sacred perfection attained perfection by negation, by negating contact with the profane world, with the understanding that by negating the world, the believer was moving towards the sacred. A dyadic structure is assumed:

God—world
Sacred—profane

Given the theonomic patriarchal promise, all the world is a defilement. Thus purification is an act of negation whereby what is identified as a desecration is removed or abandoned. In the first instance in the exclusionary text, this negation is enacted by those seeking sacred perfection 'withdrawing' from the world. In the second instance the negation is enacted by those seeking sacred perfection 'expelling' those believers who associate with the defiled.

Ricoeur contends that the symbolic structure of defilement is neither reflective nor representational. Rather, it is 'acted out'.

> One can catch sight of it in the act of purification and go back from the act that suppresses to the 'thing' suppressed. It is the *rite* that exhibits the symbolism of defilement; and just as the rite suppresses symbolically, defilement infects symbolically.[5]

The removal of defiled members from the community is the rite that simultaneously exhibits the symbolism of defilement *and* the symbolism of purification. Within this symbolic structure, defilement is infectious, while the sacred is not. The rites of sacred perfection serve to suppress, limit or quarantine the contamination from those seeking sacred perfection. Ricoeur continues:

> It [the act of ablution] is always signified in partial, substitutive, and abbreviated signs: burning, removing, chasing, throwing, spitting out, covering up, burying. Each of these acts marks out a ceremonial space, within which one of them exhausts its significance in immediate and, so to speak, literal usefulness. They are acts which stand for a total action addressed to the person taken as an undivided whole.[6]

It is assumed by Ricoeur that the rites that suppress defilement are a response to the epidemic of defilement, and that the symbolic rites of purification provide for the limitation of defilement and the chaos and violence that the profane 'issues'. Ricoeur is in good company on this point. But Paul is not a member of that company.

I argue that, for Paul, *the rite of expulsion simultaneously exhibits the sacred and the desecrated*. In the ritual act of self-purification, whether individual or communal, the sacred and the desecrated are presented as totalities. As undivided, uncompromised totalities, both the pure and the defiled enjoy clarity of identity and solidarity with their own kind. In this way, the ritual of expulsion *institutes* the establishment of the differentiation of the sacred and the desecrated, with the complexities of each identification reduced to a totality.

If perfection is an act of negation, then the division of the sacred and the profane is an act of differentiation and identification by which those seeking sacred perfection symbolize another as *evil* and simultaneously symbolize themselves as *sacred*. In the ritual differentiation, the *other* becomes a defiled totality in opposition to *one's own self* becoming a sacred totality. One's own purification is yielded by the desecration of the other. Therefore the identifications of the pure and the impure are inseparable.

5. Ricoeur, *Evil*, p. 35.
6. Ricoeur, *Evil*, p. 35.

Rites of *con*secration are acts that simultaneously *de*secrate. Rites that identify something or someone else as a desecration simultaneously identity oneself as a consecration. Exclusionary rites in which the desecration is to be removed from contact with those who seek consecration, or rites in which the desecration is to be removed, are acts that simultaneously consecrate. The ritual of consecration must of necessity symbolically enact a desecration. In opposition and in measure, the act of con/desecration yields totalizing identities—the sacred and the desecrated, the pure and the impure. In this way, one is purified only to the extent that another is corrupted. And one is desecrated only to the extent that another is purified.

Those seeking sacred purification enjoy their consecration by negating, by desecrating, another. 'To desecrate' commonly means 'to profane, to violate, to make unholy'. It can also mean 'to dedicate or devote to something evil'.[7] In this context, I take it that those seeking sacred perfection must desecrate, as in 'to dedicate another as evil', in order to consecrate themselves as sacred. Paul's accusation that the exclusionists have corrupted others stands as a judgment that the rites of purification 'defile' or 'corrupt' the one who is abandoned or expelled by the community seeking sacred purification. And the agents of 'defilement' are those members of the community who seek sacred perfection through the rites of identification, that issue in the differentiation and abandonment or expulsion of others as defilements.

Paul has not defiled, desecrated or corrupted another because Paul has not vilified another in order to gain sacred perfection. Thus, if we return to v. 2, the three-fold contention that 'No one have we wronged, no one have we corrupted, no one have we taken advantage of' may be read as a defensive declaration that Paul and company are *not* seeking consecration. Remember, consecration entails the desecration of another. The implied accusation at v. 3 confirms that the faction that disassociates itself from all unbelievers and expels all believers who continue to associate with unbelievers is seeking sacred self-perfection by defiling, desecrating or corrupting others. In the progression from separation to isolation to purging, those who 'differ' are increasingly vilified while those who are identified as seeking sacred perfection become increasingly consecrated. The consecration of the believers is dependent upon the desecration of the unbelievers. The de-conciliation or the de-at-onement of believers and

7.   *OED*, III, p. 239.

unbelievers leads to the separation of the sacred and the desecrated, measure for measure.

Paul's deconstruction of the matrix of the sacred and the profane renders self-identity with the sacred an impossibility. The act, the sacred rite of classifying another *as* a desecration, is a corruptive act that corrupts the one who enacts the rite of purification.

Within the dyadic economy of western religious thought and practice sacred transcendence is envisioned as the total and complete overcoming of desecration. While salvation and the utopian visions and social policies of religious communities obsessed with sacred purification are presented as singular and exclusive, such conceptions are inscribed in binary terms.

Sacred	Profane
One	Many
God	World
Identity	Difference
Clarity	Confusion
Presence	Absence
Light	Darkness
Pure	Impure

The sacred are sacred in opposition to and in negation of the profane. The rites of purification—sacred withdrawal from the world, communal self-purification by the expulsion of contaminated members—differentiate and occasion the binaries. Without clear differentiation between binary terms, the sacred and the profane cannot be identified. The rites of purification occasion and clarify the differences in which the desires of sanctity seek satisfaction. Without such clarity the promise of sacred salvation will remain forever elusive.

Taylor contends, 'It is against just this hierarchy that so many modern thinkers rebel.'[8] 'If hierarchical oppression and repression are to be overcome, it is necessary to *pass through* a phrase of inversion. But reversal can remain caught within the dyadic economy of conflictual opposition.'[9] For Paul simply to reverse the charge that the self-righteous faction in Corinth is the *source* of contamination that defiled the unbelievers and those believers who associate with unbelievers would be for Paul to remain caught within the dyadic economy of the sacred and the profane. But Paul does not seek transcendence within the sacred/desecrated economy. No call is made by Paul for believers to achieve

8.   Taylor, *Erring*, p. 9.
9.   Taylor, *Erring*, pp. 9, 10.

sanctification once and for all. Instead, for Paul, transcendence comes in deconstructing the dyadic economy, in reversing the hierarchy not in order to establish a new hierarchy, but to overcome or empty the economy so as to move beyond the obsession with the sacred. What follows from Paul's critical reversal and the subsequent release ('I do not say this to condemn you') is an occasion for atoning in which the conflicting opposites are understood and appreciated as being mutually dependent, if not mutually originating. Paul's move to configure the sacred/desecrated as mutually originating suggests that, for Paul, the designations do not make onto-logical or metaphysical reference. Rather, *the sacred/desecrated distinction and the identities differentiated are empty of reference.* This is not a minor point.

In so moving, Paul subverts an important strategy in western religious thought and practice. The subversion of the methods for establishing a sacred hierarchy forfeits the possibility of sacred self-identification (for that matter, desecrated identification as well). By this forfeiture, Paul critiques salvation as purification.

Each increases as 'profane' or 'sacred' in equal measure, in opposition to one another. Those groups intent upon ritual purity seek to establish a totalizing social arrangement in which the desire for pure identity drives the community to seek ever-controlled arrangements. The community thus establishes its identity by the continued process of excluding those who corrupt the purity of the community. This totalizing desire for purification exposes itself in the continuing process of restriction and repression of differences. In effect, the circle of convictions and ritual practices that are acceptable grows tighter and more exclusive as more and more is brought into scrutiny. It might also be the case that greater convectional coherence and clearer limits are sought, thus purging the community of those that were once accommodated. The purity of the community manifests itself in the rite of exclusion that establishes the boundary of inside/outside.

The act of reconciliation violates the boundary. The violation of the boundary occurs in one sense by the growth of the community from with-out. However, the process of exclusion clarifies the boundary in a radical manner. Isolation establishes the boundary marking the difference between inside and outside, while the act of exclusion substantiates the line, bring-ing clarity and focus by sharpening the differences that establish identity.

The sacred exclusionists called for an acceptance of the promise that they interpret as an appeal for the cleansing of those who have been defiled in body and soul through association with unbelievers. Such an appeal yields a community that has excluded all who are not seeking sacred perfection in the fear of God. In other words, those who refuse to dissociate themselves from unbelievers must be expelled from the community in order to meet the demands of the promise.

No one have we taken advantage of.

The desire for self-purification in the hope of unity with the sacred is a program, a fantasy, that is self-absorbed. Those who seek to become consecrated in order to 'belong' to the Lord seek their *own advantage* in an economy of sacred scarcity. In their striving for sacred purification, those who seek to become the sons and daughters of the Lord seek their own advantage over those whom they assess, whom they dedicate to evil.

The language of purity glorifies the individual who seeks purification. The perspective of the 'other', the experiences, the humiliations, the degradations of the one consigned to the impure and improper, cannot be entertained. What matters is the relation of the self to God. And so purity gives rise to an objectification of the 'other' and the 'pious self'. Salvation, union of self and the sacred, comes only in closing off one's self from the world, breaking off all contaminating encounters. Salvation becomes a totalizing endeavor in which all others who compromise the fulfillment of pious desire are demonic. Only the pious self and the desire for union with the Lord are sacred.

If the three-fold defense/accusation at 7.2 is a judgment that the sacred exclusionists have wronged, corrupted and taken advantage of others, then, given the plea by those seeking sacred perfection for the removal of all defilements, one might expect Paul to return the call and reply that the exclusionists be cleansed from the community for having violated others. Those believers seeking sacred perfection should be removed from the community because they are the agents of defilement. But instead of replying to the call for the expulsion of the self-identified, sacred perfectionists who have wronged, corrupted and taken advantage of others, Paul writes:

> I do not say this to condemn you, for I said before that you are in our hearts, to die together and to live together (2 Cor. 7.3).

Paul's inclusive comments at 7.3b-c continue the theme of 6.12:

> [6.12]You are not restricted by us, but you are restricted in your own affections. [7.3]...for I said before that you are in our hearts, to die together and to live together.[10]

10. Furnish notes that (7.3) 'to die together and to live together' is interpreted as a formula of abiding friendship, Paul's pledge to his readers that he is bound to them, whether in death or in life. Furnish, *II Corinthians*, p. 367.

Paul's point is that the exclusionary faction is not excluded from the *ecclesia*. The exclusionists exclude and isolate themselves. By vilifying others and judging them to be corrupt, and by withdrawing or expelling, the exclusionary faction restricts its own associations. They, not Paul, withdraw and restrict their own free and candid participation with other believers.

The qualification at v. 3a provides the means Paul sought to stop the dynamics of sacred exclusion and violence. The qualification that he is not condemning and that they are all to enjoy reconciling community serves to counter the totalizing identity by which one's righteousness or innocence or purity happens in opposition to another's being identified as evil or guilty or impure.

> [2]No one have we wronged,
> No one have we corrupted,
> No one have we taken advantage of.
> [3]I do not say this to condemn you, for I said before that you are in our hearts, to die together and to live together (2 Cor. 7.2-3).

The sacred/desecrated distinction is deconstructed. Each identification is understood as a necessity for the other. There can be no sacred without the profane. Purification is understandable only in relation to what is impure. Only in opposition do the terms have meaning. Paul's quick moves to indict the sacred perfectionists, followed by the quick withdrawal of the condemnation, serve to deconstruct the binary opposition of the sacred/desecrated distinction.

The confrontation at 6.12 and 7.2 affronts the sacred faction in Corinth. In these verses, convictions of the sacred cult are reversed and used by Paul *against* them. They have charged that they are being restricted or cramped, presumably by Paul, his ministry of reconciliation and his re-conciling *ecclesia*. Paul reverses their charge—and replies that they are the cause of their own restriction. Those seeking sacred perfection have charged that believers who associate with unbelievers are agents of defile-ment who contaminate the temple of God. Paul reverses their assessment and charges those who seek sacred perfection with being the agents of contamination.

Paul accuses the accuser and so reverses the system of purification and defilement. It is assumed in all sacred economies that a desecration is a desecration by virtue of its being made a desecration by contaminating contact with another desecration. The assumption is that when an entity is desecrated, that which is itself already a desecration is the source of desecration. The same produces the same. But Paul's critique of desecration deconstructs the identity of fault. In this instance he deconstructs the identification that something is a desecration by contending that the immediate source of desecration is not a desecrated entity in a string of contamination that connects and makes all the same. For the exclusionists, only the desecrated can desecrate in the economy of perfection and fault.

Instead, Paul contends that the source of desecration is the sacred. Those who seek sacred perfection 'make' their 'other', and in so differentiating between the sacred and the desecrated identify the desecrated and the sacred. Identity as sacred or desecrated is codependent and cooriginating.

The indictments at v. 2b-d turn the tables. The sacred exclusionists, not the believers who associate with unbelievers, are corrupting the community. The sacred exclusionists, not the believers who associate with unbelievers, 'restrict' (RSV) or 'cramp' (Furnish) themselves.

It is assumed that the faction in question, by its exclusion, has wronged, corrupted and taken advantage of others. The act of classifying persons as sacred or desecrated is assessed or assumed by Paul to be immoral. Those who regard themselves as enjoying sacred perfection in opposition to others, who are assessed as being profane, are responsible for the desecration. The self-proclaimed perfectionists are the agents of imperfection who wrong, corrupt and take advantage of others. The very act of sacred self-identification is itself a desecration of another.

But the accusation and condemnation of 7.2 is quickly withdrawn at 7.3. The purpose of this maneuver by Paul is to call the exclusionists into an awareness of the mechanics of purification and defilement.

The language of piety is filled with self-absorption and self-affection. The pious are porous. And they desire to control their openness by social manipulation so that they come into contact only with those who, like themselves, are seeking sacred perfection.

To be porous with another who is not pious, to be affectionate with another who is not pious, is to become *other* than pious, to become impious. Piety gives rise to the objectification or disaffection of all who are not sacred. For to be open, to be porous, to share affections with any who are not seeking sacred perfection, is to be in sympathy with the ungodly and to forfeit sacred salvation. Love of the other, love of a desecration, forecloses the possibility of being loved as the sons and daughters of God. The sacred is a jealous father who is limited in affection and can love only what is like 'himself', his own sacred children. Obsessed with their own identification, the pious fortify themselves so as to become disaffectioned, disassociated from any and all who are not the same, who are not seeking sacred perfection.

Paul's affronts are decisive. They cut at the very core convictions of the sacred exclusionists, in that Paul attacks their most rudimentary assumptions of causation. The indictments at 7.2 (and 6.12 for that matter) serve the purpose of halting the self-righteous condemnations of the sacred exclusionists in order to *invoke* a response. Paul invokes those who seek sacred perfection *to care for* those whom they have harmed, wronged and corrupted by their sacred project. If those seeking sacred perfection come to share affections for those assessed earlier to be corruptions, then the sacred project is rendered void. Pious desires for identity with the sacred are reassessed by those obsessed and self-absorbed with their own project. The deconstruction of the economy of perfection occasions an alt-onement between those who have been separated by the dividing walls of sacred hostility and violence. Thus the quick moves from the invocation ('Open!') to the condemnation and affront to the withdrawal of the condemnation serve as an occasion for the possibility of alt-onement. For Paul to do anything less than to seek alt-onement with the exclusionists would be for Paul to seek his own advantage, and to fail to seek salvation with his opposite in Christ.

Chapter 9

SACRED DECEPTIONS: SACRED DESTRUCTION

I mentioned at the beginning of our study of de/secration that I assessed
1 Cor. 3.16-17 to be a quotation that Paul critiques in the subsequent verses.
The text is preceded by verses in which Paul elucidates how he and all
others are servants for God, who work as laborers in a field or as craftsmen
constructing a building. 'For we are God's fellow workers, you are God's
field, God's building' (1 Cor. 3.9). I want to begin with the temple discourse of vv. 16-17 and then consider the framing verses.

First the quotation:

> [16]Do you not know that you are God's temple, and that God's spirit dwells
> in you? [17]If any one destroys God's temple, God will destroy him. For
> God's temple is sacred, and that temple you are (1 Cor. 3.16-17).

Paul's reply is forthright and cutting:

> Let no one deceive himself (1 Cor. 3.18).

To deceive is an action or practice of concealing the truth for the purpose of misleading—to defraud, cheat or trick. It is not a deception to
conceal the truth or to be wrong. Deception must include as well an intended harmful effect. Now, the point could be made that to mislead
another regarding the truth is itself an act of deception. Thus the act of
concealing the truth without *intent* to harm is nevertheless deception, for
concealing the truth is the harm, the trick, the fraud.

The quoted vv. 16-17 are a mix of propositional types that might give
the reader or listener the impression that a convincing argument is being
made. Verse 16 is an informative rhetorical question that assumes a
negative first response. 'Do you not know that you are God's temple, and
that God's spirit dwells in you?' Response, 'No, I did not know that I am
God's temple, or that God's spirit dwells in me!' The content of the
question calls for the reader to infer identification. If the rhetorical
question at v. 16 were successful, then the negative first response would

not be repeated if the question were issued a second time. The reader's first response, 'No', would be followed by an affirmation. 'No. I did not know that I am the temple of God. But now I do.' The identification that the assumed reader is God's temple, an identification that the negative rhetorical question of v. 16 serves to inform, is forthrightly stated in the final clause of v. 17b: 'you are that temple'.

Between the informative negative rhetorical question of v. 16 and the emphatic identification of the assumed reader with God's temple at the end of 17b is strung a hypothetical and a categorical proposition. The categorical claim '*For* God's temple is sacred' is so stated as to suggest that it is to be read as a conclusion. But what it concludes is not evident. The characterization of God's temple that we may cull from these verses is that God's temple is sacred, that the assumed reader is God's temple and that God's spirit dwells in the assumed reader. We may infer as well that the assumed reader is sacred (although this is never stated directly). But as a rhetorical device, the declaration of the characterizations and assertion of identification of the temple and the reader are not descriptive but prescriptive. The purpose of these verses is to move the assumed reader to make the self-identification as God's sacred temple.

While we might assess that the intent of the author is to manipulate the assumed reader to accept the identification as the temple (and presumably to not make contrary identifications), the issue as to whether or not such a identification conceals the truth or is a downright lie might occasion a lively discussion. But, given the subject matter, one might be hard-pressed to demonstrate that the identification was 'harmful', let alone 'masochistic'. Yet, sandwiched between the rhetorical questions of v. 16 and the categorical claims of v. 17b, is a hypothetical contention dealing with a complex array of violence and sacred revenge.

> If any one destroys God's temple, God will destroy him (1 Cor. 3.17).

Thus, given the identification between the assumed reader and the temple preceding and following the hypothetical proclamation of sacred revenge, those who accept the identification as 'God's sacred temple' may now live with a confidence that comes with knowing that they are so valued by God that God will avenge their destruction. This is an odd form of the mutually assured destruction policy practiced by the superpowers in the Cold War and parodied in the film *Dr Strangelove*: if you destroy me you will put into play the means for your own annihilation. But in the case of the claim quoted in v. 17a, the declaration is not the public policy of a state. Rather, the declaration 'If any one destroys God's temple, God will destroy him' is addressed not to anyone who might destroy God's temple but to those who presumably make the self-identification as God's temple. In other words, the declaration is not a public presentation that would serve to forestall aggression against the community. The conviction that one's sacred community has the most powerful divine avenger is a private declaration that may serve to invigorate those who identify themselves as the temple community of God to act irresponsibly in relation to the political and military powers of the age. A cultic group that is weak and vulnerable to the power of an empire may be seduced by their complex delusions of self-importance and an avenging God to act irresponsibly and initiate their own destruction at the hands of the powerful empire.

Beginning with v. 18, there is a shift in the content and perspective that I judge to be a demarcation between the material quoted by Paul and his reply.

> [16]Do you not know that you are God's temple, and that God's spirit dwells in you? [17]If any one destroys God's temple, God will destroy him. For God's temple is sacred, and that temple you are (1 Cor. 3.16-17).

In reply, Paul writes:

> [18]Let no one deceive himself. If any one among you thinks that he is wise in this age, let him become a fool that he may become wise. [19]For the wisdom of this world is folly with God. For it is written,
> 'He catches the wise in their craftiness',
> [20]and again,
> 'The Lord knows that the thoughts of the wise are futile'.
> [21]So let no one boast of men. For all things are yours, [22]whether Paul or Apollos or Cephas or the world or life or death or the present or the future, all are yours; [23]and you are Christ's; and Christ is God's (1 Cor. 3.18-23).

In opposition to those who claim to be the temple, Paul quotes from Job 5 at 1 Cor. 3.19:

> [11]he sets on high those who are lowly, and those who mourn are lifted to safety. [12]He frustrates the devices of the crafty, so that their hands achieve no success. [13]*He takes the wise in their own craftiness*; and the schemes of the wily are brought to a quick end. [14]They meet with darkness in the daytime, and grope at noonday as in the night (Job 5.11-14).

And at 1 Cor. 3.20 Paul quotes Ps. 34.11 in which the Lord is the one who knows that the thoughts of the wise are futile. The wise do not yet know.

While the vitalizing possibilities of being God's temple may be convincing to those who are frustrated by the limits of their economic, political and cultural circumstances, in the end the convictions are judged by Paul to be harmful—in fact, deadly. To act upon the presumption that God will avenge your destruction may well be self-destructive. For if you go forth in the world self-assured that you enjoy God's privilege and that God's partiality for you is a sure 'protection' (for who would dare destroy a people whom God will avenge?), you may act in ways that will assure your own destruction. If 1 Cor. 3.18-22 is a reply to the preceding vv. 16-17, then the presumption that a community is God's temple and that God will avenge the destruction of 'the temple community' is a powerful and complex theocratic fantasy that Paul judges to be self-destructive.

Convictions about sacred vengeance are futile. And if you have been persuasive and others are wooed by your vision of being God's sacred temple that God will avenge, then your wisdom explicated in v. 17a-b is nothing more than a deadly scheme that proffers an illusion of privilege and security, but that in the end may draw you into harm's way.

An interesting characteristic of the arguments in the exchange is that both those who declare that they are God's temple and Paul's assessment that such a conviction is deceptive support their claims by an appeal to the future. Those who maintain they are God's temple that will be avenged by God if destroyed employ a weak form of eschatological verification. If those who declare they are God's sacred temple are destroyed, and God avenges the destruction of his temple, then their belief that they were God's temple would be substantiated. Thus the boast would be falsified in a most horrible chain of events. Those who identified themselves as God's temple and believe themselves to enjoy God's protection might be deceived to act in such a manner as to incite their destruction. Thus, acting on the self-identification as being sacred may become the means of one's own destruction and de/secration. For in the destruction without sacred revenge, the claim to sanctity would be found to be nothing more than an empty boast.

It is Paul's contention that those who claim to be God's sacred temple employ no craft, build or edify no community, but are crafty in their rhetoric and their supposed wisdom. Contrary to the contentious rhetoric of those who believe themselves sacred, contrary to those who would institute a theocratic hierarchy Paul counters with an egalitarian claim: 'For all things are yours.' No one person or group is sole possessor of the means for attaining superiority over others in the *ecclesia*. The concluding comment, 'and you all are Christ's and Christ is God's', is not a repetition of the earlier 'I belong to Christ'. The most that could be said is that '*we all* belong to Christ' and, as such, Christ cannot serve as the means for social division or stratification. For if we all belong to Christ then there is no partiality in the distribution.

Paul returns to comment again on the self-proclamations of belonging quoted at 1 Cor. 1.12, when he notes that he has applied his critical comments to himself and Apollos for the benefit of the Corinthian community, to the end 'that none of you may be puffed up in favor of one against another' (1 Cor. 4.6). Here he raises three questions:

> For who sees anything different in you? What have you that you did not *receive*? If then you *receive* it, why do you boast as if it were *not* a gift? (1 Cor. 4.7).

The second question, 'What have you that you did not receive?', is a negative rhetorical question that is similar to the negative rhetorical question at 1 Cor. 14.36, where Paul questions the chauvinistic assumption of those who believe that men are somehow the source of the gospel and conclude that women are to be silent in church. Paul critiques the assumption that the men of Corinth or some faction of men are the source of the gospel. Paul's critique at 14.36 serves to counter the assumed superiority of those men who believe that the word of God came to them exclusively and that women are to be silent in the church in worship. Here, too, at 4.7 Paul raises a critical question suggesting that given that everyone who receives the gift of grace is not the origin of the gift but a receiver, then the one who receives such a gift is equal with everyone else who receives the gift. Such a critical query calls into question the causal and ontological presuppositions of those who assume that they enjoy some special sacred status. If they are not in themselves sacred, but enjoy such status by virtue of another's graciousness and generosity, then *no one* who receives the gift has a reason for boasting. This returns us to the first question at 4.7: 'For who sees anything different in you?' The difference referred to here has to do with whether anyone enjoys a different status (theological or theocratic) from anyone else in the community. Another way of drawing out the nuances of the question might be to ask, 'Is it evident to anyone that you are different from the rest of us?' No one in the community is the creator, or their own source, of the gift of the gospel. All receive the gift from another. All are dependent upon another human person for the gift. None is the source. 'Who sees anything different in you?' The assumed answer is 'No one!' And no one received preferential treatment from God because, Paul declares, God shows no partiality and no human flesh may boast of being selected by God. Therefore, concludes Paul, 'none of you may be puffed up in favor of one against another' (4.6).[1] Paul's contention is that hierarchy, theological and theocratic stratifications are from the beginning unfounded. No one is independent of another. No one is the cause or source of the gospel. Each and everyone is dependent, inter-dependent, upon others for the gospel. My point is that Paul is concerned that no one pretends to be more than merely human, or to believe and act as if they enjoyed some special relation to God or Christ that establishes their advantage over another. The negative rhetorical question at 4.7a is strikingly similar to Paul's critique of the pillars of the *church* at Jeru-salem in Galatians 2, who, Paul reported, were *reputed* to be *something* but who made no difference to Paul because 'God shows no partiality'.

In his confrontation with those who sought to become the temple of God in 2 Cor. 6.14–7.2, Paul's call for openness was insistent. The exclu-sionists appear to have charged that Paul's ministry of reconciliation was 'confining'. Reconciliation compromised their aspirations to attain sanctity and to fulfill the theonomic promise. Paul's reply to the charge was that 'you are not confined by us, but you are confined in your own affections' (2 Cor. 6.12). It is a rather simple point. Those who desire their own sanctity, those who in their desire for their own advantage lack affection for others, are self-confining. Paul's openness violates their very identifi-cation as sacred and confines their fulfillment of the theonomic promise. Those who seek to become the sacred family of God are themselves being called to accept responsibility for their own affections and disaffections.

Following his presentation and critique of the 'spiritual' in 1 Cor. 3.15–4.7, Paul introduces the claim made by a faction in Corinth that they are God's temple. Traditionally, interpreters have assumed that Paul is making the claim at 1 Cor. 3.16-17 that Christians are the temple of God and, further, that at 2 Cor. 6.14–7.1 Paul enumerates the social responsibility to seek perfection for those who have sought to become God's temple. How-ever, I argue that Paul is *not* making the claim that Christians are the temple of God in either 1 Cor. 3.15–4.7 or 2 Cor. 6.14–7.1. Rather, Paul is quoting or presenting those who do make the claim for a temple com-munity in order to identify and critique the temple community conceptions

1.   There is much to be said about 'puffed up' (*phusiousthe*) that we will consider in detail below when the term appears again in 1 Cor. 8. Let it suffice to say at this point that to suggest that those who seek their own favor over another is to be 'puffed up' is a partially correct translation, which may suggest that those who seek their own advantage are full of gas and that, being puffed up, they will blow out!

as a contentious and self-deceptive boast that may be self-destructive.

In both of the extended passages in which Paul addresses the conception of a Christian temple community, Paul employs a common cynical method of critique. Those who make a claim express their own valuations and desires for which they are responsible. Rather than move quickly to a discussion or debate or argument over the status of the 'objects' desired or valued, Paul addresses the affections, desires, fears and the like of those who assert their privilege. When Paul confronts the extended quotation at 2 Cor. 6.14–7.1, he does not debate the validity of the theonomic promise but appeals to those who desire to fulfill the promise to open themselves to consider their affections or loss of affection for those who will be harmed by their convictions and activity.

In both passages that address the theme of a Christian temple community, those who are the 'waste' or who are 'excluded' are identified by Paul as the means by which those who seek sacred purification are purified. There can be no sanctity without the removal of a defiling waste, an off-scouring or scum. Purification is the outcome of a purging that differentiates the pure and the impure. Prior to the expiation, there is only the undifferentiated that is assessed by those seeking perfection to be a defilement.

Those who seek their own purification are the agents of defilement; they make defiling waste in their bid for purification. Paul's critique is that those seeking sacred perfection are the 'source' of defilement for the defiled. Those who seek sacred perfection are intimately and necessarily dependent upon desecration.

In a fashion similar to the critique at 1 Cor. 1.28, when the unity of those of ignoble and noble birth are both brought to nothing, the coorigination of the sacred and of desecration brings the desire for achieving sacred perfection to nothing. For in seeking one's own advantage by means of purification, one corrupts another.

For Paul, the fault lies not in being defiled but in defiling another in one's bid to become God's sacred family. Fault lies in the contentious practices that establish *hierarchy*. Paul's *via negativa* is not just an intellectual negation of a claim to know God but is a negation that notes the emptiness of the social structures of Christian theocratic privilege.

In the exclusionary presentation, those who would be sacred are vulnerable to contamination. Their vulnerability is demonstrated in that a believer seeking sacred perfection may be easily desecrated by contact with the world. While direct contact with the world contaminates, the desecration is assumed to be such a powerful contagion that it may be passed along by the host to others through association. While there may be factors that influence the assessment that an association fulfills the criteria for desecrating contagion, such as the degree of intimacy or the length of time of the association, the community seeking sacred perfection is assumed to be vulnerable to the highly contagious desecration.

In Paul's Epistles it is the holy that is characterized as a powerful contagion passed on by association. A believer sanctifies the unbelieving or nonbelieving spouse and children. The faithful spread the holy contagion by association.

These differences with respect to the topic of contagion between Paul and those who desire to be God's sacred temple have significant social implications. Only a society that is free of contaminating associations can fulfill the criteria to become the 'temple' community of God. For those seeking sanctification, the vulnerability of the sacred to worldly contamination posits a society consumed with such terror of their 'other' as to motivate extreme exclusionary and expulsionary practices.

The assumption is that in so far as those who are seeking perfection are God's chosen, then God's chosen enjoy shelter. Theocracy, and the promise of theonomy, holds forth the promise that with divine connections there is at least the power of being in God's abiding shelter. Social order, in this case the totalistic order of a community that is seeking radical conformity, promises extreme social well-being. This is a powerful image (if believed) for those who lack power and influence in relation to the imperial powers. So those who are vulnerable to the institutional power and military force of the empire seek refuge in their fantasies that if they attain perfection God will protect them from harm. Instead of acknowledging their own helplessness in the midst of the powers and principalities of the world, those who seek sacred perfection make their own doing the means by which they may attain safety from the imperial storm. Thus, when those who seek to become the temple of God are assailed by the empire, when the community refuses to accommodate the empire and survive, their destruction would be not because they were helpless, not because the community was a powerless minority group in a vassal state within an oppressive empire, but because the community was unable to attain perfection. As such, the community seeking sacred perfection must conclude that they have failed if God does not protect them from annihilation or avenge their destruction. Their endeavor to attain perfection was not enough to become the sacred temple of God and to enjoy sacred protection from the powers and principalities of the world. Instead of being helpless, with no potential for the enhanced sense of security that comes with worldly power, those who would become the sacred temple of God would be guilty of having failed to attain perfection.

I suspect that the transcendence hoped for by those seeking to become the temple of God was a sacred theonomy in Judea. God would take up residence among a people who had attained sacred perfection and live as a father in direct and immediate contact with and control of his family. As a 'utopia' the hoped-for theonomy stands in powerful defiance of the oppressive socio-political circumstances of Judea and the holy city of Jerusalem in the Roman empire. The loss of perceived status and power, the sense of helplessness—helplessness in the face of the enormous power and strength of Roman military, social, cultural, economic and religious institutions—fueled the isolationists' fantasies and their desire to attain clear demarcations between the 'sacred' community and the empire. The Kingdom of God became a hoped-for society that would stand in sacred isolation from the Roman empire and the many cultures within its domain.

The promise held forth by those seeking theonomy offers sacred bliss, ecstasies of perfection, the transcendence of human politics in a regime of divine, benevolent, patriarchal authority, and the security of dwelling in a sacred fortress. It does not take much imagination to begin to see the relation between the utopia of sacred perfection and the status of Judea in the Roman empire. From the vantage point of those who sought to be the temple of God, Paul's ministry of reconciliation and the *ecclesia* would appear to be little more than a religious compromise. No! Paul's *ecclesia*, from the vantage point of the convictions and fantasies of those who would become God's sacred dwelling, would be viewed as 'collaboration' with the powers and principalities of the devil and an invitation to self-annihilation.

Sacred value is bestowed by sacred violence. The sacred integrity of those who sought to become God's sacred temple was bestowed by the exclusion and expulsion of those who were corrupted. In the fantasy of those who would become God's temple their value as 'sacred' was imme-diately conveyed in the ritual acts of exclusion and expulsion. And this value, which came with the removal of others, served as the model for understanding the ecstasy promised with complete and total perfection.

In seeking atonement with God, the community seeks to fashion itself into a totality in the hope of occasioning a theonomy. But if God does not come to dwell in the community of those seeking sanctification, the only explanation that might be entertained within the perimeters of temple convictions would be that the community continues to be desecrated by some less obvious association with a contaminate. Failure to invoke the theonomy indicts the community for its lack of total purification. Those who are consumed by the passion for purity and the fantasy of non-mediated sacred authority will seek to identify and expel those who desecrate the community. Driven to simultaneously fulfill the conditions of the promise and out of fear of contamination, the community will be motivated to seek even greater purification, thus 'wasting' or declaring more of its associates to be desecrations. If this desire continues unabated, if the purification project is not reinterpreted into another project or abandoned, then the obsessive seeking for sacred perfection may yield the destruction of the community in its bid to discern and purge desecration. And since theonomy cannot be obtained, the exclusion and expulsion of all desecrating associations offers no final satisfaction. Thus, so long as God is a no-show, the community will continue its rituals of exclusion and expulsion in a frantic bid to attain sacred perfection. The force and violence that erupt from those who seek to fulfill the promise nevertheless fails to invoke God's change of venue.

But, of course, no matter who is purged theonomy will not and cannot be established. Instead the community seeking sacred perfection might turn its gaze outward. If the external contaminates can be annihilated beyond the limits of the community, then desecration may become moot. Of course, given the power and prevalence of the contagion, one might have to destroy so very much.

Customarily, however, the fantasy of sacred perfection through expulsion and the attainment of theonomy are exchanged in an odd economy of accommodation for a theocratic project and social institutionalization. Thus, just short of the destruction of the community or the annihilation of the world, or the disillusionment with the fantasies of sacred perfection, the theonomic enterprise is exchanged for theocracy. The theocracy may promise the invocation of a theonomy in the future, but the desire to create a temple society for God's dwelling and disclosure is deferred. God's disclosure is deferred and effectively abandoned for the time being. And in its place a theocracy provides the community with a degree of sanctity and social stability. Nevertheless, a promise deferred does not mean that the promise is dead. Rather, the totalizing fantasy for sanctity and theonomy may serve to refresh, among other things, the authority of the theocracy.

Paul's critique sprang from his refusal to separate those seeking their own perfection from the social context and consequences of their contentious desires and actions. Self-saving, self-serving, gratuitous immoral activity, not perfection, was endemic in the temple project. And those in the Christian community assessed as being defiled would pay the price for those seeking their own perfection. Those who seek perfection corrupt others in their own self-interest.

I find the political implications of Paul's critiques innovative. For Paul, the mutual origination and mutual dependency of opponents overcome theocracy and yield in their wake the mutual domination of members in the body of Christ. The theocratic hierarchy is dismantled by the assembly of members reconciled with one another in the body of Christ. Extreme reconciliation empties theocracy of its 'hierarchy'.

Chapter 10

AN *A*/THEOCRATIC CONCLUSION

By negation, order reaffirms itself.[1]

The Question of Order

> I appeal to you brethren, by the name of our Lord Jesus Christ, that *all of*
> *you* agree and that there be no contentions [*schismata*] among you, but that
> you be *united* [*katērtismenoi*] in the *same* disposition and the *same* accord
> (1 Cor. 1.10).

Mitchell argues that Paul's urging the Corinthians to end their factional
competition and re-establish a unified political community draws upon
Greco-Roman political oratory and treatises. In particular, she contends
that Paul employs the technical language of Greco-Roman *homonoia*
rhetoric in 1 Cor. 1.10 to serve his own political agenda.[2]

A repeated theme of *homonoia* speeches is the call for the weak and
sometimes the strong to yield to the other, giving up one's private interest
for the sake of the common good. But such calls for momentary yielding,
especially when the strong and powerful were called to yield to the weak,
constitute no challenge to the hierarchy of the political body. Martin writes:

> Indeed, there existed in the Greco-Roman world a conservative ideology
> that maintained social hierarchy by urging the lower class to submit to those
> in authority and the higher class to rule benevolently and gently, accom-
> modating its own demands in order to protect the interests of those lower
> down the social scale.[3]

The ideology of benevolent patriarchalism avoided the extreme alter-
natives of democracy, depicted as the chaotic rule of the masses and the

1. Ricoeur, *Evil*, p. 43.
2. Mitchell, *Paul*, pp. 68-80.
3. Dale B. Martin, *The Corinthian Body* (New Haven: Yale University Press,
1995), p. 42.

enslavement of the upper classes, and tyranny, portrayed as the harsh and unbending rule of an oligarchy or dictator without sufficient concern for the interests of the entire political body, including the masses. 'But when the stronger rules the weaker with restraint and the weaker submits to the stronger in self-control, the interests of the entire city are protected, and everybody lives happily ever after.'[4] As the mean between democracy and tyranny, benevolent patriarchalism neither reversed the social hierarchy nor excessively oppressed the masses, both actions assessed in the ideology as courting destruction of the political body.

What is at issue for critical scholars is whether Paul's appeals for social unity entail an overcoming of 'conflict' that does not address the inequalities assessed to foster such conflict in the first place. To end competition between contending groups and individuals without resolving the underlying inequalities is tantamount to a declaration that the established social and political inequalities are 'proper' and 'natural', and should be *peacefully* accepted as such by all parties for the good of society. Such appeals to political and social unity are deliberated speech designed to simultaneously 'restore' the peace and 'restore' power and authority to the established parties.

Paul's appeal to the Corinthians to enjoy the same disposition and the same accord and so to overcome their contentiousness and be reconciled is taken by Mitchell as Paul's imitation of conservative Roman political rhetoric. Paul seeks peace and unity at the expense of those who may have just claims for a greater distribution of benefits. On Mitchell's reading, those who are seeking their own advantage are presumed to be those individuals who would benefit from a more egalitarian distribution of benefits and responsibilities in the Corinthian community. So assessed, Paul is no friend of those who value liberty and equality. Rather, Paul is the protector of patriarchy and social hierarchy. Mitchell contends, 'The term *katartizein* (in the passive "to be reconciled or united") as used by Paul in [1 Cor.] 1.10 is an exact counterpart to the other political term used, *schisma*, "faction/division" '.[5] Paul's appeal and his choice of terms are characterized by Mitchell as deliberative political rhetoric. She contends that *katartizein* was an appropriate choice for Paul because the term often meant the bringing of warring factions back together again.

4. Mitchell, *Paul*, p. 42.
5. Mitchell, *Paul*, p. 74.

> The verb *katartizein* ... is used in discussions of political division and unity
> in antiquity. The basic meaning of the root is to 'adjust, put in order, re-
> store' (LSJ 910). The word is used in a literal sense as a medical term, de
> noting the knitting together of broken bones or dislocated joints (Apollon.
> Lit.2 (1st century BCE): 'Dislocations are manifest...it is thus prescribed to
> set right (*katartizein*) one after another', *Concerning the Study of Joints*.
> Perhaps the clearest example of the root meaning is found in the work
> *Definitiones medicae* by Galen (c. 129-199 CE) in which the abstract
> substantive *katartismos* is defined. '*Katartismos* is a moving of a bone or
> bones from (an) unnatural position into a natural position.'[6]

Mitchell's thesis is that Paul's appeal for social unity in 1 Corinthians may be categorized according to Greco-Roman rhetorical genre as a deliberative letter that urges 'concord' and employs the strategies and *topoi* of *homonoia* speeches.[7]

It is not uncommon for critical biblical scholars to note similarities and suggest influence between Plutarch's Alexander and Augustus, and Paul's Christ on the subject of 'reconciliation'. Georgi argues that while Paul was about the task of establishing a 'theocracy' that was influenced by Roman imperial political theology, Paul modified the propagandistic language of imperial political theology with its ideology of reconciliation and peace.[8] Plutarch wrote of Alexander that he

> came as a heaven-sent governor to all, and as a mediator for the whole
> world; those whom he could not persuade to unite with him, he conquered
> by force of arms, and he brought together into one body all men every-
> where, uniting and mixing in one great loving-cup, as it were, men's lives,
> their characters, their marriages, their very habits of life. He bade them all
> consider as their fatherland the whole inhabited earth, as their stronghold
> and protection his camp, as akin to them all good men, and as foreigners
> only the wicked.[9]

---

6.   Mitchell, *Paul*, p. 74.

7.   Mitchell contends that, while the word *homonoia* is not used by Paul, 'There is no reason to doubt that Paul knew the word. Paul's extended literal paraphrase of the term with the prepositional phrase *en tō autōnvoi* in the *prothesis* to the argument of 1 Corinthians, probably to avoid reference to the pagan goddess and her cult, does not mask the allusion to the realistic need for *homonoia*, political or social unity.' Mitchell, *Paul*, p. 74.

8.   Dieter Georgi, *Theocracy in Paul's Praxis and Theology* (Philadelphia: Fortress Press, 1991), pp. 64-66.

9.   Plutarch, *On the Fortune or the Virtue of Alexander* 329C (*Alexandri Magni fortuna aut virtute*) translated with Introduction by Frank Cole Babbitt in *Plutarch's Moralia*, IV (The Loeb Classical Library; London: William Heinemann, 1936), p. 399.

For Plutarch, ever since Augustus, the Caesars assumed the role of Alexander the Great and fulfilled what Alexander had begun. Rome's political and military successes were the means of overcoming factionalism and establishing a single state in which all would be governed under a single justice and obey a single purpose.

Georgi argues that Paul's modification of the propagandistic language of Roman imperial political theology 'is in critical antithesis to the Hellenistic society based on success, which claims to pursue equality'.[10] Georgi continues,

> Everywhere, and above all in the Caesar religion...this society singles out the individual set apart by success—allegedly for the benefit, but in fact at the expense of the whole. Paul, however, asserts that since Jesus, humankind is not intrinsically controlled by competition and success, superiority and inferiority, superordination and subordination. Rather, humanity is controlled by the mutual solidarity of a life born out of a common death... It is in this solidarity—not in success or power or fame—that righteousness and justice are to be found.[11]

Unlike the reconciling unity and peace of Rome successfully wrought at the hands of the legions to subdue the peoples of the world, Paul's Christ occasions a reconciling unity in his own death.

Other differences between Roman political theology and Paul's become clearer when we consider the problem of how the many are one. The singularity of the world, the metaphorical single pasture in which all dwell, provides for the bases upon which all are one in Roman imperial political theology. The singularity that the empire seeks to bring the peoples entails an overcoming of non-Roman identity. Roman reconciliation is presented in terms of a movement from differences to the progressive integration of the individual as Roman. The state sought to 'reconcile' the peoples of the world by assent to the supremacy of Roman law and political authority.

Reconciliation so conceived served the political ambitions of the empire to mingle the people to such an extent that the social and cultural distinctions that divided the empire might be overcome. Non-Roman social groupings and cultures were devalued as incidental. Such reconciliation served to overcome the influence and authority of political and cultural identifications that might disrupt the peace and authority of Rome.

While it is clear that Paul employs some of the terminology of 'reconciliation' associated with the political-theological rhetoric of the Roman

10. Georgi, *Theocracy*, p. 71.
11. Georgi, *Theocracy*, p. 71.

empire, Paul's social theology differs from the political theology of the empire in significant ways. The unity that the empire brings to the various peoples is principled and ruled by law. And the peoples of the world are to be so *mingled* as to overcome the distinctions that divide the empire into peoples. First, Paul does not appeal to an assent to law or tradition as the provider of social order. Secondly, and related to the first point, Paul does not seek to establish social order by the demise or obliteration of the various social identifications and differentiations. Roman 'reconciliation' is possible only in a process of individualization whereby previous identifications, such as the identification with one's ancestral societies, communities and cultures, are severed. Thus the reconciliation of the various peoples conquered by Rome is a process whereby individuals are disassociated, if not alienated, from their identifications with ancestral society and culture, so that they may come to 'identify' with the Roman state exclusively.

Instead of seeking to eradicate social identification, and instead of downplaying opposition in the communities, Paul *exaggerates* opposition in order to make all the more clear the coorigination of identities and the unity of opposition in the body of Christ. The 'reconciliation' of various opponents in Virgil's Augustus came as the conclusion of a process of alienation and disassociation. Reconciliation in Christ was the at-oning of those who stood in opposition, not of those whose identifications were no longer viable.

I argue that Mitchell's assessment that Paul employed the strategies and *topoi* of *homonoia* is inadequate. True, Paul's appeal for the contentious factions in Corinth to become 'united' was an appeal for social unity, but I contend that Paul's conception of 'order' differs from the social unity sought in Greco-Roman *homonoia* rhetoric. I find Mitchell's thesis is over-dependent on critiquing the traditional translations and interpretations of the letter, habits of translation and interpretation that I argue are inadequate. While I agree with Mitchell that 1 Cor. 1.10 contains technical language, I argue that this verse, especially the second clause of the verse, employs technical terminology that *does not support* her general claim that Paul employed 'stock phrases from Greco-Roman antiquity' or her more specific contention that Paul's appeal employed *homonoia* rhetoric in order to maintain patriarchal 'order'.

In particular, I do not think Paul was concerned with 'order' in the way that Mitchell assumes. Or, at least, Paul's conception of social order (and cosmic order, for that matter) is significantly different from the 'stock options from Greco-Roman antiquity' and, I might add, the 'stock options' of Christendom. While her analysis is forceful and insightful, Mitchell's argument is with those interpretations of the letter that were employed to serve the *homonoia* political agendas of emergent Christendom. Mitchell's thesis is flawed to the extent that she accepts as a given the customary interpretive practices of reading Paul's Corinthian replies as *homonoia*. And so I argue, against Mitchell and company, that Paul's appeal for unity among the Corinthian Christian community was not a simple appeal for *homonoia*. Instead, the means by which 'unity' is to be restored is the outcome of his critique of theocratic privilege. Paul introduced the 'methodology' that would accomplish his stated thesis to reconcile the contentious factions in Corinth in the concluding verses of 1 Corinthians 1:

> [26]For consider your call, brethren; not many of you were wise according to worldly standards, not many were powerful, not many of noble birth; [27]but God chose what is foolish in the world to shame the wise, God chose what is weak in the world to shame the strong, [28]God chose what is low and despised in the world, even things that are not, to bring to nothing things that are, [29]so that no human being might boast in the presence of God. [30]He is the source of your life in Christ Jesus, whom God made our wisdom, our righteousness and sanctification and redemption;[31]therefore, as it is written, 'Let him who boasts, boast of the Lord' (1 Cor. 1.26-31).

In this passage opposition deconstructs hierarchy and, in particular, it 'negates' the means by which one group establishes its theocratic superiority over another. The deconstruction of the hierarchy of theocracy is declared by Paul to be an act of God whereby the distance between God and flesh is re-established in the nullification of the privilege of those who count themselves wise, powerful and/or of high birth. Those things that are 'contemptible' or 'scandalous' (*ezouthenmena*) negate and bring those who are boastful to nothing.

Martin points out that *homonoia* rhetoric seeks social concord without addressing the socially established inequities. In *On the Cosmos*, Pseudo-Aristotle explains what he means by the *synkrisis* of the elements of the cosmos by making an analogy with the apparently more common notion of social concord. He writes:

> It is as if men should wonder how a city survives, composed as it is of the most opposite classes (I mean rich and poor, young and old, weak and strong, bad and good). They do not recognize that the most wonderful thing of all about the harmonious working [*politikēs homonoias*] of a city-com-

munity is this: that out of plurality and diversity it achieves a homogeneous unity capable of admitting every variation and degree.[12]

Martin comments that:

It is worth nothing that in the joining of these hierarchically arranged opposites the hierarchy itself is not challenged. In fact, since opposites are necessary for each other's existence, it would appear that the weak and the poor are necessary to balance the strong and the rich in the city as well as the cosmos. Homonoia has as its aim not equality or strength for all members but the preservation of the 'natural' relations of strength to weakness.[13]

The issue for Paul is not the harmoniously working (*politikēs homonoias*) city community or the Roman empire. The social unity that concerns Paul is the small group of persons who voluntarily associate as members of the *ecclesia* in Corinth. The issues for Paul are the claim to theocratic authority made by factions who warrant their privilege by appeals to their wisdom, power and/or natural-family connections. Instead of reading Paul as calling upon the 'strong' to moderate the excesses of their natural and legitimate power in order to preserve the social status quo, we read Paul as asserting that the scandalous—the foolish, the weak and the common—are chosen by God to nullify, to violate, to empty those who claim wisdom, power and family connections. In bringing the strong 'to nothing', no human being may boast of being in the presence of God. Theocratic hierarchy is deconstructed.

However, the low and contemptible do not change places with the wise, the powerful and those of high birth. There is no revolution, no reversal of fortune. The low and contemptible are chosen by God in order to nullify theocracy because the theocratic projects, or those who seek to forward themselves with a theocratic project, assume that their promoters enjoy some special allocation or association with the sacred that warrants their own rank and privilege.

And so the intent of the negative rhetorical question at 1 Cor. 1.13a as a critical reply to v. 12d is all the more clear: 'I belong to Christ', that is, 'I enjoy kinship with Christ as his bloodbrother or cousin', or 'I am a member of the household of Christ as one of his chosen disciples.'

---

12. Aristotle (Pseudo-), *On the Cosmos* 5.396 (translated with Introduction by D.J. Furley in E.S. Forster and D.J. Furley, *Aristotle On Sophistical Refutations, On Coming-to-be and Passing-Away, On the Cosmos* [The Loeb Classical Library; Cambridge, MA: Harvard University Press, 1955], pp. 377-79).

13. Martin, *The Corinthian Body*, p. 41.

'Has Christ allocated himself (1 Cor. 1.13a)?'

Christ has not allocated or distributed his authority or sanctity to some and not others. No one is in the presence of God. There can be no theocracy.

The body of Christ is not a beautiful, balanced body (as Martin argues) in which the various identities find and accept their place in the established social hierarchy of the community. The body of Christ is not the mean between the extremes, in which the tension finds formal equilibrium. Paul does not call for 'order' that holds all in place and provides stasis to the whole. Paul does not call for a balance between the various parties in order that the body may not be destroyed by an imbalance. Nor is the body of Christ a third party in which those who oppose one another find resolution as predicates joined to a subject. Rather, for Paul the body of Christ is presented as the domain, the context and the domicile in which opposing identities are disclosed as mutually dependent and without substance, without essential identity, without cosmic designation, without theological reference. Christ is 'the accommodation' for meeting, in which all who are gathered are to understand their identifications as mutually originating and mutually dependent upon those from whom they are differentiated.

The body of Christ is the carcass of one who was crucified by the powers that be from the sacred, political and military powers of the age. The body of Christ is a dead body, emptied of all sanctity, in which those who are in contention may find at-onement. Christ is that divinity who, negating himself, emptied of rank and position, was humiliated and crucified (Phil. 2.7). Selfless, humiliated and crucified, Paul's Christ is the gathering of the differences that preserves them as such *in itself*, a self that in the end is no self at all but the corpse of at-oning, of holy gathering.

Martin points out that the ideology of the presentation of the natural relation of strength to weakness in a social unit is evident in the *topos* of the state of the household.

> The household lives harmoniously when the different members—paterfamilias, wife, children, slaves—all occupy their proper positions with mutual respect but submission to those above them in the familial pyramid. The necessity of interdependence and mutuality between the different members does not in any way imply equality.[14]

---

14. Martin, *The Corinthian Body*, p. 41.

On Martin's terms, the opposite of *homonoia* is equality. But Martin fails to elaborate what he means by equality, what equality might have meant in a Greco-Roman city in the first century CE, or what political options were available at the time.

In 1 Corinthians 7 Paul directly addresses the issue of ecclesial order by delineating the proper relations between members of a household, predominantly the relation of heterosexual mates, but also the status of children, nonbelieving family members and slaves, as well as a brief discussion of the status of the circumcised and uncircumcised.

The seventh chapter begins with a quoted slogan from the Corinthian letter to Paul to which he immediately replies:

> [1]Now concerning the matters about which you wrote. It is well for a man not to touch a woman. [2]But because of the temptation to immorality, each man should have his own wife and each woman her own husband. [3]The husband should give to his wife her conjugal rights, and likewise the wife to her husband. [4]For the wife does not rule over her own body, but the husband does; likewise the husband does not rule over his own body, but the wife does. [5]Do not refuse one another except perhaps by agreement for a season, that you may devote yourselves to prayers; but then come together again, lest Satan tempt you through lack of self-control (1 Cor. 7.1-5).

Paul proceeds in a manner that undercuts the assumptions of the position posed to him. The phrase from the Corinthian letter assumes a hierarchy between the genders in which men are vulnerable to corruption in sexual contact with a defiling woman. The flow of v. 1 shifts at the beginning of v. 2, breaking from the quotation that asserts male asceticism and proceeding with an argument for marriage based upon the interdependence and mutual domination of husband and wife.

Thus we find Paul replying to the ascetic dictum 'It is well for a man not to touch a woman' with a discourse based on the mutual dependence and mutual rule of husband and wife. Paul's response is conspicuously egalitarian. Robin Scroggs notes that 1 Corinthians 7 as a whole cannot be understood as advocating the supremacy of men and the subordination of women (a traditional interpretation).[15] Scroggs argues, 'Paul in almost every instance addressed himself explicitly to *both* men and women in order to show that each sex has the same freedom and the same responsibility'.[16]

15. Robin Scroggs, 'Paul and the Eschatological Woman', *JAAR* 40 (1972), pp. 283-303.

16. Scroggs, 'Paul and the Eschatological Woman', p. 294. Hurd (*Origins*, pp. 65-66) concurs.

Verse 7.4 ('For the wife does not rule over her own body, but the husband does, likewise the husband does not rule over his own body, but the wife does') occurs as the basis for Paul's repudiation of 7.1b ('It is well for a man not to touch a woman') with 7.3 ('The husband should give to his wife her conjugal rights, and likewise the wife to her husband'). Verse 7.4 asserts the codomination of husband and wife, thereby relativizing the presumption of male asceticism expressed in the quoted verse at 7.1.

Paul clearly does not assume 'equality' between the heterosexual mates if by equality one means the liberty and independence of each individual in the association. Instead, the husband *rules* his wife's body and, in direct opposition to this formal relation, the wife *rules* her husband's body. This is clearly not the simple interdependence of the ruler and the ruled, wherein the ruler needs someone to rule to be a ruler, and so the one who is ruled is necessary for the preservation of the social order of the paternalistic heterosexual marriage. Paul contends that the male has authority over the body of the female in the marriage *and* that the female has authority over the body of the male in the marriage. But is this equality? Yes and no! True, each mate enjoys similar authority and power over the other, but the arrangement is not between two independent entities that are *self-ruling*. If Paul was proposing simple equality as understood in modern democratic societies, then he could have the wife and husband ruling over *their own* individual bodies. But he clearly rejects this interpretation in vv. 4a, c when he contends:

> For the wife does not rule over her own body … likewise the husband does not rule over his own body (1 Cor. 7.4a, c).

'Ruling the body' may refer to sexual positions and action, as in which mate is on top during intercourse, or which mate directs the sexual activity of the other, or which mate has license to seduce or request sexual activity or stimulation from the other. Or the passage may bespeak the desire or passion that rules one, so that the one who is desired or pursued rules the other by virtue of being able to sexually arouse the mate, or the one who is aroused rules in persuing sexual relations and so comes to rule the body of the mate who is desired. However, if the intent of Paul's codomination of husband and wife is to relativize the presupposition of male superiority and purity with respect to female inferiority and impurity, then the sexual codomination of a heterosexual couple would clearly violate such household order and possibly violate as well the socio-cultic and cosmic orders of gender and purification assumed by some in Corinth.

Men and women are depicted in 1 Cor. 7.8-16, 25-40 with respect to various household arrangements and different sexual and marital statuses. One of the aspects of these verses I find interesting is that Paul gives the same advice to men and women who are in similar circumstances. There is no gender double standard. Paul's reply to the prohibition of a man touching—having sexual relations—with a woman clearly violates and disregards the prescription that such contact with a woman will desecrate the man. Paul's response serves to relativize the political status of heterosexual mates, with each ruling the other.

In an earlier study I argued that the extended text of 1 Cor. 10.31–11.16 included a quotation from a text sent by a faction in the Corinthian community (1 Cor. 11.3-10) to which Paul offered a countersystem of causation (11.11-12), followed by another quotation (vv. 13-15) to which Paul offered a concluding critique of the custom of veiling women.

The first section of the text begins with the presentation of a hierarchical cosmology that ranks 'God', 'Christ', 'man' and 'woman' in descending order. Assuming the hierarchy, the text proceeds to elaborate further the relationship of man and woman, and to draw conclusions as to the proper head attire for women in worship. The hierarchical text reads:

> But I want you to understand that the head [*kephalē*] of every man is Christ, the head of a woman is her husband, and the head of Christ is God (1 Cor. 11.3).

Assuming the hierarchical cosmology of v. 3, vv. 4-10 proceed to address the social religious issue of proper head attire for men and women when they participate in worship.

> [4]Any man who prays or prophesies with his head covered dishonors his head, [5]but any woman who prays or prophesies with her head unveiled dishonors her head—it is the same as if her head were shaven. [6]For if a woman will not veil herself, then she should cut off her hair; but if it is disgraceful for a woman to be shorn or shaven, let her wear a veil. [7]For a man ought not to cover his head, since he is the image and glory of God; but woman is the glory of man (1 Cor. 11.4-7).[17]

17. Elisabeth Schüssler Fiorenza writes that, 'Archeological evidence…shows that female devotees of Isis usually wore long hair "with a band around the forehead and curls falling on the shoulders", while the male initiates had their hair shaven' (Schüssler Fiorenza, *In Memory of Her* [New York: Crossroad, 1992], p. 227; see S. Kelly Heyob, *The Cult of Isis among Women in the Greco-Roman World* [Leiden: E.J. Brill, 1975], p. 60). Fiorenza concludes, 'Hence, Paul's sarcastic statement in vv. 5ff' (Fiorenza, *Memory*, p. 227). I take it that the position of 11.4-7 is not Paul's but is held by a faction in the Corinthian church. It could be that those who argue for Christian

It is interesting to note that the cosmological/social hierarchy of v. 3 does not in itself establish rites of gender differentiation. Verse 7 details the relation between God, man and woman in terms of the concepts of 'image' (*eikōn*) and 'glory' (*doxa*), providing theological justifications for the veiling of women and the uncovering of the heads of men: 'For a man ought not to cover his head, since he is the image and glory of God; but woman is the glory of man.' This is immediately followed in vv. 8-9 with an elucidation of the meanings of 'head' (*kephalē*) suggested in the hierarchy at v. 3: '⁸For man was not made from woman, but woman from man. ⁹Neither was man created for woman, but woman for man.' Verse 8 contends that man is the source of woman and not vice versa. Verse 9 asserts that woman was created *for* man, that is, woman was created to be ruled by man and not vice versa. The section concludes that

> That is why a woman ought to have a veil on her head, because of the angels (1 Cor. 11.10).

But v. 7 goes beyond the already clear ranking and ordering of gender present in v. 3, when theological connection and the status of human genders are presented. In v. 7, man is the image and glory of God, while woman is the glory of man. Woman does not enjoy the same status as man of being a presentation, image or likeness (icon, *eikōn*) of the sacred. Man is the *icon* of *God*, but woman is not. Woman is not even the *icon* of *man*, for that matter. This lack of an iconographic connection between man and woman has significant implications given the value of icon in the text. For if woman were the icon of man, then, in so far as woman is the icon of man who is the icon of God, then woman would be an icon of an icon of God. But not even this play of presentation of the sacred is accorded woman.

The Greek term *doxa* carries a number of meanings.[18] But in the phrase

---

women covering their hair in worship are fearful that female Christian worshippers with loosened hair might be mistaken for followers of the pagan god Isis. Or, if those who argue for women covering their hair in worship are Jewish in thought and custom, their reasoning might be that loosened hair is a sign of uncleanness (Joseph A. Fitzmyer, 'A Feature of Qumran Angelology and the Angels of 1 Cor. 11.10', *NTS* 4 [1958], pp. 48-58).

18. Greek *doxa* meant 'I., a notion, opinion; a sentiment, judgment (especially a philosophic opinion); a mere opinion, as opposed to knowledge; a fancy, vision; II., the opinion others have of one, one's reputation (good report, credit, honor); glory, splendor' (Liddell-Scott, *Lexicon*, p. 444). *doxa* is offered for no fewer than 25 Hebrew words in the LXX (*TDNT*, II, p. 242).

at 11.7, *doxa* has commonly been translated into English as 'glory'.[19] It has been assessed by translators and interpreters that the meaning of *doxa* in this instance conveys the sense of glory as praise, honor, majesty and splendor attendant upon a manifestation. And so 'man' is the praise, honor, majesty and splendor attendant upon a manifestation of God, and 'woman' is the praise, honor, majesty and splendor attendant upon a manifestation of man.

Given the structure of the text as an epistle that replies, the query I put forward is this. Who is making the statement that 'man' (and not 'woman') is the 'glory'—the honor, majesty and splendor—of God? Who is making the statement that 'woman' is the 'glory'—the honor, majesty and splendor—of man? I do not think this is a trivial inquiry. For if it is the case that a faction in Corinth are asserting that they 'as men' are the *glory* of God, and that the women in the community—and in the cosmos, for that matter—are 'their' (male) *glory*, then it seems to me that the verse is expressive of a contentious group that seeks its own advantage to the disadvantage of others. *Men* contending that '*man* is the glory of God and that *woman* is the glory of man' serves to further stratify the gender hierarchy presented in v. 3 by marking the division between men and women as the limit of sacred presentation and value. Men are connected to the sacred, whereas women are not.

Man is the *icon* of God and woman is not. That man is the *glory* of God while woman is the *glory* of man reads as a *boastful* self-description and self-evaluation in service to the contentious desires and designs of those seeking their own advantage at the expense of 'women' in the community. The sacred 'iconography' of 'man' is upon closer inspection a vanity, a male vainglory for sanctity.

Verses 8 and 9 continue to elucidate gender inequalities, drawing out the two common meanings of *kephalē*, translated 'head' in v. 3, as source and ruler.

---

19. The term *glory* carries diverse meanings in English, including: '1., subjectively, the disposition to claim honor for oneself; 2., objectively, exalted praise, honor or admiration accorded by common consent to a person or thing; 3., something that brings honor and renown; 4., praise, honor and thanksgiving offered in adoration; 5., in Biblical phraseology: *the glory of God*: the majesty and splendor attendant upon a manifestation of God; 6., resplendent beauty or magnificence; 7., the splendor and bliss of heaven; 8., a state of exaltation and splendor; 9., the circle of light represented as surrounding the head, or the whole figure of the savior, the Virgin, or one of the saints' (*OED*, IV, pp. 229-30).

⁸For man was not made from woman, but woman from man. ⁹Neither was man created for woman, but woman for man.

Verse 8 contends that man is the *source* of woman and not vice versa. Verse 9 asserts that woman was created *for* man, that is, woman was created to be *ruled* by man and not vice versa. Verse 10 concludes the section with 'That is why a woman ought to have a veil on her head, because of the angels'.

So, the veiling of women in worship is based upon a cosmological model of causation that is presented as offering structure and justification for the hierarchical stratification of gender in which the sacred is not presented or glorified in 'woman'. Only 'man' is a sacred *icon* in the world. Only males can serve as the presentation of God in worship.

However, v. 11 begins rather oddly:

¹⁰That is why a woman ought to have a veil on her head, because of the angels. ¹¹*Nevertheless*...

With the beginning of v. 11 we are led to anticipate a shift. And in fact, vv. 11-12 shift so completely from the flow of the text that precedes them that many modern translations have marked these verses as parenthetical. What is it about vv. 11-12 that they should be marked as parenthetical?

¹¹Nevertheless, in the Lord woman is not independent of man or man of woman; ¹²for as woman was made from man, so man is now born of woman. But all things are from God.

In v. 11, Paul asserts that in the Lord, man and woman are codependent, and in v. 12 that man and woman cooriginate from one another, each in turn, but that all things are from God. Verses 11-12 offer an alternative explanation of the origin and status of gender differentiation from the one put forward in v. 3 and evaluated in vv. 8-9. In v. 3 the creation of the 'second sex' occurs at the far end from the sacred. The origin and purpose of woman are inferior to and subservient to man. But, in Paul's reply in vv. 11-12, gender deconstructs. The opposites are mutually originating and mutually dependent. Paul breaks his tracing of the Corinthian ply with *plēn*, at the beginning of 11.11, where in quick fashion he takes issue with the assumptions of vv. 3-10. Paul's counterproposal (11.11 and 12a) leads him to arrive at a position (11.16) that rejects the conclusion drawn in the Corinthian correspondence (v. 10).

In opposition to gender stratifications expressed in both the 'head/ruler' and 'source' presentations of vv. 3, 8 and 9, Paul contends in v. 11 that *woman is not independent of man*, that is, *she was made 'for' man*, and *'from' man*, and *man is not independent of woman*, that is, *man was made 'for' woman*, and *'from' woman*. In a strange sort of way, v. 11 relativizes the gender hierarchy, but neither by rejecting 'hierarchy per se' nor by simply reversing the hierarchy and concluding with an inversion of the positions. Paul relativizes the hierarchy by setting up male and female in hierarchical relationships in which each is the *head* of the other. And in so doing gender hierarchy plays out power relations in a manner that defers conclusion.

To the theocratic stratification of gender, wherein man is the *icon* and *glory* of God and woman is the *glory* of man but not the glory of any sacred personage, and wherein woman is not in the *iconographic* play of representation, Paul responds in his alternative explanation that in the Lord male and female are mutually dependent and mutually originating. And all things, male and female, are from God.

Paul concludes his response to the contentious ritual demarcation of gender by the veiling of women (11.10) based on the stratification of gender presented in 11.3-9 with a clear and sharp denunciation.

> If any one is disposed to be contentious, we have no such custom, nor do the churches of God (1 Cor. 11.16).

Verse 16 is Paul's final word on this matter of veiling women in worship. 'If any one is disposed to be contentious (*phileikos*)…', that is, if any one is disposed to be quarrelsome in their love of victory and domination, '…we have no such custom'. We do not practice the veiling of women, 'nor do the churches of God'. Given Paul's assertion regarding the codependence of women and men in the Lord, and their coorigination in one another, then the attempt to subjugate women by imposing rules of dress in service to a speculative hierarchy wherein the sacred finds presentation and glory *only* in 'man' and not in 'woman' gets the unsurprising response that such a custom has no place in the churches of God. Paul does not argue or make the counterproposal to the gender hierarchical claim that men are icons of God and women are not icons of anything by declaring that both men and women are icons of God. Instead, male and female are cooriginating and codependent. What is prior to the production of human males and females is not a primordial source from which male and female are the duplication of some essence or gene. What is prior to male and female is nothing, undifferentiated. Male and female emerge out of undifferentiation and become male and female in their mutual differentiation. It is not that one or the other or both together are icons of God. Instead, neither male nor female is an icon of God. The gender difference—in fact, gender per se—is emptied of iconic significance.

The public–private distinction, evident in much of the ideology of social order in Greco-Roman society, and the prescriptions of proper gender roles in public domains assumed by some groups in Corinth are clearly called into question in Paul's critical reply to the probation against women speaking in public worship. A faction in Corinth maintains that female silence in worship is expressive of women's subordination to men as is established by the law. Paul draws from their letter to him in his reply to them in order to make clear exactly to which position he is responding.

> [34]The women should keep silence in the churches, for they are not permitted to speak, but should be subordinate, as even the laws says. [35]If there is anything they desire to know, let them ask their husbands at home. For it is shameful for a woman to speak in church (1 Cor. 14.34-35).

To this quotation from the Corinthians' letter to Paul, he replies:

> What! Did the word of God originate with you, or are you the only ones it has reached (1 Cor. 14.36)?

Paul's reply is a two-fold negative rhetorical query introduced with the particle *eta* that emphatically refutes the subordination and silencing of women. Here too Paul does not seek to substantiate the gender hierarchy and preserve patriarchy in the cult. Women and men have received the word of God. And no one in Corinth may boast by declaring that the word of God originated with himself. All are dependent upon another for the word of God.

If Paul is seeking to maintain and defend the social order of the empire, why does he so forcefully critique the defense of the social status quo? What we find in our study of these verses is not the simple development of a theme or concept. Rather, in each instance Paul is engaged in a confrontation, analysis and critique of the various metaphors and concepts employed by those seeking their own advantage in the Corinthian community to subordinate women. Gender is deconstructed as the means for political advantage and disadvantage within the community. Paul's use of opposition serves as the means by which he critiques those who seek to establish their own power and authority in the community as males. The use of opposition in *homonoia* rhetoric serves to maintain hierarchical social arrangements, not to critique and deconstruct hierarchy.

I have argued that Paul's replies in the Corinthian Epistles are for the most part in response to the authority and the social agenda of the *church* and its influence on the religious community of Rome-Corinth. And so I find the contention that Paul employs *homonoia* arrangements to order the *church* misleading and confusing. Paul is precisely not seeking to order the *church*, that is, 'the community of those who belong to the Lord'. And clearly, his ordering is in distinction to the order of the *church*. For one thing, it appears that no one in Corinth rightly 'belongs' to the Lord as a member of the Lord's family or as a member of the Lord's household by virtue of having been called as a disciple by the Lord. No one in Corinth has such means or connections about which to boast. But it may be the case that some in Corinth assume identification or association with those who are in the Lord's family and/or household as a means for their own theocratic authority. Paul is critical of those who have sought or seek to establish 'relations' with the family or household of the Lord.

But the contention by Mitchell is that it is Paul who employs *homonoia* rhetoric, and that in response to the conflict at Corinth it is Paul who employs Greco-Roman political rhetoric, in particular imperial political rhetoric, to attain authority similar to the authority desired by Rome in the empire. I think such an interpretation and assessment of the Pauline letters are mistaken, and for many reasons.

Clearly, the 'order' that Paul proposes is unlike the 'order' of the *church*, where the rites of inclusion/exclusion are dominant. And, further, Paul is preoccupied throughout 1 Corinthians 7 with overcoming what appear to be various differentiations between the pure and the impure. But the question raised by Mitchell is whether Paul seeks to establish social order along the lines of the Roman empire. I answer no. I argued earlier that the church of Jerusalem as Paul presents it instigated, or at least influenced, the conflict. Further, I contend that Paul's conception of 'reconciliation' differs in significant ways from Roman conceptions. This conflict is not between Jerusalem and Rome, the *church* and the Empire.

In the discussion of 'identifications' in 1 Corinthians 7, Paul's discussion of 'slavery' appears to run counter to his advice that everyone should remain in the life that the Lord has assigned and to which God has called them. After declaring 'neither circumcision nor uncircumcision counts for anything', Paul states the conclusion that naturally follows from the declaration: 'Everyone should remain in the state in which he was called' (1 Cor. 7.20). This is followed by a question (v. 21a), 'Were you a slave when called?' Paul's answer to this question is straightforwardly clear (v. 21c): 'But if you can gain your freedom, avail yourself of the opportunity.' But this is contrary to the stated rule at v. 20. And Paul indicates in the text that he is mindful that he will now offer advice contrary to the stated rule to remain in the state one is in. Everyone should remain in the state they are in. Were you a slave? Never mind the rule. If you can gain your freedom, do so. This is immediately followed by an odd set of phrases:

> For he who was called in the Lord as a slave is a freedman of the Lord. Likewise he who was free when called is a slave of Christ (1 Cor. 7.22).

The christological reversal of the socio-politico-economic hierarchy of slave/free is curious. Clearly, in v. 21 Paul suggests that it is better for any one who is a slave to attain his or her freedom. This valuation is reiterated in v. 23b, 'do not become slaves of men'. But given the contentiousness within the Corinthian community, Paul may have attempted in v. 22 to override any possible attempt by free persons in Corinth to establish their privilege over slaves in the Christian community armed by what Paul has just written (v. 21) that it is better to be free than a slave. Paul earlier critiqued the hierarchical order of the community. He advises those who are not circumcised to not seek circumcision (contra the *church*), and Paul advises those who are circumcised to not seek to remove the marks of the rite because, he argues, ritual demarcations count for 'nothing'. Members should stay in the *state* that they are in because such states are empty. Given Paul's encounter with the *church* and the authority of James and the disciples, then clearly those who are circumcised may belong in the *church* while those who are uncircumcised are not. Yet for Paul the rite is unfounded. Circumcision is emptied of its privilege, and so neither the circumcised nor the uncircumcised are granted privilege.

However, unlike the circumcision/uncircumcision distinction, the differences between slave and free is not a ritual demarcation of communal inclusion/exclusion or cultic rank, although it could become such a demarcation. So what Paul seeks to accomplish in the discussion of slavery is to support those who have the opportunity to become free to do so without suggesting that the slave/free differentiation can serve as the means for establishing political authority in the Christian community of Corinth.

If Paul were making *homonoia* rhetorical claims, I would expect to read something to the effect that slaves should obey their masters and not seek their own freedom. Or Paul might employ a stoic argument that it is the slave *as* a slave who is *truly* free. But Paul does not employ these rhetorical options. If Paul was as well-versed in *homonoia* rhetoric as Mitchell claims, then we might assume that Paul was aware of these options of argumentation available to one seeking to maintain the status quo.

I argue that Paul is not calling for a revolt, the 'overcoming' of social differences and the attainment of some common designation to be enjoyed by all, as if there were a common nature hidden beneath or behind the various social 'identifications' just waiting to be liberated. Hebrews are to remain Hebrews, Gentiles Gentiles, men men, women women, so on and so forth. There is no move to annihilate the differences in order to disclose some hidden, common identity—not in this age or in an age to come. The differences are to continue as differences.

So, we may ask, what has changed?

If, as I have suggested, Paul is critical of the attempts to seek theonomy or establish theocracy, it could well be that Paul is making such moves to disconnect or disassociate the relations that support such privilege because he does not enjoy such connections himself. James, the brother of the Lord, and the disciples of Jesus enjoy connections on which they founded their theocratic authority. Paul critiques the household of the Lord and rejects theocracy. His critique is warranted in large part by his negative evaluation of sacred boasting, which he judges to be unethical and theologically inadequate.

Was it the case that the family and household of the Lord politicized its relations with Jesus to establish their authority among Christian groups? Or was the authority of the family and the household inchoate, emergent and vague both to those in the family and household and to those beyond? Would members of the family have declared that since they were of noble birth their decisions on a matter were final? Or was Paul's presentation of the *church* and its presumptions of authority a more formal statement, his rendering, of what he took to be the source of their advantage, their authority and power? Such sources may have appeared clearly to Paul because of his subordinate status relative to the *church*. What he lacked and they possessed might appear to Paul to be the source of the hierarchy. Family relations would explain the discrepancies, the inequalities of power relations. Thus Paul may have sought to 'politicize' the family of the Lord in order to make their inchoate theocratic authority evident. And once evident, once named, such authority could be examined, compared, with other modes of authority and opened to criticism.

I argue that Paul's conception of order occasioned by deconstructing sacred identification and reconciling opposites is not an imitation of Greco-Roman *homonoia* rhetoric and the benevolent patriarchal ideology common in Greco-Roman society. But neither is Paul's project a sustained, direct engagement with such rhetoric and ideology. Paul's foremost concern is to counter the rhetoric of authority employed by those 'who belong to the lord'.

It was in opposition to the *church* that Paul constructed his alternative, critical vision of community. From the perspective of the *church*, Paul's *ecclesia* would be a dystopia.[20] From the perspective of the *church*, the *ecclesia* would forward the very social arrangements that the *church* identified with the desecrating, the immoral and the ungodly. If believers acted in accordance with Paul's ministry of reconciliation, then the temple/ family of the *church* would be further compromised and deferred.

Paul's privileging of the crucified Christ over the historic person may have been a means by which he furthered his critique of the power and authority of the *church*. The community as the body of Christ, the corpse of Christ, did not rely upon the familiar relations of the living Lord. The metaphor of community as 'the body of Christ' (much discussed by Martin) has an edge. The social metaphor 'the body of Christ' plays upon the theme of the body as crucified corpse that is not to be confused with the rhetoric of 'the household of the Lord' that established a transfer or association of authority between the living Lord and his siblings and disciples. The social metaphor 'the body of Christ' signifies a break with the living Jesus, for the 'body' in which Jews and Gentiles, male and female, slave and free, circumcised and uncircumcised are gathered is the *corpse* of Christ, the body crucified and yet resurrected. And while it is fashionable in some academic quarters to align Paul with Roman social and political conceptions, if not Roman convictions and rhetoric, over against the 'original' Christian movement influenced by the family and disciples of the historic Jesus, to do so is to downplay if not gloss over Paul's critical edge. But then again, downplaying or glossing over Paul's critical edge is a well-established habit.

Negating Theocratic Authority

The negation of sacred identification that overcomes the contentious differentiations is the salvific work of Christ. In Christ, all the opponents are one, opposites are one, the many are one. Paul's negation serves to deconstruct the identifications of privilege and to assess that those who seek their own advantage, those who desire superiority over another, are themselves the agents of corruption who, by their identification of another

---

20. An imaginary place or condition in which everything is as bad as possible.

as impure, are themselves the cause of the desecration, defilement, corruption of another.

However, the negation is not a means of reversing the differentiations, of deciding that those who are seeking their own advantage are 'really' the desecrated. To proceed in such a way as to privilege those who are of low birth, foolish, weak, female, poor, and so on, would be to 'substantiate' contentious desire—albeit in reverse of the characteristics employed by those seeking their own privilege as identified by Paul, but a contentious desire for theocratic privilege nonetheless. To be a fool for God, or the poor of the poor as an expression of one's own perfection or sanctity, would be a ritual act of identification that establish one's privilege in the political hierarchy of theocracy. Paul's negation serves to empty the active means of contentious desire for position in theocracy.

Paul does not seek to liberalize theocratic hierarchy. He does not make the counterproposal to the claim that men are the icons of God while women are not the icons of anything by declaring that both men and women are icons of God. Instead, male and female are cooriginating and codependent. What is prior to the production of male and female is not a primordial source from which male and female are the duplication of some identity or the substantiation of an essence. What is prior to male and female is nothing, is undifferentiated. Male and female emerge from this undifferentiation and become male and female in their mutual differentiation. It is not that one or the other or both together are icons of God. Instead, neither male nor female is an icon of God. The gender difference and therefore any particular gender are emptied of all iconic significance.

The negation of the various modes of exclusion brings the contentious desire for superiority to rest, wasting the differentiation, ending the division and emptying the hierarchy that is erected ritually through acts of 'sacred withdrawal' that instigate and differentiate a desecration, or the 'sacred expulsion' of those not seeking perfection, or the social stratification according to political privileges determined by household membership or sibling relations, or theological knowledge, or sacred (apostolic) authority, or wealth or privileged gender.

The negation of the contentious differentiations and stratifications in Paul's ministry of reconciliation in which the various opponents are brought into unity in the body of Christ is salvific. The dismantling of the constructions of identifications that establish an economy of privilege yields reconciliation in the body of Christ.

The dismantling of the constructions of identification is not a means of reversing the differentiations, of reversing the economy of privilege, by which those who previously sought their own advantage are 'really' the desecrated or powerless. The negation of identification is not the means of a reversal of fortune with the economy left intact.

Calling into question the designations of family belonging, claims to knowledge, righteous self-evaluation, male iconic representation and the desire for self-purification, Paul sought to dismantle the differentiations and identifications that were in play in the construction of theocracy. Paul's letters from Ephesus exceeded theocracy and violated the passions and fantasies for hierarchy by critically engaging the constructions of identification that established the economies of authority and power.

Concluding Comments

A/theocracy does not arise outside of theocracy, but is inscribed from within theocracy. Paul's thinking *a*/theocratic is disciplined by his efforts to maintain the questionableness of all theological significations. Such questionableness is played out in the letters sent from Ephesus to Corinth in which Paul plays intimately within and often at the parameters of the text and reports sent to him in his replies. His engagements were not an anti-Christian attack on emergent Christian communities, thoughts or institutions. Rather, Paul traced out the means by which theocratic authority was composed, exposing the construction of theocratic value as a mundane quest for power and authority that was always and already empty of theocratic signification.

Dynastic theocratic authority collapses not by a critique external to theocratic thought and discipline, but by means of theocratic privilege. Theocratic privilege serves to collapse theocratic privilege in a manner that is complete in that it works from within such thought, convictions and discipline to empty theocratic thought, conviction and discipline. Paul's questioning of theocracy was not a manner of indifference and ignorance. Time and again Paul sought the authority of the very persons and institutions that he placed in question. And yey, despite his appeals for *the church's* sanction, he nevertheless sought to subvert the extra-ordinary authority of the very persons and institutions to which he submitted.

Paul's questioning theocracy is obscure for a number of interrelated, and dare I say, interdependent reasons. Theocracy is such a part of the process and structure of Christian values that the idea that Paul's letter to the Corinthians might critique theocracy would be unthinkable. How would a set of texts, some of the oldest and among the first to be evaluated as Christian scripture, be in opposition to a fundamental organizing principle and value of Christian thought and practice? To rethink what is ordinarily taken for granted is to think in ways that appear to be unwarranted, un-justified, if not simply unthinkable. So pervasive are the habits of theocracy in Christian thinking, institutions, interpretations and ethical action that the very idea that Paul questioned theocracy would appear to be a ludicrous proposal, an interpretative hypothesis without merit.

One might conclude at the end of this study that domination, totalization (i.e. incipient fascism), and subjection are inevitable in the traditions of Christianity no less and no more than any other western cultural power.[21] But this study is not a genealogy of Christian theocracy, at least not to any great extent. My concern is to read a few pages from a couple of letters that addressed and questioned domination, totalization and subjection. And yet, the historical context of the exchange and critical engagement is difficult to identify, for inevitably our assessments bespeak cultural powers and genealogies of self-formation in which we, ourselves, nevertheless circulate.[22]

Paul's *a*/theocracy bespeaks something other to theocracy. Paul assesses that the sacred identification that is necessary for theocratic power rela-tions is an expression of everyday, mundane, mortal life. Such identifi-cations enjoy no transcendence. In such moves, theocracy is emptied of its 'significance' and becomes *just politics*. What it means for Christian 'belonging' to be other than theocratic and hierarchical, let alone a 'com-munity', is a topic beyond the limits of this study.

An irony (or is it a tragedy?) is that while the themes of reconciliation were drawn upon and developed in Christian thought and practice, they were formulated and interpreted in differentiation from Paul's critique. Without Paul's critical engagements, Christian conceptions of reconcilia-tion came to mimic Imperial *homologia* rhetoric and to imitate Roman social institutionalization in the establishment of Christian theocracy. It is my conclusion that reconciliation without deconstructive *a*/theocracy yielded authoritarian, totalistic institutions.

---

21. Charles E. Scott, *On the Advantages and Disadvantages of Ethics and Politics* (Bloomington: Indiana University Press, 1996), p. 7.
22. Scott, *Ethics and Politics*, p. 115.

BIBLIOGRAPHY

Aristotle (Pseudo-), *On the Cosmos* (translated with Introduction by D.J. Furley in E.S. Forster and D.J. Furley, *Aristotle On Sophistical Refutations, On Coming-to-be and Passing-Away, On the Cosmos* [The Loeb Classical Library; Cambridge, MA: Harvard University Press, 1955]).

Barthes, Roland, 'From Work to Text', in J.V. Harari (ed.), *Textual Strategies: Perspectives in Post-Structural Criticism* (Ithaca, NY: Cornell University Press, 1979), pp. 73-88.

Betz, Hans Dieter, *Galatians: A Commentary on Paul's Letter to the Churches in Galatia* (Hermeneia; Philadelphia: Fortress Press, 1979).

Bruce, F.F., *1 & 2 Corinthians* (London: Oliphants, 1971).

Bultmann, R., *Primitive Christianity in its Contemporary Setting* (New York: Meridian Books, 1956).

Collins, Raymond F., *First Corinthians* (Sacra Pagina Series, 7; Collegeville, MN: Liturgical Press, 1999).

Conzelmann, Hanz, *1 Corinthians* (Philadelphia: Fortress Press, 1975).

Derrida, Jacques, 'Freud and the Science of Writing' (trans. Jeffrey Mehlman), *Yale French Studies* 48 (1972), pp. 74-117.

—*Of Grammatology* (Baltimore: The John Hopkins University Press, 1974).

—*Writing and Difference* (trans. Alan Bass, with an Introduction and Additional Notes; Chicago: University of Chicago Press, 1978).

Douglas, Mary, *Purity and Danger: An Analysis of Concepts of Pollution and Taboo* (New York: Frederick A. Graeger, 1966).

Elliott, Neil, *Liberating Paul: The Justice of God and the Politics of the Apostle* (Maryknoll, NY: Orbis Books, 1994).

Fitzmyer, Joseph A., 'A Feature of Qumran Angelology and the Angels of 1 Cor. 11.10', *NTS* 4 (1958), pp. 48-58.

Funk, Robert W., *Language, Hermeneutics and the Word of God* (New York: Harper & Row, 1966).

Furnish, Victor Paul, *II Corinthians* (The Anchor Bible; trans. with an Introduction, Notes and Commentary; Garden City, NY: Doubleday, 1984).

Georgi, Dieter, *The Opponents of Paul in Second Corinthians* (Philadelphia: Fortress Press, 1986).

—*Theocracy in Paul's Praxis and Theology* (Philadelphia: Fortress Press, 1991).

Girard, René, *Violence and the Sacred* (trans. Patrick Gregory; Baltimore: The John Hopkins University Press, 1972).

Heidegger, Martin, *An Introduction to Metaphysics* (trans. Ralph Manheim; New Haven: Yale University Press, 1959).

—*Essays in Metaphysics: Identity and Difference* (trans. Kurt F. Leidecker; New York: Philosophical Library, 1960).

—*Early Greek Thought* (trans. David Farrell Krell and Frank A. Capuzzi; New York: Harper & Row, 1975).

Heyob, S. Kelly, *The Cult of Isis among Women in the Greco-Roman World* (Leiden: E.J. Brill, 1975).

Horsley, Richard, *1 Corinthians* (Abingdon New Testament Commentaries; Nashville: Abingdon Press, 1998).

Hurd, John C., *The Origins of 1 Corinthians* (New York: Seabury, 1965).

Kirk, G.S., *Heraclitus: The Cosmic Fragments* (Cambridge: Cambridge University Press, 1954).

Klein, E.A., *A Comprehensive Etymological Dictionary of the English Language* (New York: Elsevier, 1966).

Klinzing, George, *Die Umdeutung des Kultus in der Qumrangemeinde und im Neuen Testament* (Göttingen: Vandenhoeck & Ruprecht, 1971).

Lacan, Jacques, 'Seminar on "The Purloined Letter" ' (trans. Jeffrey Mehlman), *Yale French Studies* 48 (1972), pp. 38-72.

Levine, Baruch A., *In The Presence of the Lord* (Leiden: E.J. Brill, 1974).

Liddell, Henry and Robert Scott, Revised and Augmented by Henry Jones, *A Greek-English Lexicon, Ninth Edition with Supplement* (Oxford: Clarendon Press, 1940).

Lifton, Robert Jay, *The Broken Connection* (New York: Simon & Schuster, 1979).

Martin, Dale B., *The Corinthian Body* (New Haven: Yale University Press, 1995).

Martyn, J. Louis, *Galatians: A New Translation with Introduction and Commentary* (The Anchor Bible; New York: Doubleday, 1997).

Mitchell, Margaret, *Paul and the Rhetoric of Reconciliation* (Louisville, KY: Westminster / John Knox Press, 1991).

Moffatt, James, *An Introduction to the Literature of the New Testament* (New York: Charles Scribner's Sons, 3rd edn, 1929).

Neusner, Jacob, *The Idea of Purity in Ancient Judaism* (Leiden: E.J. Brill, 1973).

Odell-Scott, D.W., 'Let the Women Speak in Church: An Egalitarian Interpretation of First Corinthians 14.33b-36', *Biblical Theology Bulletin* 13.3 (July 1983), pp. 90-93.

—'In Defense of an Egalitarian Interpretation of First Corinthians 14.34-36: A Reply to Murphy-O'Connor's Critique', *Biblical Theology Bulletin* 17.3 (July 1987), pp. 100-103.

—*A Post-Patriarchal Christology* (American Academy of Religion, Academy Series 78; Atlanta: Scholars Press, 1991).

—'Paul's Skeptical Critique of a Primitive Christian Metaphysical Theology', *Encounter* 56.2 (1995), pp. 127-46.

—'Editor's Dilemma', *Biblical Theology Bulletin* 30.2 (May 2000), pp. 68-74.

Onions, C.T. (gen. ed.), *Oxford English Dictionary* (Oxford: Clarendon Press, 1966).

Painter, John, *Just James: The Brother of Jesus in History and Tradition* (Columbia, SC: University of South Carolina Press, 1997).

Patte, Daniel, *Paul's Faith and the Power of the Gospel: A Structural Introduction to the Pauline Letters* (Philadelphia: Fortress Press, 1983).

Plummer, Alfred, *A Critical and Exegetical Commentary on the Second Epistle of St. Paul to the Corinthians* (Edinburgh: T. & T. Clark, 1975).

Plutarch, *On the Fortune or the Virtue of Alexander* (*Alexandri Magni fortuna aut virtute*) translated with Introduction by Frank Cole Babbitt in *Plutarch's Moralia*, IV (The Loeb Classical Library; London: William Heinemann, 1936), pp. 379-487 (326D–345B).

Ricoeur, Paul, *The Symbolism of Evil* (New York: Harper & Row, 1967).

—*Interpretation Theory: Discourse and the Surplus of Meaning* (Fort Worth: Texas Christian University Press, 1976).

—'Philosophical Hermeneutics and Theological Hermeneutics: Ideology, Utopia and Faith', in W. Wuellner (ed.), *Protocol of the Colloquy of the Center for Hermeneutical Studies in Hellenistic and Modern Culture* (Berkeley, CA: The Center, 1976).

—*Lectures on Ideology and Utopia* (ed. George H. Taylor; New York: Columbia University Press, 1977).

Schüssler, Elisabeth Fiorenza, *In Memory of Her: A Feminist Theological Reconstruction of Christian Origins* (New York: Crossroad, 1971).

Schwartz, Regina, *The Curse of Cain* (Chicago: University of Chicago Press, 1997).

Scott, Charles E., *The Language of Difference* (New York: Humanities Press, 1987).

—*The Question of Ethics* (Bloomington: Indiana University Press, 1990).

—*On the Advantages and Disadvantages of Ethics and Politics* (Bloomington: Indiana University Press, 1996).

Scroggs, Robin, 'Paul and the Eschatological Woman', *JAAR* 40 (1972), pp. 283-303.

Shipley, Joseph T., *The Origins of English Words: A Discursive Dictionary of Indo-European Roots* (Baltimore: The Johns Hopkins University Press, 1984).

Taylor, Mark C., *Deconstructing Theology* (New York: Crossroad, 1982).

—*Erring: A Postmodern A/theology* (Chicago: University of Chicago Press, 1984).

—'The Eventuality of Texts', *Semeia* 51 (1990), pp. 215-40.

INDEXES

INDEX OF REFERENCES

BIBLE

INDEX OF AUTHORS